PREHISTORIC
GLOUCESTERSHIRE

To the memory of the late Wilfred L. Cox (1919–1986)

W.L. Cox beside grooved stone at Campden Lane, Hawling, Spring 1979.
[Photograph: Author]

PREHISTORIC
GLOUCESTERSHIRE

Timothy Darvill

ALAN SUTTON &
GLOUCESTERSHIRE COUNTY LIBRARY
1987

The County Library Series is published jointly by Alan Sutton Publishing Limited and Gloucestershire County Library. All correspondence relating to the series should be addressed to:

Alan Sutton Publishing Limited
30 Brunswick Road
Gloucester GL1 1JJ

First published 1987

British Library Cataloguing in Publication Data

Darvill, T.C.
    Prehistoric Gloucestershire.
    1. Man, Prehistoric—England—
    Gloucestershire   2. Gloucestershire—
    History
    I. Title
    936.2'41   GN806.G56

    ISBN 0-86299-460-8

Printed in Great Britain

Contents

Preface

Gloucestershire and the surrounding area is extremely rich in prehistoric remains. It is justly famous throughout Britain, and indeed north-west Europe, for its numerous visible field monuments, for example the long barrows, hillforts, round barrows, enclosures and ditch systems, and for some very fine objects on display in our local and national museums.

In the last decade or so much new and exciting evidence has come to light through excavation projects and fieldwork, and this, coupled with recent research, allows new and vivid insights into the lives of the people who inhabited the area before the Roman conquest of AD 43. This book brings together what is known about Gloucestershire in prehistoric times. It is aimed primarily at the interested layman, and accordingly concentrates on setting the evidence visible in the countryside and our museums into its context. Some of the qualifications which must in all honesty be attached to our understanding of prehistory have been omitted in this so that the evidence can be presented simply and without the clutter of academic debate. For readers wishing to look deeper into the prehistory of the county, the notes that accompany the text will lead to specific references listed in the bibliography.

The present county boundary is of course a recent feature defined for modern administrative purposes. It had no meaning to prehistoric people living in the area, and for this reason no apology is made for referring to sites which lie just outside the present county proper.

Because of the very long period of time covered by this book an essentially narrative account is presented, starting with the first appearance of Man in the area and working through to the Roman conquest. There are no documents to provide a chronological framework for prehistory and so most of what we know about the age of things is based on radiocarbon dating. Throughout this book radiocarbon dates are expressed as years BC. Dates after about AD 1 are, however, derived from the more familiar historical calendar that we still use today. A list of radiocarbon dates so far available for the Gloucestershire area is given as Appendix A. There are not very many as yet, but of course dates from elsewhere also have a bearing on material from Gloucestershire and can therefore provide additional pegs from which to hand the local chronological framework of prehistory.

Our understanding of life in prehistoric times is still far from complete. Research both within the county and elsewhere continues, and in time will bring about new insights and new interpretations. This is perhaps one of the fascinations of archaeology, but it should not distract us from making good use of the evidence currently available.

This book is dedicated to the memory of the late Wilfred Cox, probably one of Gloucestershire's last true antiquaries, who will no doubt be remembered by many, both old and young, as a fine teacher, enthusiastic archaeologist, and ever-popular lecturer and author.

Timothy Darvill
Midsummer's Day, 1987
Gloucester.

1

In Search of Gloucestershire's Prehistory

Introduction

The area now known as Gloucestershire has been inhabited by human societies for over a quarter of a million years. Generation after generation carved out a living for themselves, and in so doing left behind numerous traces of their activities, which, with patient study, can reveal something of the lifestyles, economy, and beliefs of these long-vanished communities. Medieval abbeys, deserted villages, Saxon churches and Roman villas are all familiar features of the countryside, but older still than these are the equally impressive camps, barrows, dykes, ditches, caves and hillforts; remnants of the time before written history. This book is the story of those ancient times, from Man's first arrival in the area during the last Ice Age down to the Roman invasion of AD 43. It is a story of slow change from groups of nomadic hunters to settled farming communities living in tribal groups, punctuated by episodes of conflict and turmoil. It is a story of ups and downs, of good times and bad.

The quality and quantity of upstanding prehistoric sites and monuments in and around Gloucestershire is quite exceptional. Traces of settlements, the farms and the villages used in prehistory, abound. There are also burial monuments, such as the long barrows built about 3000 BC, and sacred places such as stone circles, henges and standing stones. For every visible standing monument there are perhaps a score of sites buried beneath the ground which are only revealed when the soil is disturbed. All contribute to our understanding of the prehistory of the area.

The development of interest in prehistory

Scholars have known for a long time that Britain was inhabited before the Romans arrived here because writers such as Caesar and Strabo described the indigenous population – the Ancient Britons as they became known.[1] Yet, strange as it may seem, the accurate identification of the remains of these pre-Roman communities has only relatively recently been achieved.

1

Beech Pike round barrow, Elkstone. A fine Bronze Age burial monument probably built
c 1500 BC. [Photograph: Author]

Among the general public, ignorance of the true origin of mounds and earthworks was concealed by the invention of myth and folklore. Some of this is perpetuated in the names still attaching to sites, for example Nan Tow's Tump near Didmarton allegedly contains the burial of a local witch named Nan Tow, while Money Tump, a burial mound near Bisley, is said to contain buried treasure.[2]

From the mid 17th century interest in the early history of Britain grew as inquisitive minds sought to explain mysterious features of the countryside and unravel their secrets. The development of antiquarian interest was a national phenomenon, but Gloucestershire was in the vanguard of the movement and events within the county represent a microcosm of the wider picture.

As long ago as 1586 the wealth of Gloucestershire's ancient remains was recorded by William Camden (1551–1623) in his *Britannia*, which was in effect the first guidebook to the antiquities of Britain.[3] Later, about 1665, John Aubrey (1626–97) included details of no fewer than 28 monuments within the county in his *Monumenta Britannica*, but the manuscript of this volume languished in the Bodleian Library in Oxford until its publication in 1982.[4] Various other travellers and map-makers did, however, publish their work during their lifetime, and among those who referred to sites in Gloucestershire were William Stukeley (1687–1765) and Isaac Taylor (1730–1787).[5]

One of the earliest known excavations of a prehistoric site in Gloucestershire took place about 1700 at the large long barrow near Leighterton which is known as West Barrow. The excavator's name was Matthew Huntley but few details of his work were recorded except that the barrow 'contained three vaults arched over like ovens, and at the entrance of each was found an earthen jar containing burnt human bones, but the skulls and thigh bones were found unburnt'.[6]

During the 18th and 19th centuries many more excavations took place, usually on upstanding monuments. Among the famous men who worked in Gloucestershire at this time were John Thurnam, a Wiltshire antiquary who excavated at Hetty Pegler's Tump, Uley, near Dursley in 1854,[7] and Canon Greenwell from Durham who journeyed outside his home area in the East Riding of Yorkshire to excavate a number of sites around Swell, in the north Cotswolds, usually in the company of George Rolleston and the Reverend David Royce.[8] Rolleston was Linacre Professor of Anatomy and Physiology at the University of Oxford and, being well known for his interest in the physical anthropology of prehistoric people, it was he who studied the human bones found by Greenwell.[9] In contrast, David Royce was the rector of Lower Swell from 1850 to 1902, and in addition to helping with a number of excavations he amassed a collection of over 5000 flint artefacts from around the area, mostly by paying farm labourers a small reward for bringing him anything they found while working in the fields.[10]

Sufficient interest in geology, botany, zoology and archaeology had developed in the county by 1846 for the formation of the Cotteswold Naturalists Field Club, and thirty years later archaeology alone commanded sufficient following for the Bristol and Gloucestershire Archaeological Society to be established.[11] Both these groups sponsored and promoted excavations, but perhaps more importantly they both issued journals in which accounts of finds, investigations, and research could be published. Among the early presidents of the Bristol and Gloucestershire Archaeological Society, in 1892, was General Pitt Rivers, one of the founding fathers of modern archaeology.

The Reverend Royce was typical of many antiquaries in that he combined the life of the church with an interest in the ancient past. But not all antiquaries of this period were clergymen, and one especially notable exception was George Witts, a civil and railway engineer by profession but a dynamic man who carried out a number of excavations in Gloucestershire during the late 19th century. This was a time when much new archaeological material came to light because the countryside was being opened up by the construction of new roads and railways. Something of the excitement of making new and spectacular discoveries can be glimpsed from Witts' own writings. He records, for example, that in July 1880:

> 'I was on horseback, and in taking a short cut through Buckholt Wood, with my mind intent on archaeology, I suddenly saw before me a huge mound! I rode to the top of it, and around it, and after a careful examination, came to the conclusion that it was a long barrow, and a very perfect one. Before many hours were past, in fact before I returned home that night, I had obtained permission . . . to have it opened and examined and had also obtained . . . promises of funds sufficient, at any rate, to commence the work'.[12]

The excavation which ensued is probably the earliest in Gloucestershire to have been recorded by photography, and it is a measure of the enthusiasm of George Witts that the excavation was promptly published in 1881. Two years later he published his *Archaeological handbook of the county of Gloucestershire*.[13] This volume, which remains an invaluable source of information to this day, lists some 278 prehistoric sites in the county and provides a short account of each.

The single biggest difficulty facing these early antiquaries was that of determining the age of the sites and finds they were dealing with. It was appreciated that much of the material was pre-Roman, but it was not until after the mid 19th century that the oldest material began to be distinguished from the less old and a basic prehistoric calendar began to be constructed.

West Tump long barrow, Brimpsfield. Neolithic long barrow under excavation in 1883, showing the burial deposits in the entrance to the chamber on the south side of the mound.

The turning point came with the development by the Danish archaeologist Christian Thomsen of what has since become known as the Three Age System.[14] In this scheme three divisions of the pre-Roman period were proposed on the basis of the technology used for toolmaking during each. The earliest was the Stone Age, before the use of metals, and this was followed in turn by the Bronze Age and the Iron Age. Of course it was some time before this basic framework was widely adopted, and it was not until the early years of the present century that these terms became at all widely used in the archaeological literature or everyday speech. The term 'prehistory', meaning before written history, was also an invention of the mid 19th century and was first used in print by Daniel Wilson in his book entitled *The archaeology and prehistoric annals of Scotland* which was published in 1851.

Even with the Three Age System as a framework there was no real idea of when each period began or ended in years before Christ. Thus prehistoric studies in the first half of the 20th century became preoccupied with fitting as much visible evidence as possible into its correct period, and guessing at the chronology and duration of each period. The Stone Age was an early casualty of this attention because it was found to be too large a category.

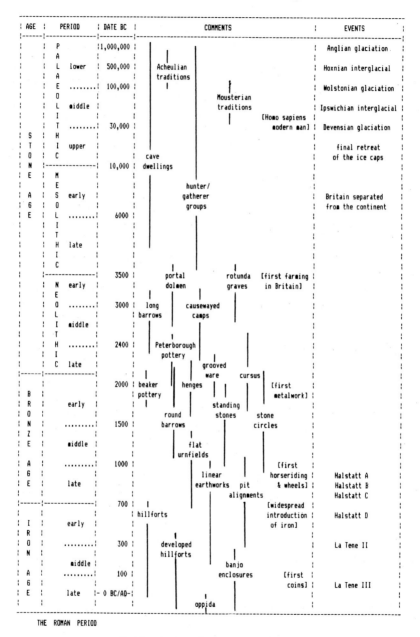

THE ROMAN PERIOD

Prehistoric time-chart (not to scale).

Accordingly it was subdivided into three periods known as the Palaeolithic (old stone), Mesolithic (middle stone), and Neolithic (new stone) ages. These terms, like Bronze Age and Iron Age are still in common use today as a short-hand for specific periods of prehistory, much as we might talk of the Victorian era or Georgian times. As will be discussed shortly, however, the development of radiocarbon dating from the late 1940s now makes it possible to determine the absolute age of certain archaeological finds without reference to the Three Age System.

Excavations continued to be undertaken during the first half of the present century, all the time developing and improving techniques of recovery and recording established by pioneers such as General Pitt Rivers in the late 19th century. Among the most active archaeologists in Gloucestershire during the period 1930–1965 were Elsie Clifford and Helen O'Neil. Between them, these two ladies excavated and published over 30 prehistoric sites within the county, not just barrows like those which had so dominated archaeological interest in the 19th century, but also settlements and camps which added a new dimension to existing knowledge.[15]

In parallel with excavation, a strong tradition of fieldwork developed in the county as another way of finding out about the past. Careful document-ation of surface features through written descriptions, plans, and maps has provided a valuable record of sites and monuments as they were before modern agriculture accelerated their denudation and erosion. Among the many outstanding fieldworkers this century mention may be made of Dr O.G.S. Crawford who published the first detailed survey of Neolithic tombs in the area[16] and Leslie Grinsell who in the 1950s visited, measured, and recorded all the known Neolithic long barrows and Bronze Age round barrows in the county, a total of over 425 sites, for the most part walking to each location and staying overnight in Youth Hostels.[17]

The focus of much early archaeological work in Gloucestershire was the Cotswold uplands. The Severn Valley and the Forest of Dean attracted rather less attention, perhaps because in general the evidence preserved there is less spectacular, although as we shall see later, no less important. One exception was Dr Charles Scott-Garrett who, between about 1914 and the late 1960s, made many discoveries and undertook both excavation and fieldwork in the triangle of land between the Severn and the Wye in west Gloucestershire.[18]

By the mid 1960s, the face of prehistoric archaeology both nationally, and in Gloucestershire, was changing. Radiocarbon dating was beginning to resolve some of the outstanding problems of the chronology of prehistory, and for the first time the true antiquity of many sites became clear. Furthermore, the building boom of the later 1960s and 1970s brought to light a wealth of new evidence in the form of previously unknown sites and large quantities of stray finds. At the time there was much public outcry over the speed at which ancient and fascinating sites were being lost to the bulldozers. As a result more public money was spent on archaeology and the professional side of the discipline expanded rapidly.[19]

Perhaps one of the most vivid and unexpected insights into the wealth of archaeological evidence in Gloucestershire came in 1969 and 1970 when the M5 motorway was constructed along the whole length of the Severn Valley from Bristol in the south to Tewkesbury in the north. Some 40 sites were recorded along the 55km of motorway in present-day Gloucestershire, an average of one site every 1.33km. Not all these sites were of prehistoric date but the density of evidence is nonetheless impressive.[20]

With the new information about the nature and extent of prehistoric settlement gathered during the 1960s and 1970s to hand, the last decade or so has seen many traditional interpretations revised and new ideas put forward. These are the matters covered in Chapters 2–7 of this book, but before embarking on a detailed discussion of what is now known, it is perhaps helpful to pause briefly and look in a little more detail firstly at the main methods and techniques used by prehistorians today, and secondly at what is known of the environment and landscape of the Gloucestershire area during prehistoric times.

Dating the past

Arguably the single most important development in prehistoric studies during recent decades has been the widespread application of radiocarbon dating. This technique, which was developed during the late 1940s by the American nuclear physicist Dr Willard Libby, provides a way of determining the absolute age of any organic matter – such as bone or charcoal – which is preserved on archaeological sites. It works by measuring the amount of the radioactive isotope carbon 14 (^{14}C) relative to the non-radioactive isotope carbon 12 (^{12}C) in the samples submitted for analysis. All plants and animals absorb minute quantities of ^{14}C from the atmosphere, and while they are alive a relatively constant level of ^{14}C is maintained. However, at death no new ^{14}C can be taken in, and, because ^{14}C is a radioactive isotope, that which is already present begins to decay. The rate of decay is fairly even, and after about 5568 years half of the ^{14}C which was present at death will have been lost. Thus by finding out the level of ^{14}C remaining in an ancient sample it is possible to calculate how much time has elapsed since death, and accordingly its age.[21]

The methods by which radiocarbon dates can be determined are complicated and varied. Moreover, several of the assumptions made when the technique was being developed have since proved incorrect and it is now clear that radiocarbon dates do not correspond exactly with solar years or

Radiocarbon dating laboratory at Oxford University. [Photograph: J. Gowlett]

calendar years as we know them today. For this reason a number of calibration methods are currently being developed, but until a particular curve can be universally accepted dates have to be given in radiocarbon years BC. All dates Before Christ given in this book are based on the radiocarbon calendar (see Appendix A for select list of dates). It is also important to realize that radiocarbon dates are simply estimates of the actual age of the material tested. Accordingly, dates are usually quoted with a standard deviation (eg. 2000 ± 70 BC) expressing the statistical concept that the actual date has a 66% probability of lying within the limits specified either side of the mean value (in this case within the range 2070–1930 BC). Doubling the standard deviation raises the probability level to 95.5%.

Tools for reconstructing the past

Alongside radiocarbon dating there are many other tools and techniques available to the archaeologist wishing to investigate the prehistoric period, some of them simply developments of existing techniques, some new innovations.[22]

Excavation remains the main source of detailed information about the prehistoric period. Sites can be slowly and methodically taken apart to see what they contain, how they came about, how objects relate to structures and how, over a period of time, one set of activities was replaced by another. In recent years the scale of excavations has increased. Large areas are now investigated wherever possible in order to get a representative picture of the pattern of activities within a given site. More attention is paid to retrieving evidence such as plant remains, snail shells, seeds, insects, small animal bones, and tiny chips of worked stone. Only by doing this can a detailed picture be built up of life at and around a site, what food was being consumed, what pests, parasites, and animals were around at the time, and what the environment of the site was like.

Excavation is, however, only useful for the examination of relatively small parts of the landscape at a time, usually places which were intensively used, for example camps, settlements or burial sites. For the study of much larger areas of landscape fieldwalking provides a wealth of information, albeit less detailed. Fieldwalking allows the identification of those areas used intensively for settlement, and also the areas used rather less intensively for fields or grazing animals. Gaps in the distribution of settlement at any given time can also sometimes be glimpsed.

Fieldwalking involves systematically scanning the surface of ploughed fields or other disturbed ground, carefully noting the presence or absence of artefacts such as flint tools, worked stone, or pottery. By plotting the recorded distribution of finds onto large-scale maps differences in the density of past activities can be detected. Several fieldwalking projects have been undertaken in Gloucestershire over the last few years among them the Birdlip survey,[23] the Cotswold survey[24] and the Forest of Dean survey.[25]

Another technique for looking at wide areas of the landscape to detect sites otherwise invisible on the ground is aerial photography. Sites with very denuded earthworks sometimes show more clearly from the air late in the day or in winter when low sunlight throws the features into relief. A light snow fall accompanied by moderate winds has the same effect because the snow collects in the lee of the slightest surface undulation.

A further use of aerial photographs is to record cropmarks. Crops growing over silted-up ditches or pits tend to grow more vigorously and in the case of cereals ripen more slowly than those on thin soils over natural bedrock. Colour differences, growth patterns, and parch marks in ripening crops often betray the presence of buried features. Naturally, some soils are more responsive than others, and in Gloucestershire the most spectacular results come from areas of gravel sub-soil, for example in the upper Thames Valley between Cirencester and Lechlade.[26]

Geophysical surveys are a relatively new innovation in archaeology. Two particular methods are widely used, resistivity survey and proton magneto-

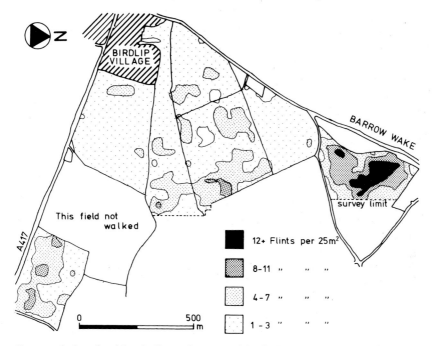

Contoured plot of prehistoric flintwork recovered by fieldwalking at Birdlip. The darker areas represent concentrations of worked flints indicating former settlement/activity sites.

meter survey.[27] In the first an electric current is passed through the soil between an array of electrodes. The resistance of the soil to the flow of current is measured and plotted in a systematic way. This leads to the definition of areas of high and low resistance which in turn can be interpreted as characteristic of particular types of feature below ground level, for example ditches, pits or walls. In contrast, the proton magneto-meter measures areas of anomalous magnetism such as might be produced by a heavily burnt hearth or even a ditch filled with soil of a different magnetic intensity to the surrounding bedrock. Again, by systematically working over a given area, a map of high and low readings can be built-up and converted into a picture of what lies beneath the ground surface.

Technical studies of prehistoric artefacts can reveal much of interest about their origin and manufacture. Petrological analysis of prehistoric stone axes has been widely used to determine which rock outcrops provided the raw materials. In Gloucestershire, for example, it seems that axes used during the Neolithic period were largely imported from the Lake District, North Wales and Cornwall (see below Chapter 3).[28] Pottery can be analysed in the same way, the clay sources identified, and the techniques used to manufac-

Aerial photograph of cropmarks at Langford (Oxfordshire). Land boundaries, house sites, and enclosures can be seen in the foreground, a trackway approaches the site from the top of picture. [Photograph: Author; Pilot: Ron Locke]

ture the pot determined.[29] For metal items analysis of trace elements and their chemical composition can identify pieces from particular workshop areas.[30]

One final area of interest which has developed rapidly in recent years is the concern for a theoretical base to archaeological reasoning. The prehistoric world is, after all, no longer available to be observed in action; it survives only as the material remains of a wide range of different, but interrelated, activities. The first step in interpreting archaeological evidence therefore requires a set of assumptions which relate material remains to incidents and activities in the past. These assumptions can then be used to construct 'models' of the past. Such models are nothing more than conceptual pictures of some aspect of the behaviour of a past society based largely on what is actually known, but filling in any gaps in our knowledge with experiences derived from elsewhere, perhaps for example comparisons with modern-day primitive societies. By using such approaches prehistorians can step outside the 20th century world, with all its particular values and philosophies. The evidence can then be interpreted in a context appropriate to the kinds of small scale societies which left it behind.[31]

Landscape and environment

The basic topography of the Gloucestershire area changed very little in the last 10,000 years, and four distinctive geographical zones can be identified.

The first, in the far west of the county, is the upland plateau of Dean, rising to 215m above sea-level, and dominated by hard sandstones and carboniferous limestones.

The second distinctive area is the Severn Valley running south-west to north-east across the county. This low lying area is dominated by heavy clays sporadically overlain by alluvial gravel islands. The river itself is now confined to its course by artificial banks; in prehistoric times a more braided and constantly changing river course must have existed.

On the eastern side of the Severn Valley is the third zone, the Cotswold Hills which form the backbone of the county. These limestone uplands reach a maximum height of 310m at Cleeve Cloud near Cheltenham and are

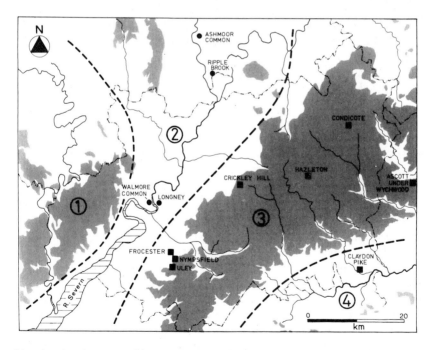

Map showing the extent of the main geographical zones referred to in the text, and the locations of sites studied for environmental sequences in the Gloucestershire area. (1) = Forest of Dean uplands; (2) = Severn Valley; (3) = Cotswold uplands; (4) = upper Thames Valley. Squares indicate environmental deposits from archaeological deposits, dots indicate deposits from natural accumulations. On this and subsequent maps, land over 200m is shaded.

edged by an impressive, and in places precipitous, westward facing escarpment. The dip slope of the Cotswolds descends gradually eastwards. Geologically it is dominated by Jurassic limestones, interspersed with outcrops of fullers earth (a marly clay), but where rivers have cut through the limestone, Lias clays may be exposed.

To the east of the limestone uplands is the fourth main topographic zone in the county, the upper Thames Valley. Here the headwaters of the River Thames – the Evenlode, Windrush, Leach, Coln and Churn – flow south-eastwards to join the Thames proper near the eastern border of the county. Geologically the upper Thames Valley is, like the Severn Valley, dominated by heavy clays, in this case the Oxford clays. Large areas are, however, overlain by river gravels, and these were prime areas for prehistoric settlement.

Against this fairly stable landscape must be set the dramatically changing pattern of soil fertility and vegetation cover. Ideally these changes need to be documented in each of the four geographical areas already discussed

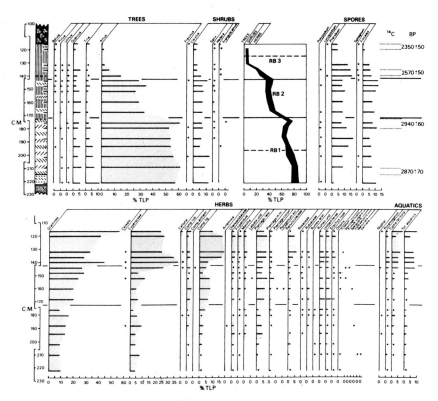

Pollen diagram showing changes to the vegetation cover between about 1000 BC and 300 BC around Ripple Brook, near Twyning.

because soils and vegetation are closely linked with geology and topography. At present, however, detailed environmental evidence derived
from dated pollen sequences only exists for the Severn Valley; elsewhere
our knowledge of the prehistoric environment is based on samples of pollen
and snail shells recovered during the excavation of settlements and burial
monuments.

For the very early periods of human settlement in Gloucestershire,
between about 250,000 BC and 10,000 BC, relatively little is known of the
environment (see below Chapter 2). From about 10,000 BC, however, after
the ice caps of the final glaciation had retreated, all of the southern Britain
became covered in woodland. This in turn gave rise to thick humus–rich
soils and provided browsing for many animals, among them red deer,
aurochs (wild cattle), wild pig, and wild horse.

Detailed investigations of pollen trapped in peat and sediments which
slowly accumulated in old channels of the River Severn from about 5000
BC onwards, provide a vivid insight into conditions in the valley. Three
sites in Gloucestershire and its immediate area have been studied by Dr
Tony Brown over the last few years[32] with interesting results. All three
sites show that lime was the dominant tree species on the river terraces
during early prehistoric times, with lesser quantities of oak and elm,
possibly with an understory of hazel. On the river bank itself alder was
dominant.

Around the Ashmoor Common study area to the north of Tewkesbury,
the first changes to the composition of the native woodland began perhaps
as early as 3500 BC. At that time levels of elm pollen declined and this may
indicate the creation by Man of small clearances in the woodland (see
Chapter 3 below). Major episodes of woodland clearance are not, however,
represented in the Severn Valley at the sites so far investigated until about
1750 BC, the same time that cereal pollen first appears.[33]

Clearance did not take place all at once, it was a cumulative process and
certainly continued in later prehistoric times. At Ripple Brook, again near
Tewkesbury, evidence indicated that between about 920 and 400 BC the
whole character of the vegetation in that part of the Severn Valley changed
from being a heavily wooded area punctuated by a few, probably pastoral
clearings, to a landscape almost cleared of trees and intensively farmed with
a good proportion of arable land.[34] Further support for this change in
land–use and vegetation cover during the later Bronze Age and early Iron
Age may be found in the Avon Valley between Tewkesbury and Stratford,
where the pattern of sedimentation along this stretch of river changed
markedly about 650 BC. This is thought to result from a major increase in
the amount of deforestation taking place along the valley sides.[35]

When the Cotswolds began to be cleared is not known at present.
However, it is notable that two sites of Neolithic date, the Hazleton long

barrow near Northleach, and Condicote Henge near Stow-on-the-Wold, were both situated in woodland clearings rather than in open country, at least according to the evidence provided by the species of snail shells recovered during recent investigations.[36] A rather different picture is revealed by studies of the environment round the Neolithic long barrow at Ascott-under-Wychwood, on the Oxfordshire Cotswolds. Here clearance of the woodland probably took place before about 3000 BC, some two or three centuries before the barrow itself was built.[37] From such disparate evidence it must at present be concluded that there was a considerable degree of variation in the speed and date of clearance in different parts of the Cotswold uplands. Much of the woodland which covered the area in early prehistoric times had, however, almost certainly been cleared away by the middle Iron Age (see Chapter 6).

In the upper Thames Valley no pollen sequences have yet been published in detail, but, as in the Avon Valley, sediments and alluvium suggest widespread woodland clearance in later prehistoric times.[38]

Prehistoric climate is rather more difficult to reconstruct. That it was, at some periods at least, rather different from today is certain, but how different is a matter of some debate.[39] Early prehistoric climate cannot be determined with accuracy, but from 10,000 BC, with the disappearance of the glacial ice caps, it is generally thought that the climate gradually became warmer and drier, reaching a peak about 4000 BC when average air temperatures may have been as much as 2 degrees Celsius warmer than today. After this, during the later part of the Neolithic period temperatures declined slightly and the climate became more continental. An improvement during the early and middle Bronze Age was followed by a deterioration, with noticeably increased rainfall, from about 1000 BC. During much of the Iron Age the climate was probably very much like that of today.[40]

It is against this backdrop of a changing environment that the prehistoric inhabitants of Gloucestershire lived. Of course most of the changes which seem clear to us today were not perceptible to individuals at the time, they took place much too slowly for that.

2

The Earliest Inhabitants (to c 3500 BC)

Early Man and the Ice Age

The earliest inhabitants of Gloucestershire were probably small bands of hunters visiting the area in pursuit of wild animals which would have provided an important source of food and raw materials. The only remaining traces of these people are a few flint tools, and even these are difficult to date as they have all come to light by chance rather than as finds recovered during controlled excavations.

It is, however, clear that Man arrived in Gloucestershire during what geologists call the Pleistocene Ice Age, which is currently dated to the period between about 2 million years ago and about 12,000 years ago.[1] The Ice Age was not, however, a single expansion and retreat of the polar ice-caps; rather there were at least four successive advances and retreats. At periods of maximum glaciation, ice covered most of Britain, but the periods between glacial advances, interglacials as they are called, were much like today, if not warmer, with well developed soils, mixed-species woodland, and open plains which hosted a wide range of animals. Even within glacial episodes there were warmer periods, interstadials as these are called.

Fluctuations in sea-level, and concomitant changes in coastline, accompanied these glacial advances and retreats, but generally speaking Britain was an island during the interglacials and variously connected to the continental mainland during the colder spells when so much sea water was locked-up as ice in the enlarged polar ice-caps.[2]

Only the first two glacial advances, the Beestonian and the Anglian glaciations, covered parts of Gloucestershire; the later two advances, the Wolstonian and the Devensian glaciations respectively penetrated rather less far south, leaving the Gloucestershire area during these periods rather like today's arctic tundra.

Understanding the nature and extent of early settlement in Gloucestershire, and indeed in Britain as a whole, is made difficult by the disturbance of archaeological sites during the successive episodes of glaciation. As the ice-caps advanced across the landscape almost all traces of earlier occupation were wiped away; swept up and moved around by the ice together with thousands of tons of soil and rock. When the ice melted all this debris was deposited as moraines which, in many areas, were then sorted by fast-flowing swollen rivers to form the gravel terraces which still dominate our major river valleys. For this reason, except where special conditions of protection are found, such as in caves, only the most robust remains of early Man survive, mostly just flint tools and a few of the more resilient bones. From what little that does survive, however, at least an outline of early settlement can be reconstructed even if the details are vague.

According to available evidence it was after the Anglian glaciation that Man first moved into western Britain, probably during the early part of the Hoxnian interglacial sometime about 400,000 BC.[3] Occasional use of the area continued during the more mild spells within the penultimate, Wolstonian, glaciation and through the Ipswichian interglacial. During the height of the final glacial period, the Devensian, Britain was largely deserted, and it was not until the landscape had begun to recover from the effects of this glaciation after about 12,000 BC that the area was again resettled.

Hoxnian and Wolstonian settlement

The tools from western England which were used by Man during the Hoxnian interglacial and the Wolstonian glacial phases – the lower and middle Palaeolithic in conventional archaeological terminology – belong to what is called the Acheulian tradition.[4] Such tools are found widely over northern Europe and are best characterized by fine pear-shaped handaxes. These were made by taking a piece of stone, usually flint, and then flaking off unwanted pieces from both sides (bifacial working as it is called) until the desired shape and finish was achieved.

Acheulian handaxes are known in a variety of sizes and appear to have been multi-purpose tools useful as knives, saws, choppers and cleavers in both domestic and hunting activities. Other tools which are sometimes associated with these handaxes include 'ovates' and points of various sorts.[5]

Acheulian tools have been found at 14 findspots within Gloucestershire, of which five are on the gravels east of Gloucester and eight lie on the gravels beside the upper Thames and its north bank tributaries. Generally, these gravels are poorly dated, but were probably deposited or restructured during the Devensian glaciation, so the tools included in them must belong to an earlier period.[6] One further implement, from Charlton Abbots on the Cotswolds, may also belong to this period, although its exact provenance and details of the circumstances under which it was found are rather vague.[7] Finds of quartzite and flint handaxes and worked flakes are also known from

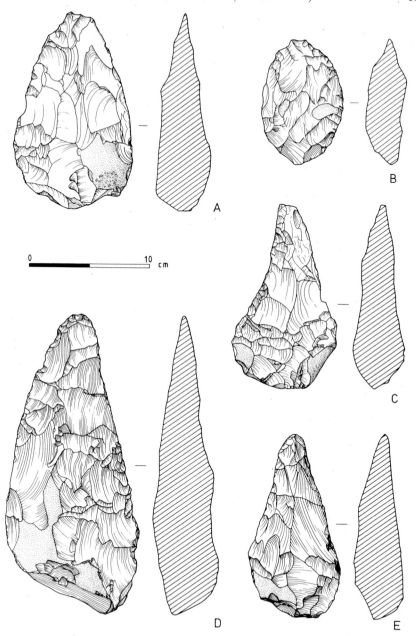

Acheulian tools and weapons from Gloucester. (A) Meyseyhampton; (B) South Cerney; (C) Longlevens, Gloucester; (D) Brockworth, Gloucester; (E) Halford Quarry, South Cerney.

the gravel deposits along the Avon Valley around Twyning in the north of the county but these have not yet been fully published.[8]

Just outside the county important finds of Acheulian implements have come to light near Beckford (Hereford and Worcester),[9] and along the Bristol Avon near its confluence with the Severn.[10]

In the Severn Valley the most prolific site yielding Acheulian implements is at Barnwood on the east side of Gloucester.[11] Here, a bed of locally derived oolitic gravel representing the third main terrace of the Severn has been recognized in two adjacent gravel pits, Lillies Field, off Upton Lane, and Forty Acre Field. Two handaxes have been found in this gravel, together with several worked flakes which are probably of the same period. The animal bones present include the remains of mammoth, musk ox, horse and woolly rhinoceros, but it is far from certain that they are of the same period as the flint tools.[12]

Other tools in the Acheulian tradition from the Barnwood area include an implement from a gravel pit at Great Witcombe,[13] a handaxe of late Acheulian type found during the construction of a sewer trench at Brockworth,[14] and another handaxe (ficron- type) found in gravel beneath the garden of a house in Longlevens.[15]

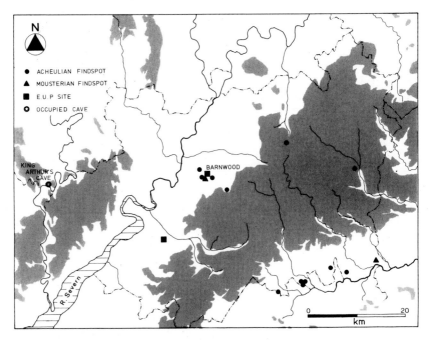

Map showing the findspots of tools and weapons dating to before c 12,000 BC.

To the east of the Cotswolds lower Palaeolithic tools are well represented in the gravels of the upper Thames Valley.[16] Handaxes have been found during gravel extraction at Cerney Wick,[17] Meyseyhampton,[18] Poole Keynes,[19] South Cerney,[20] Fairford,[21] and the area south of South Cerney.[22] The last mentioned find is the most recently discovered specimen, and a close examination of place where is it was found revealed that the gravel from which it derived was laid down in the mid Devensian period; the handaxe is therefore older than 40,000 years BC.[23]

Gravels along the north bank tributaries of the Thames also contain Palaeolithic tools, as shown by the find of an Acheulian handaxe at Santhill Gravel Pit near Bourton-on-the-Water in 1963.[24] The cutting edge of this specimen is heavily abraded, perhaps by much use in antiquity.

The Acheulian industries of northern Europe are usually associated with an early species of Man known as *Homo erectus*.[25] Occupation sites of this period suggest hunting camps, and it is generally thought that at this time small communities, or bands, roamed widely over the north European Plain following their prey.[26] As climatic conditions allowed, different species were available within any given area. During cold periods mammoth, woolly rhinocerus, bison, wild horse and reindeer would be dominant while in warmer periods fallow deer, giant ox, horse, straight-tusked elephant, rhinocerus, bear, lion, jaguar and sabre-toothed tiger would be available.[27] It should not, however, be assumed that these early hunters always tracked down and killed their prey themselves. Some, if not all communities, may have obtained their meat supplies simply by scavenging the left-overs remaining from kills made by other animals.[28] Plant foods, generally far easier to procure than meat, may indeed have constituted the major part of the diet at this time, but such activities leave very little trace in the archaeological record.

The evidence from Gloucestershire, as we have seen, does not provide any details about the life-style of these people in the area. However, the fact that the tools recovered from the county are generally in a fairly fresh condition hints that the ice did not move them far from where they were first deposited and it can therefore be suggested that at least the major river valleys in the area were being used as hunting grounds, or as routeways between the uplands to the north and west, and the open plains to the south and east.

The Ipswichian interglacial and the age of Neanderthal Man

The later part of the middle Palaeolithic period in Britain, broadly corresponding to the Ipswichian interglacial, is characterized by the introduction of implements of the Mousterian tradition of toolmaking.[29]

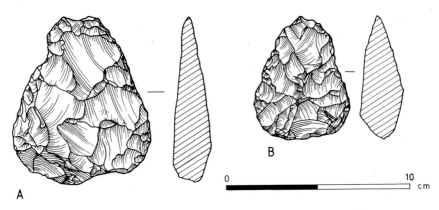

Mousterian handaxes from Gloucestershire: (A) Barnwood, Gloucester; (B) Lechlade.

Mousterian handaxes are distinctive because they are more triangular in outline than their Acheulian predecessors. More important, however, was the development of a much wider range of tools, some of them made on small flakes of flint or stone. For the first time it was scrapers, knives and points rather than handaxes which dominated most tool-kits.

From Gloucestershire, a possible Mousterian handaxe came to light during gravel extraction at Lechlade,[30] and one of the Barnwood handaxes already mentioned lies on the borderline between the Acheulian and the Mousterian traditions.[31] A small triangular-shaped handaxe and Mousterian flake tools have also been found at Barnwood.[32]

On the continent, Mousterian tradition tools have long been associated with *Homo Neanderthalis*, Neanderthal Man[33] and recently firm traces of this species of early Man have been found in Britain.[34]

The changes in tool design seen so clearly in the development of the Mousterian industries may indicate changes in economy, and it is perhaps from this period that the skills of hunting as distinct from scavenging really came to the fore as a means of providing food.

Caves, camps and the arrival of modern Man

About 40,000 BC modern Man, *Homo sapiens sapiens*, first appeared in northern Europe.[35] This marks the transition to what is known archaeologically as the earlier upper Palaeolithic, and with modern Man comes new flintworking technology and new tool types.[36]

The flintwork characteristic of this period is very fine compared with earlier products. Flintworkers of the earlier upper Palaeolithic had learnt how to make long narrow flakes – blades as they are properly called – by

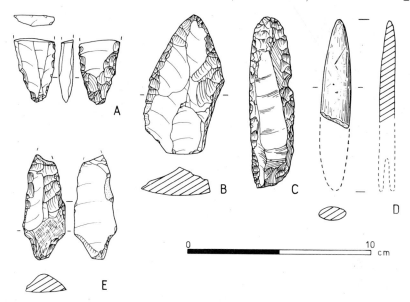

Selection of tools and weapons of earlier upper Palaeolithic date. (A) King Arthur's Cave, Whitchurch (Hereford and Worcester); (B), (D) and (E) Forty Acre Field, Barnwood, Gloucester; (C) Eastington Gravel Pit.

carefully shaping a block of raw flint into a core so that thin slivers could then be detached by applying pressure with a soft punch, in many cases probably a piece of bone. The flint blades created in this way were then made into tools such as knives, points, and scrapers by retouching the edges of the flint blade to blunt them or to shape the tool for hafting.

In Gloucestershire, evidence of activities during this period is just as scarce as for earlier times. The Barnwood gravels again provide the best material, and in Bed 3 at Forty Acre Field a range of objects came to light in the 1930s and 40s.[37] These appear to represent the remains of a small open encampment of the earlier upper Palaeolithic; the implements recovered included two blades, one of which was possibly a tanged point, three scrapers, and an ivory point.

Another possible open campsites of the period may be represented by finds from an old gravel pit beside the A38 at Eastington near Stroud. One find is an elongated blade retouched along both sides and from its condition it seems clear that it derived from the gravel deposits at the pit.[38] Less satisfactory is a second piece from the same area if not the same pit. This specimen is again a flint blade made into a tool, but the retouch is much more extensive and its fresh condition gives grounds for doubting its affinity with earlier upper Palaeolithic flintwork.[39]

King Arthur's Cave, Whitchurch (Hereford and Worcester). [Photograph: Author]

At least some of the caves in the Wye Valley were occupied during the earlier upper Palaeolithic. The most extensively documented is King Arthur's Cave, Whitchurch, (Hereford and Worcester) on the west bank of the Wye above Symond's Yat. This cave is about 100m above the present level of the River Wye and consists of two chambers, the largest about 12m deep. Excavations both inside and outside the cave were carried out by W.S. Symonds in 18709–1,[40] and Herbert Taylor in 1925–7.[41] At least two levels of occupation were found, of which the earliest comprised a cave earth containing bones of wooly rhinocerus, mammoth, hyaena, horse, bison, the great Irish Elk and reindeer.

The onset of colder conditions associated with the last glacial episode, the Devensian, made much of northern Europe unattractive to hunter-gatherer groups, and during the height of the glacial advance, from about 25,000 BC down to 12,000 BC Britain seems to have been unoccupied, or at least visited by small bands only very occasionally.[42]

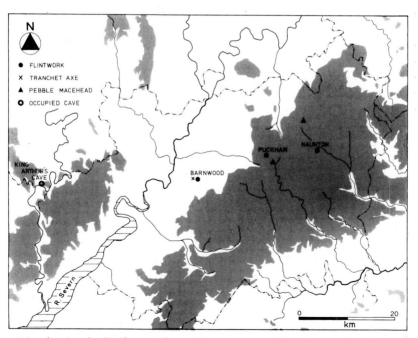

Map showing the distribution of recorded early post-glacial settlements (later upper Palaeolithic and early Mesolithic).

Early post glacial times

With the retreat of the last ice sheets of the Devensian glaciation, and the accompanying climatic improvement about 10,000 BC, the Gloucestershire area was transformed from a tundra environment to one in which woodland predominated.[43] The sea-level rose as water which had been locked up in the ice-caps melted. By about 6000 BC the English Channel had formed and Britain took on something of its present outline.[44]

Occupation in Gloucestershire from the closing stages of the Devensian glaciation at the end of the Palaeolithic through into the earlier stages of the Mesolithic period was scant according to present evidence.[45]

King Arthur's Cave beside the River Wye was reoccupied in the late upper Palaeolithic, as shown by the presence of Creswellian type flint tools which were found in the upper occupation level, separated from the earlier levels by stalagmite and sterile red sand.[46] Elsewhere in Gloucestershire settlements must have existed, but as yet they remain illusive.

Claims that cave paintings had been discovered in a small rock shelter in the Wye Valley[47] have since proven bogus,[48] but it should not be forgotten

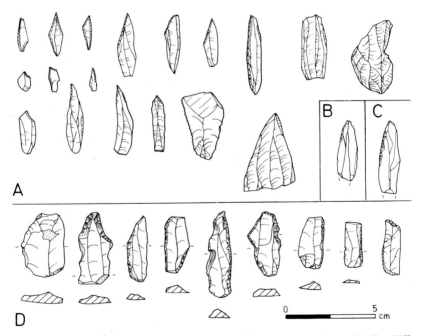

Selection of late upper Palaeolithic and early Mesolithic tools and weapons. (A) Tog Hill, Cold Ashton (Avon); (B) Naunton; (C) Puckham, Sevenhampton; (D) King Arthur's Cave, Whitchurch, (Hereford and Worcester).

that the late glacial period was one of great artistic expression, as shown most clearly by the well known cave paintings of the Dordogne. Decorated and ornamented animals bones of this date are known from cave sites on the Mendips and the Pennines.[49]

Over the county boundary in Avon, a flint scatter at Tog Hill, Cold Ashton,[50] contains a few distinctive tools of earlier Mesolithic type, including early forms of microlith which probably date to the seventh or sixth millennium BC.[51] These microliths are small flint blades, often blunted along one side, which are thought to have been mounted as barbs in wooden or bone harpoons. Large, obliquely blunted, points are also common at Tog Hill and are found elsewhere in Gloucestershire, for example at Naunton and Sevenhampton on the Cotswold uplands,[52] although on their own these pieces are very difficult to date precisely.

One axe of Mesolithic (tranchet) type has so far been reported from Gloucestershire, probably from Barnwood, Gloucester, although the exact provenance is uncertain.[53] If an authentic find, this example lies on the periphery of the distribution of such tools; most are from south-eastern England.

Perforated pebbles are also rather poorly represented in the county. These implements, some of which might have been weights for digging sticks, are usually natural pebbles which have been perforated by grinding or pecking a hollow on both sides until they join, thus producing a hole with an hour-glass profile. Two examples are known from the county, one from Temple Guiting[54] the other from Andoversford.[55]

One possible explanation for the paucity of evidence for this period is that sites in river valleys and sheltered coombs were used for settlement but have since become sealed beneath layers of soil and rock of more recent date so that now their identification is most difficult. Only further research backed up by excavation will tell.

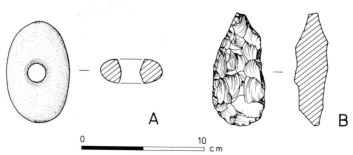

A   B

0   10
cm

Mesolithic tools. (A) Pebble hammer from Temple Guiting; (B) Tranchet axe from Barnwood, Gloucester.

The deer hunters

From about 6500 BC the early settlement of Gloucestershire comes into sharper focus because many more sites can be recognized. These belong to what is known as the later Mesolithic and are characterized by the presence of geometric microliths, including triangular forms, and tool made on small, narrow, flint blades.[56]

Flint is not native to the Cotswolds and all the pieces used in prehistoric times must have been brought in from elsewhere. Many assemblages are characterized by a variety of different types of flint, and it is likely that most groups obtained their supplies from outcrops encountered during their annual cycle of movements following migratory herds of animals and making best use of seasonal resources known to be rich in particular areas. In some cases, however, groups may not have encountered flint during their everyday existence and it is possible that even at this early date nodules of raw flint or finished flint tools were passed from group to group through some form of simple exchange system or trading arrangement.[57] Everywhere, flint was used very frugally at this time. Tools tended to be

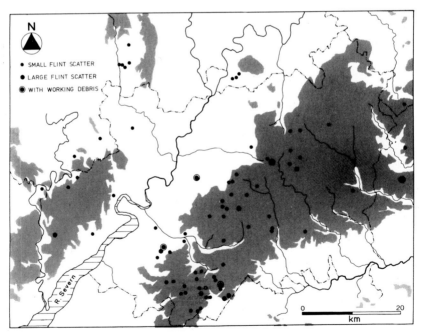

Map showing the distribution of recorded later Mesolithic settlement (*c* 6500 – *c* 3500 BC).

small which may be a product of both the need to minimize weight when on hunting trips, and the reworking of broken pieces rather than using new flint.

Over 40 sites in the county have yielded late Mesolithic flint tools, mostly on the Cotswolds, but some on gravel spreads in the Severn Valley and along the Leadon up into Hereford and Worcester, and also on the higher ground to the west of the Severn in the Forest of Dean. Sadly, no sites of this period have been investigated through excavation except where chance finds have been encountered during the course of work on later sites, as for example at the Hazleton North long barrow, the Syreford Mill Iron Age and Romano-British site, Whittington, and the Frocester Court Roman villa.

At some sites very extensive scatters of late Mesolithic flintwork extending over several hectares have been recorded. Around Troublehouse, Cherington, for example, fieldwalking by Arthur Witchell identified a scatter of Mesolithic flintwork which yielded over 37 microliths of different sorts together with scrapers, awls, hollow scrapers perhaps for shaving arrow shafts to get them straight, serrated blades, and knives. In addition to the tools, many discarded cores and waste flakes were collected.[58] The assemblage was not confined to flint, which was mostly brought in from the chalk downs to the east, but included upper Greensand chert, Portland chert, water-worn flint pebbles, and a rather unusual honey-coloured flint.[59] This may illustrate the range of connections fostered by the people living in the area, or perhaps the radius of their wanderings.

Another similar site is known at Long Newnton. Here, late Mesolithic flintwork is scattered over three fields, which total over 20ha in extent, overlooking the upper Thames Valley.[60] Fieldwalking brought to light over 5400 pieces of flint, including 23 microliths, and a variety of retouched flakes, scrapers, knives, points and awls. Working debris and spent cores were also found, and it may be noted that again a variety of different kinds of flint and chert had been used for the manufacture of tools.

Possibly the largest assemblage of late Mesolithic flintwork in Gloucestershire comes from Syreford Mill, Whittington. It was recovered during the excavation of an Iron Age and Romano-British site under the direction of Wilfred Cox. No certain Mesolithic features such as postholes or pits were recorded, probably because the whole area had been heavily disturbed in later prehistoric and Roman times. Preliminary analysis[61] suggests that the assemblage includes over 100 cores and commensurate quantities of waste debris. Over 56 microliths were also recovered, including a wide variety of different forms. The manufacture of microliths at the site is illustrated by the presence of 14 microburins – small blade-ends snapped off during the production of microliths. The most likely interpretation of this assemblage is that it represents a manufacturing focus which also served as a settlement. The situation of the site on a sheltered and

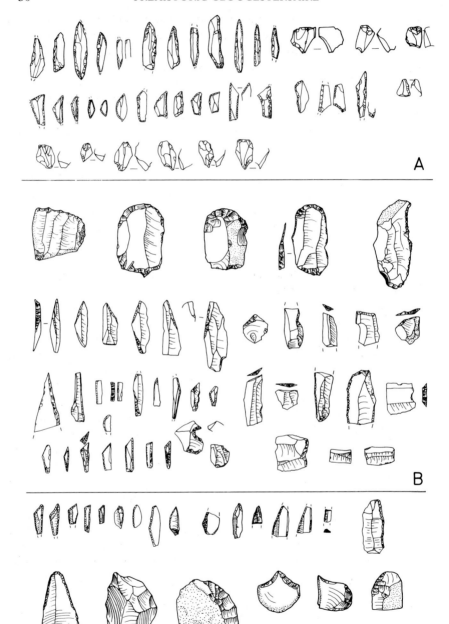

Selection of tools and weapons of late Mesolithic date. (A) Syreford Mill, Whittington;
(B) Troublehouse, Cherington; (C) Long Newnton.

well-drained gravel spread beside a small stream would be ideal for such a purpose, and would also allow easy access to the surrounding uplands.

A recently recovered assemblage of late Mesolithic flintwork from beneath the Hazleton North long barrow, contains at least 55 microliths, in a similar range of shapes to those from Syreford.[62] Preliminary work on environmental samples from this sites suggests that the Mesolithic occupation was focused in a woodland clearing.[63]

On the eastern side of the Cotswolds at Ascott-under-Wychwood (Oxfordshire), Mesolithic flintwork of fifth millennium BC date from beneath another Neolithic barrow presents a broadly similar picture. Here environmental evidence suggests that the Mesolithic community established itself in an area of open woodland, perhaps a small clearing, which after they left became more shaded as the tree canopy closed in.[64]

Large collections of Mesolithic flintwork are rare in the northern Cotswolds, although stray finds of microliths from surface collections and fieldwalking serve to confirm the presence of some activity in the area at this time. A microlith from Cow Common, Swell,[65] belongs to a class of tool characteristic of late Mesolithic assemblages in central England,[66] and may again indicate the distances over which these groups travelled.

West of the Severn, intensive fieldwalking has recently brought to light a number of late Mesolithic flint scatters, some of quite large size.[67] At Nedge Cop, Bearse Farm, St Briavels, for example, an area of high ground investigated in 1984–5 has yielded 12 microliths, scrapers, a core, and nine retouched blades.[68]

Clearly there are several different types of assemblage represented by the collections of flintwork currently known, and these probably relate to a range of sites where different sorts of activity would have been undertaken. Research into this sort of variability is still at an early stage and it would be premature to propose any sort of rigid site classification. It is, however, possible to differentiate two very general types of site. First, there are extensive flint scatters which contain a wide range of tool types and working debris. These are usually set in sheltered spots, often near a permanent water supply and on the junction between different types of environment. Such sites may tentatively be interpreted as base camps occupied for perhaps several months at a stretch where tools, weapons, clothes and many other everyday items would be made or repaired and a wide range of domestic activities undertaken. In contrast, the second identifiable type of sites are rather smaller in size and the finds from them consist mostly of weapons and small amounts of working waste. These sites are often in extreme locations, for example high in the uplands or down in large river valleys, and may tentatively be interpreted as hunting camps used for perhaps only one or two nights by small groups of people, and where broken tools and weapons could be quickly repaired.[69]

Because no late Mesolithic sites in Gloucestershire have been explored by excavation it is difficult to reconstruct the economic background to settlement in the area at this time. Microliths are known to have been parts of composite tools, usually barbed spears and harpoons used for hunting animals and probably also fish. On the coast, Mesolithic communities relied heavily on the collection of shellfish and off-shore fishing. Inland, evidence from elsewhere in Britain suggests that hunting and gathering were still the main sources of food.

The woodlands which clothed the Cotswolds during late Mesolithic times would have been ideal for deer to browse, and wild pig and wild cattle would also have been widely available. Hazlenuts were certainly among the fruits collected.[70]

No burials of Mesolithic date have been reported from the area, indeed very few are known from Britain as a whole. Because of this, nothing can be said of the physical anthropology of any individuals, or of the population as a whole. The density of settlement was probably fairly low, with perhaps as few as two or three small communities based in the area at any one time.

By the fourth millennium BC the combined effects of several thousand years of low intensity but extensive exploitation of the countryside were probably beginning to take their toll. There were certainly small clearances in the woodland, and taking the evidence from Britain as a whole, groups may have been beginning to settle down in the sense of relying on a more restricted range of food resources while curtailing their annual cycles of movement. Coastal communities were at the forefront of this trend, but there were ample opportunities for groups in the Gloucestershire area to settle down too. Rich landscape diversity, which would have been reflected in a wealth of different foodstuffs and the abundance of permanent springs and small rivers, would have offered many ideal sites.

These changes, which peaked in the mid fourth millennium BC, set the scene for very much more far-reaching transformations in economy and society which were to take place in the centuries following 3500 BC.

3

The First Farmers in Gloucestershire (c 3500 – c 2500 BC)

The introduction of farming

From about 3500 BC, the communities living in the Gloucestershire area underwent a number of fundamental changes in their lifestyles as reliance on hunting and gathering as the main source of food was replaced by farming. The centuries following these changes are traditionally known as the Neolithic period.[1]

The farming way of life originated far away from Britain in the Near East where plants and animals were domesticated perhaps as early as 7000 BC. The idea spread rapidly across southern and central Europe because it provided a more predictable and sustainable food supply.[2] The changeover from hunting and gathering to farming in Britain is traditionally portrayed as a rapid transformation; a revolution prompted by the arrival from the continent of colonists who were well versed in farming ways and equipped with all the necessary apparatus and stock. But this view may be largely illusory.

Late Mesolithic communities in Britain had already come to rely on a relatively restricted range of resources and were a lot less mobile than their early Mesolithic predecessors. Coastal communities were undoubtedly aware of the adoption of farming on the continent and could easily have introduced cereals (wheat and barley) and sheep to augment domesticated pigs and cattle which could have been drawn from the wild fauna in Britain. Making the shift from hunting and gathering to farming may therefore have been the culmination of a long series of social changes stretching back several millennia rather than the result of colonization. Unfortunately, one of the difficulties of resolving exactly how farming was taken up in this country is that the tools necessary for the two types of subsistence are fundamentally different, even though the people using them may have been the same.[3]

Opening up the wildwood

Traces of the earliest farming groups in Gloucestershire take two forms. First there is evidence for changes to the environment, and second there are the remains of the settlements and burials of these communities.

Most of the mid-west of England was clothed in natural woodland in the early fourth millennium BC. These woods, sometimes known as the wildwoods,[4] had undergone continuous development since the regeneration of vegetation cover after the last Ice Age, and by the early Neolithic were dominated by alder, hazel, and oak, with lesser quantities of elm and lime.[5] The soils were fertile and deep, in places decalcified and enriched with windborne loess.[6] In order to realize the potential of the land for agriculture, however, one of the first tasks facing the earliest farmers was to clear areas of forest for settlements, fields and grazing plots. Evidence for this can be glimpsed in pollen samples from the region.

At Ashmoor Common, Kempsey (Hereford and Worcester), analysis of peat deposits in an old channel of the River Severn revealed declining elm pollen levels from about 3500 BC onwards, and this may indicate the creation of small areas of pasture within the woodland.[7] On the Cotswolds, analysis of pollen and the remains of snail-shells preserved in an ancient soil buried beneath a long barrow at Ascott-under-Wychwood (Oxfordshire), shows that fairly dense woodland in the vicinity of the site was cleared before about 3000 BC.[8]

The scale of these clearances should not, however, be overestimated because they would rarely have been more than a few hundred metres across; moth-holes in a blanket of wildwood. What they show is that interference with the natural vegetation was underway on a previously unprecedented scale and that Man was beginning to manipulate the environment to his own ends. In a few places, natural glades or small scale clearances made by Mesolithic groups may have provided breaks in the woodland cover which could be settled by early farming groups.

Among the many changes accompanying the development of farming was the introduction of pottery for everyday and ceremonial uses. The earliest wares were characteristically plain open bowls with a carinated or shouldered profile. These vessels were usually well made and their findspots provide a useful indicator of the position and extent of early Neolithic settlement.

At Hazleton North long barrow, on the Cotswolds north-east of Andoversford, a midden, or rubbish heap, was found sealed beneath the barrow mound.[9] Preliminary analysis of the contents of this midden indicates the presence of distinctive early Neolithic pottery together with flint tools, animal bones, quern-stone fragments, and cereal grains. Nearby was a group of postholes and a hearth which may represent the remains of a

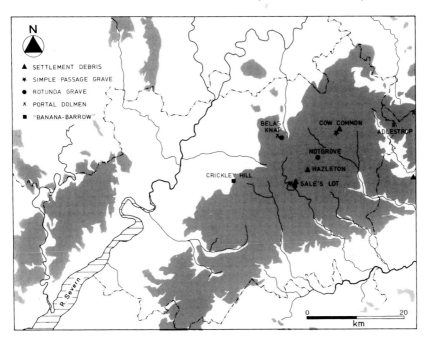

Map showing the distribution of known early Neolithic settlements and burial monuments (*c* 3500 – *c* 3000 BC).

rectangular structure of some kind, possibly contemporary with the midden. Radiocarbon dates suggest that the midden results from occupation in the period around 3000 BC.[10]

Similar evidence was recovered at Sale's Lot, Withington, where excavations in 1963–5 revealed the postholes of a structure, probably a dwelling, again apparently sealed below a middle Neolithic long barrow.[11] No midden was found, but fragments of pottery, over 80 pieces of flint, including an arrowhead and scrapers, and a sandstone rubber from the area of the building suggest a small compact settlement site. Within the building was a hearth, and scattered over the floor were a number of charred hazelnut shells.

Early Neolithic pottery was also found at the Cow Common long barrow, Swell, during excavation in the 1870s, although whether it came from a pre-barrow settlement or from the barrow itself is not known.[12] Further afield, a comparable settlement is known on the eastern edge of the Cotswolds at Ascott-under-Wychwood (Oxfordshire). Here, hearths and pits dating to about 3000 BC were accompanied by quantities of pottery, flintwork and animal bone, but how long this settlement lasted is impossible to say.[13]

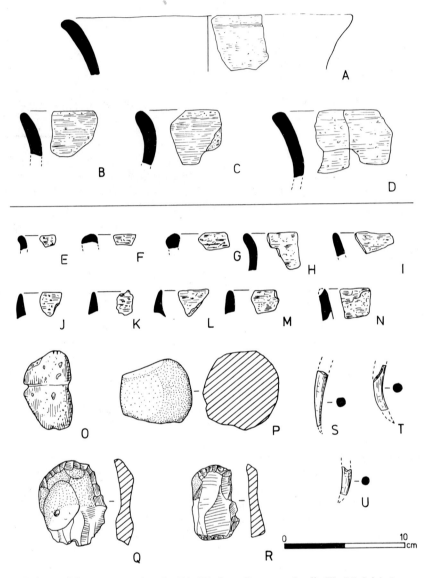

Early Neolithic pottery and tools. (A)–(D) Cow Common, Swell; (E)–(U) Sale's Lot, Withington.

Burial monuments which may be tentatively associated with early farming groups can also be recognized in Gloucestershire, often by the fact that they were later incorporated within, and thus sealed beneath, much larger structures built sometime after about 3000 BC. A number of different

Reconstruction of the early Neolithic rotunda grave at Notgrove [Drawing: Jane Timby]

types are represented and this may be a reflection of the autonomy of each individual community.

Among the most distinctive early Neolithic burial monuments are the circular structures known as rotunda graves. Most is known about the one discovered beneath the Notgrove long barrow, during excavations by Elsie Clifford in 1935.[14] The rotunda cairn measured about 7m in diameter and stood some 0.76m high. It was neatly built of local stone and at its centre was a polygonal-shaped cist, constructed from thin slabs of local limestone. Within the cist were the remains of an adult male aged about 50, together with two pieces of unworked flint. A similar structure is known at Sale's Lot, Withington, where excavations by Helen O'Neil revealed traces of a circular or oval monument some 5m across. Much of this example was destroyed before the excavation began, but traces of a burial in the form of a few human teeth and a flint leaf-shaped arrowhead remained in the centrally placed cist.[15] Yet another example may be at Belas Knap, Sudeley, near Winchcombe, where excavations in 1865 revealed a 'broken circle of stones' about 2.2m in diameter beneath the later tomb. Around this circle was a deposit of ashy soil.[16]

Portal dolmen represent a rather different type of early Neolithic tomb. These monuments are typically built from large slabs of local stone with three uprights at the front set in an H-shaped formation and another slab set several metres behind. A large roofing stone rested across the uprights.[17] The most complete portal dolmen on the Cotswolds is the Whispering Knights at Rollright (Oxfordshire). Here the four uprights are local limestone blocks, each originally over 2.0m high. The capstone, which has become displaced since Neolithic times, measures approximately 2.5m long by 1.75m wide by 0.7m thick. A low circular mound representing no more than a platform probably once surrounded the chamber, but this has long-since disappeared.[18] No burials are known from the site, but this is hardly surprising in view of the fact that it has been ruinous for many centuries.[19]

Four other possible portal dolmen tombs can be recognized on the Oxfordshire Cotswolds at the Hoar Stone at Enstone, the Hoar Stone at Langley, the Hawkstone at Spelbury, and the Hoar Stone at Steeple Barton.[20] It is also tempting to interpret the H-shaped portal setting (the so-called false-entrance) in the forecourt of the Belas Knap long barrow as the remains of a portal dolmen which was later incorporated within a larger and more elaborate tomb. The lintel stone seen today is a 19th century replacement,[21] but when the original lintel was lifted during excavations in 1863 the skeletons of a young man of less than 20 and five children variously aged between 6 months and 8 years were found within the rubble behind the portal. Also present were bones of horse and pig, several flint flakes, including a serrated blade, and fragments of coarse pottery.[22]

Whispering Knights, Rollright (Oxfordshire). A portal dolmen on the north Cotswolds. [Photograph: Author]

Another fairly common type of early Neolithic burial monument is the simple passage grave. These comprise circular mounds within which are rectangular or polygonal chambers accessible from the outside by way of a short passage.[23] In contrast to rotunda graves, these monuments contain multiple burials. A number of possible examples are known in Gloucestershire, but none have been fully excavated under ideal conditions. A large circular structure to the south-east of the rotunda grave at Sale's Lot may be a simple passage grave later incorporated into a long barrow.[24] Another example is the Swell 2 round barrow on Cow Common, Swell, which was investigated in about 1874 by Canon Greenwell. During that excavation he uncovered a roughly circular chamber approached by a passage opening from the west side of the mound. There were indications that the roof had originally been corbelled, but the chamber and the upper part of the mound had been lost through quarrying for stone during the construction of a neighbouring wall.[25] Some of the so-called 'beehive chambers' known on the Cotswolds, for example at Ablington, Bibury, and Saltway Barn, Bibury, may also be simple passage graves in origin.[26]

One final monument which might date to the early part of the Neolithic period is the so-called 'banana-barrow' found sealed beneath the causewayed enclosure on Crickley Hill, Coberley.[27] This monument comprised

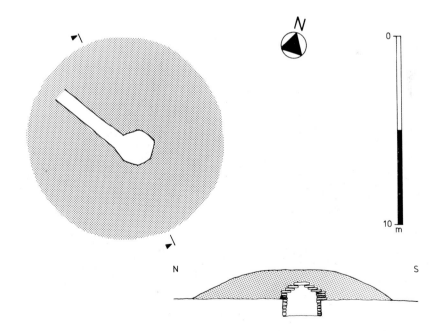

Plan and section of the simple passage grave at Cow Common, Swell.

an enclosure about 8.0m long, bounded by a series of quarry pits, and, as the name suggests, was banana-shaped in plan. Spoil from the pits had seemingly been piled up in the central area, but was removed when the causewayed enclosure was built. The purpose of the structure is unclear, although it might have been a burial monument.

Together, these snippets of evidence suggest that early Neolithic farming groups in the county were widely dispersed, largely autonomous, communities living in small settlements. Little is known about their economy, although they certainly kept livestock and cultivated cereals. To what extent the distribution of known sites of this period may be regarded as significant is difficult to assess, but it may be no coincidence that the central Cotswolds seems to have been the focus of activity in view of its position on the watershed between the upper Thames Valley and the Severn Valley.

Expansion

The earliest farming groups in Gloucestershire were evidently successful. From about 3000 BC onwards the distribution of known monuments expands to cover most parts of the Cotswold uplands, and there is evidence too of settlement in the Forest of Dean and the Severn Vale, largely in the form of stray finds of flintwork and axeheads.

Farming could support a greater density of population than hunting and gathering because settlements could be permanent and territories smaller. The evidence suggests that by the middle of the third millennium BC the population of the area was perhaps twenty or thirty times that of the early Neolithic period, with perhaps as many as 150–200 small villages and farmsteads scattered across the landscape. This increase in density took its toll on the environment, especially through the clearance of woodland.

The greater number of known sites allows more detailed insights into the lives and organization of these communities. Moreover, a number of settlements and burial sites of this period have been excavated in the county over recent years, and two projects in particular have contributed much to our understanding of the period. The first, is the research excavation at Crickley Hill which has been undertaken annually since 1969 under the skillful direction of Dr Philip Dixon. This work has brought to light a succession of enclosed settlements.[28] Second, is a rescue excavation at the Hazleton North long barrow between 1979 and 1982 under the direction of Alan Saville which has provided much exciting new evidence about the construction and use of a chambered long barrow.[29] With such a wealth of material to hand, this period can be reviewed under a series of thematic headings.

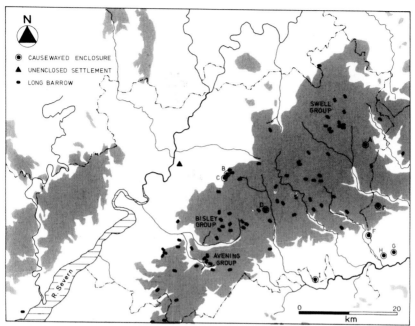

Map showing the distribution of recorded middle Neolithic settlements and burial monuments *c* 3000 – *c* 2500 BC. A = Icomb Hill; B = Crickley Hill; C = Peak Camp; D = Southmore Grove, Rendcomb; E = Signet Hill, Burford (Oxfordshire); F = Eastleach; G = Broadwell (Oxfordshire); H = Langford (Oxfordshire); I = Down Ampney.

Camps, settlements and land-use

A distinctive feature of the British Neolithic are the monuments known as causewayed camps.[30] These are enclosures bounded by a bank and ditch, in which the ditch is usually dug as a series of elongated pits, the plan of which is often compared to a string of sausages. Until the early 1970s no causewayed enclosures were known in Gloucestershire, but in the last 15 years no less than six have come to light within the county through aerial photography and chance finds; two have been excavated. Three further examples are known in eastern Oxfordshire,[31] and a possible example has been recognized through fieldsurvey at Dinedor Hill, Dinedor (Hereford and Worcester).[32]

Much debate surrounds the interpretation of causewayed enclosures, in particular whether they were settlements or ritual sites. It now seems that a variety of purposes underlies the similarities in construction technique, and that during the course of their lives the function of some enclosures

Aerial photograph of the causewayed enclosure at Eastleach. [Photograph: Author; Pilot: Ron Locke]

changed. It also seems that in western England at least, many, if not all, served as settlements of various kinds.

In Gloucestershire, causewayed camps are found in a variety of locations. Crickley Hill and the Peak Camp are situated on promontories of the Cotswold escarpment overlooking the Severn Vale. Icomb Hill and Southmore Grove, Rendcomb, are set on hilltops, while those at Eastleach and Down Ampney lie on lower ground in the upper Thames Valley. Size varies too, the largest is Eastleach with an area of 3–4ha, the smallest is Down Ampney which covers about 0.6ha. In most cases, the enclosures are situated on the junction of two or more distinct environments, for example the junction of upland and vale land in the case of Crickley Hill and the Peak Camp.[33]

At Crickley Hill the earliest enclosure comprised a double line of causewayed ditches, each with a stone rampart behind. There were at least four entrances, all provided with wooden gates. Both lines of ditches were deliberately filled, or became filled, on several occasions, and each time they were redug. After this complex had been in use for some centuries the causewayed ditches were abandoned and a new much larger ditch dug immediately outside and parallel to, the inner ditch of the earlier enclosure. Unlike the earlier arrangements, the new boundary ditch was continuous except for two causeways corresponding to the gateways through the rampart. The rampart of this second enclosure appears to have been defensive. In the interior the remains of roadways and houses have been found together with a flint-knapping area away from the living quarters.[34] Part of the site had seemingly been set aside for ritual or ceremonial

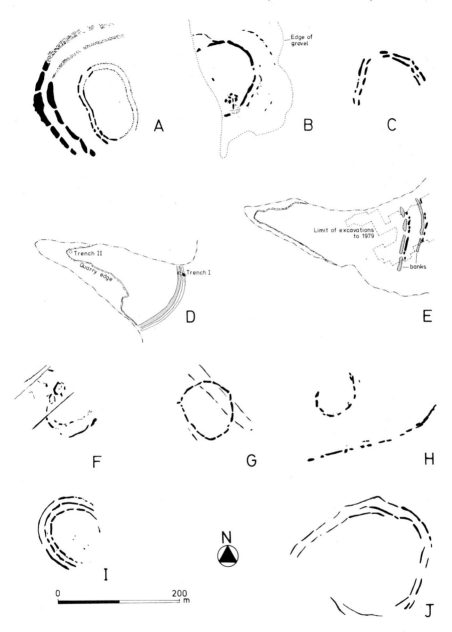

Plans of causewayed enclosures in Gloucestershire and eastern Oxfordshire. (A) Eastleach; (B) Aston (Oxfordshire); (C) Southmore Grove, Rendcomb; (D) Peak Camp, Cowley; (E) Crickley Hill, Coberley; (F) Down Ampney; (G) Signet hill, Burford (Oxfordshire); (H) Icomb Hill, Icomb; (I) Broadwell, (Oxfordshire); (J) Langford (Oxfordshire).

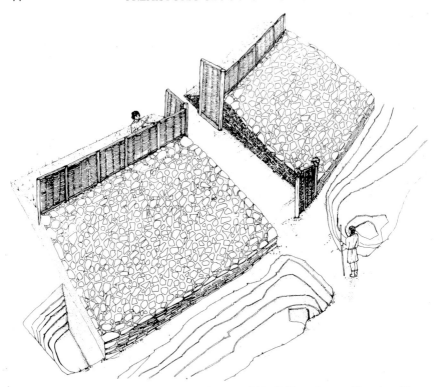

Crickley Hill, Coberley. Entrance to the second Neolithic enclosure. [Drawing: Liz Wilczynska after Philip Dixon]

purposes, the focus of which was a circular stone platform set within its own fenced enclosure and approached from the east through a gate.[35] Taken as a whole, the evidence from this second main enclosure suggests that the Crickley Hill was nothing less than a small fortified village by the mid third millennium BC.

Redigging of the ditches and remodelling of the ramparts was also a notable feature of the activities at Peak Camp, Cowley, to judge from a single section through the ramparts.[36] The range of finds from the rampart and the investigated features in the interior suggests that Peak Camp was also a settlement, and therefore all the more interesting for being less than 2km distant from Crickley Hill. The close proximity of these sites may indeed be an indication of the density of settlement at this time in choice areas. Altogether, the ditch at Peak Camp was redug no less than four times. The first stage is difficult to date, but radiocarbon dates for bone in the fill of the second episode of redigging combine to give a date of 2750 ± 45 BC;[37] phases III and IV followed some time later. The pottery from Peak Camp is similar to that from Crickley Hill and comprises mostly plain

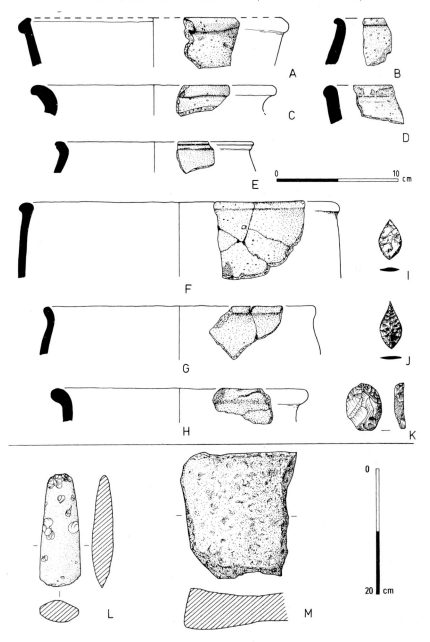

Selection of middle Neolithic tools, weapons, domestic equipment, and ornaments. (A)–(D) and (I)–(K) Crickley Hill, Coberley; (F)–(H) Peak Camp, Cowley; (L) Charlford; (M) Burn Ground, Hampnett.

round–bottomed bowls made in a variety of local fabrics. Carinated bowls typical of the pioneer farmers of the early Neolithic form a minor part of the assemblages, the most common types being straight-sided vessels with thickened and sometimes out-turned rims. Flintwork includes quantities of working waste,[38] and among the implements were scrapers, knives, axes, and finely made leaf-shaped arrowheads.

Settlement was not, however, confined to the causewayed enclosures at this time. Fieldsurveys in the north Cotswolds have brought to light many other possible habitation sites which now only survive as flint scatters.[39]

Knowledge of settlement patterns in the major river valleys is poor in comparison to the uplands. Despite the examination of large areas of terrace landscape in advance of gravel extraction, evidence for middle Neolithic activity in the upper Thames Valley is confined to the causewayed enclosures and a few stray finds of flint and stone axes.[40] Fieldsurveys have demonstrated that flint-scatter sites are rare in the Isbourne, Windrush, and Coln Valleys,[41] although some stray finds of axes and flint tools are known. In the Severn Valley stray finds are fairly abundant, and at Gloucester, traces of a possible settlement were discovered during excavations in advance of the construction of the new telephone exchange in Berkeley Street in 1969.[42] Here, a single pit cut into the natural subsoil was found to contain about one third of a middle Neolithic bowl and several pieces of flint. Such slight evidence is difficult to interpret, but if parts of the Severn Valley had been cleared of woodland for pasture at this time, the site at Gloucester could represent a herder's temporary encampment. Other similar small sites undoubtedly await discovery.[43]

The extent of settlement during the middle Neolithic is perhaps most clearly summarized by the distribution of flint and stone axes, many of which were simple woodman's tools lost or broken during woodland clearance or the collection of leaf fodder for animal feed. Over 540 axes or parts thereof have been recorded from the county to date. The main concentration lies on the Cotswold uplands, as might be expected from the distribution of known monuments. The area west of the River Severn was probably more intensively settled than the plot of axes suggests if the distribution of stray finds of other flintwork is anything to go by. When the area is subject to more detailed survey a pattern like that recorded in south-eastern Herefordshire is likely to extend down into the Forest of Dean.

The intensity of land-use undoubtedly varied greatly from place to place during middle Neolithic times. The lighter soils of the Cotswold uplands would have provided easily cultivated land suitable for arable, whereas the Severn Vale would have been better for pasture. The siting of causewayed enclosures on the Cotswolds to exploit the potential offered by contrasting environments has already been mentioned. The enclosures of the upper

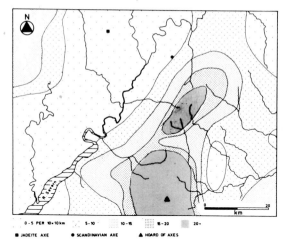

Map showing the density of recorded stone and flint axehead finds. The contours are drawn at intervals of 5 axes per 10×10km square by trend surface mapping. Total sample of axes in the analysis = 540.

Thames Valley are altogether different, however, in being situated on low ground within an homogeneous landscape. Rather than seeing these sites as permanent settlements it is tempting to interpret them as seasonal activity sites. However, until such time as they are examined by excavation these suggestions must remain speculations.

Subsistence

The early farmers relied for their food upon five basic resources: cattle, pigs, sheep, wheat (mainly emmer: *Triticum dicoccum*), and barley (mainly six-row barley: *Hordeum vulgare*).[44] Assessing the relative importance of each of these is not, however, easy. At both Peak Camp, and Crickley Hill, cattle were the dominant species according to the number of bones found, pig and sheep being less well represented. This frequency may not, however, correspond exactly to their contribution to diet since cattle may have been kept for milk, while pigs and sheep supplied meat. Indeed it is interesting to note that pig bones are more commonly represented than cattle and sheep among the finds from burial sites, possibly because of their value as meat for feasts and other ceremonial occasions.

Careful butchery of animals is evident from patterns of knife cuts noted on the animal bones from the Peak Camp, and this is a feature found at other sites of similar date in Britain.[45] Carcasses were clearly dismembered to maximize the yield of meat, hide, and bone.

Cereal production is directly represented by the charred grain which has been found at Crickley Hill, Peak Camp, and in the early Neolithic midden under the Hazleton North long barrow. Indirect evidence for the use of cereals includes crop processing equipment. Querns of middle Neolithic date have been found at Crickley Hill and among the stones used in the construction of the Burn Ground long barrow, Hampnett.[46] Flint sickles, many of which have a characteristic gloss along the cutting edge, are widespread on the Cotswolds, and a few examples are known from the Severn Valley.

Domesticated animals and cultivated cereals undoubtedly provided the staple diet of these communities, but contributions from hunting, gathering and fishing may also have been important. Wild animals, including horse, red deer, and fox, are represented by bones at a number of middle Neolithic sites in Gloucestershire, although whether they were hunted for meat or pelts, or were simply uninvited guests to the homestead must remain open to question. Hazelnuts were certainly gathered from the woods, no doubt alongside many other fruits and berries, continuing a tradition stretching back several millennia. Fish bones are hard to find on archaeological sites because of their small size so it is hardly surprising that to date none have been reported from Neolithic contexts in the county. Shellfish remains have, however, been noted in the final ditch recut at Peak Camp, and a pendant made from a dog whelk was found in the Nympsfield long barrow.[47]

Crafts and economy

The range of tools, ornaments and other objects manufactured during the middle Neolithic was considerable. Flint provided the main material for the manufacture of cutting tools. Waste flakes and spent cores at most sites of the period attest widespread flint working in the area, and it must be concluded that, with a few exceptions, raw material rather than finished items was imported from flint-rich areas to the south and east. Several flintworking floors within the enclosure at Crickley Hill have been invest-igated in detail.[48]

Leaf-shaped arrowheads are perhaps the most distinctive flint artefact of the period, but most assemblages also include a range of knives, scrapers, serrated blades, sickle pieces, axes, awls/points, laurel-leaf shaped spear tips, and notched blades. The last mentioned tools were possibly used as spokeshaves for straightening arrow- and spear-shafts.

Bone tools of various sorts are known, including spatulae, gouges, and awls. Ornaments were also made from bone, including beads, pendants, and armlets.[49]

Pottery production took place locally, probably within each community. Clay is plentiful in Gloucestershire, and scientific analysis has revealed that several different types were used.[50] Various materials were also added to the clay as tempering agents to make it easier to work and to give the finished products special properties. A wide range of vessels were manufactured, different types presumably having different functions. The careful choice of materials can be seen in the fact that 16 different mixes of clay and tempering agents were represented in the assemblage of pottery from Peak Camp. These 16 fabrics can be divided into two main groups: calcite tempered wares which would have been used as cooking and storage vessels, and limestone tempered wares which would have been storage vessels and eating/drinking vessels. Pottery with organic tempering (possibly straw or chaff), which is found in small quantities on many early and middle Neolithic sites in the west of England, may have been a special class of porous vessel for storing liquids such as milk which needs to be kept cool.

In addition to the many items that have survived, much use would have been made of wood, leather, and perhaps basketry which does not survive. Numerous woodworking tools, including adzes, axes, gouges, chisels, and wedges attest the importance of wood for houses, stock pens, tools, containers, and many other things beside. It is salutary to remember that almost all the flint and stone tools originally had wooden hafts or shafts. Wood was probably the most plentiful resource available to middle Neolithic communities.[51]

Burial and ritual

Throughout middle Neolithic times burial, ritual, and settlement were closely linked. This can be clearly seen at Crickley Hill, where not only was there a ceremonial area inside the enclosure, but also, in common with many other causewayed enclosures, human bones, especially skulls, lay in the ditches.[52]

The most numerous, and certainly the most impressive series of burials of this period are, however, those contained within monumental tombs; long barrows as they are called. These tombs have attracted attention since the earliest days of antiquarian interest in the prehistoric archaeology of the county, and have been the subject of much discussion and debate both before, and after they were made famous by Dr O.G.S. Crawford in his book *The long barrows of the Cotswolds*.[53]

The long barrows of the Cotswolds form part of a general tradition of long barrow construction found over much of Atlantic Europe during the early third millennium BC.[54] Regional styles can be identified within this overall

Aerial view of the Belas Knap long barrow, Sudeley. [Photograph: Royal Commission on the Historical Monuments of England]

distribution and one such style is the Cotswold-Severn family of tombs found on the Cotswolds, in north Wiltshire, along the western shores of the Bristol Channel in south-east Wales, and in the Black Mountains of Powys.[55] All the long barrows in Gloucestershire belong to the Cotswold-Severn group and share many features of construction and design.

About 70 long barrows are known within Gloucestershire, although more undoubtedly await discovery.[56] They are confined to the limestone uplands, mostly above the 120m contour, but their distribution is far from even and there are marked concentrations around Swell, Avening, and Bisley. No long barrows have to date been identified in the Forest of Dean, although one example is known on the western bank of the lower Severn at Heston Brake, Portskewett (Gwent), and sites are also known in south Herefordshire.[57]

Cotswold long barrows are rarely situated on hilltops as such, but usually on false crests or ridges a little way from the summits. They often command an impressive view in one or two directions. Many lie adjacent to steeply sloping ground on at least one side, but it would be wrong to place

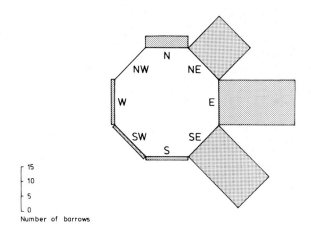

15
10
5
0
Number of barrows

Orientation of the long axis of long barrows in Gloucestershire.

undue emphasis on the impressive situation of most barrows because present evidence suggests that they were built in small woodland clearances rather than open country.[58]

There is a general tendency for the long axis of the mounds to be aligned between south-east to north-west and north-east to south-west, although there are sufficient exceptions to cast doubt on any reconstruction of specific beliefs based on common alignments. Occasionally, two barrows occur together as a pair, as for example at Hazleton North and South, and Eyford Hill and New Close, Upper Slaughter,[59] although whether such pairs were chronologically successive sites or contemporary monuments used by different communities is a matter for speculation.

In plan, Cotswold-Severn tombs have a number of distinctive features. The most noticeable element is the large mound or cairn, which is either trapezoidal or rectangular in plan. All were carefully built from stone and soil derived from quarries in the vicinity; in the case of the two barrows at Hazleton, the quarry pits lay immediately adjacent to the cairns.[60] A faced, dry-stone-wall circumscribed the cairn, and internal revetments were built in the course of heaping up the mound in order to stabilize the piles of rubble and facilitate construction. A forecourt was usually provided between two projecting horns at the wider end of the mound, perhaps to serve as a focus for rituals.

There is considerable variation in cairn size. Smaller tombs, such as Nympsfield long barrow, Frocester, are as little as 30m in length, while the largest examples in Gloucestershire, for example Colnpen, Coln St Dennis, and Lamborough Banks, Bibury, are nearly 100m long. Most lie within the range 30–60m. It should of course be remembered that a small increase in

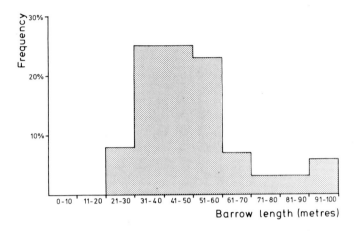

Histogram showing the recorded length of long barrows in Gloucestershire.

length actually means a very considerable increase in cairn volume, and it has been estimated that the construction of a medium to large sized tomb would require about 16,000 man-hours, or the equivalent of 10 people working an eight hour day continuously for about 7 months.[61]

Some long barrows were built over the top of early Neolithic monuments and therefore represent the enlargement and aggrandizement of earlier structures.[62] Presumably, fashion or ritual convention dictated the sort of monument a community should have at any given time. Notgrove long barrow is one of the best documented cases of a multi-phase monument where a Cotswold-Severn tomb was built directly over a rotunda grave.[63]

At Sale's Lot, Withington, the picture is more complicated as there were probably two monuments, a rotunda grave and a simple passage grave on the site before the long mound was built. Details of the exact order of events at this site are difficult to reconstruct from the records made during the excavation, but the plan gives every appearance of a rather hastily executed conversion in which rubble was piled up between pre-existing structures to form a long mound with a chamber at the tail end.[64]

Belas Knap, Sudeley, may be another multi-period tomb constructed over one or more pre-existing structures if it is accepted that the portal setting at the rear of the forecourt is the remains of a portal dolmen and the ring of stones is the remains of a rotunda grave. Such an interpretation would go some way to explaining the unusual orientation of this site which has its forecourt at the north end of the mound.

Other long barrows, possibly the majority, were built on sites which had not previously been occupied by ritual monuments, although sometimes

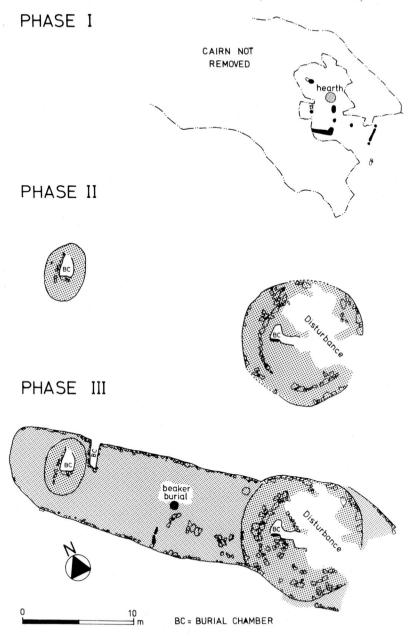

Provisional reconstruction of the main phases of activity at Sale's Lot, Withington. Phase I – settlement; Phase II – rotunda grave and simple passage grave; Phase III – long barrow incorporating monuments of Phase II.

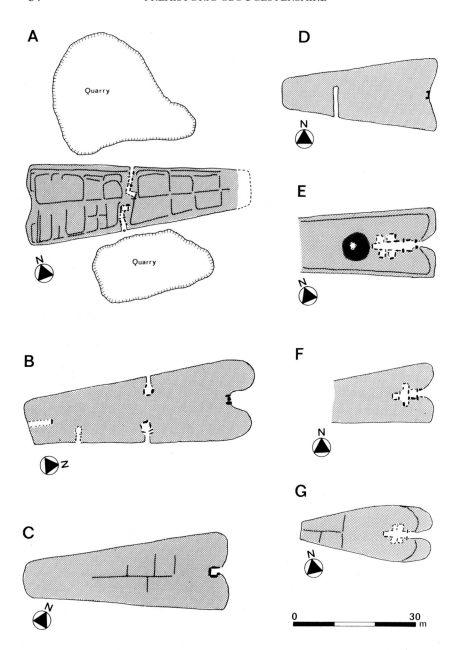

Middle Neolithic long barrows in Gloucestershire. (A) Hazleton North, Hazleton; (B) Belas Knap, Sudeley; (C) Randwick; (D) West Tump, Brimpsfield; (E) Notgrove; (F) Nympsfield, Frocester; (G) Hetty Pegler's Tump, Uley.

early Neolithic settlement debris is present. Such sites include the recently excavated monument at Hazleton North.[65] One explanation for the reuse of a former settlement area is that land was costly in time and effort to clear and that existing clearances were used over and again wherever possible.

Within the cairns of all Cotswold–Severn tombs there is one or more chambers, usually with a passage of some sort giving access from the exterior of the cairn. Large stones, or orthostats, were commonly used to make the walls of both chambers and passages, the gaps between the stones being filled with dry-stone-walling. Corbelling, or a series of large capstones, or a combination of both, were used to roof the passages and chambers. Where stones of sufficient size for orthostats and capstones were not available locally suitably large limestone blocks were transported to the construction site of a new long barrow from some distance away.

The number, positioning, and arrangement of the chambers varies greatly between sites, but in general, three recurrent arrangements can be identified: chambers placed laterally along the sides of the cairn each with a separate entrance passage leading to it (as at Belas Knap and Hazleton North); a simple box-like chamber set at the wider end of the cairn and approached through the forecourt (as at Randwick); and transepted chambers on either side of an axial passage leading from the forecourt into the wider end of the mound (as at Nympsfield and Notgrove). Hybrid monuments comprising both terminal and lateral chambers are known, for example at Burn Ground, Hampnett.[66] In a few cases the chambers were less well made, and at West Tump, Brimpsfield, and Poles Wood East, Swell, the burials were placed in what seems to be little more than a trench running through the mound.[67] Invariably, the chambers occupy only a small fraction, often less than 5%, of the total area covered by the cairn.

One common feature of all types of chamber is the presence of constricting stones across entranceways and passageways. These slabs effectively divide the passage and chamber into segments or units, and this may have been significant in the way the tomb was used. The slabs also served to restrict access, perhaps stopping people or spirits entering, or leaving, the chambers.[68] Among the most unusual constricting devices are the so-called portholes: circular holes cut through upright slabs of stone to form a very restricted entrance. The most complete examples are those at Windmill Tump, Rodmarton, but equally impressive is the specimen which can still be seen beside the driveway to the Old Rectory at Avening and which is believed to have come from the barrow east of Avening Court, Cherington.[69]

Once it was thought that the laterally chambered variety of long barrows were later than the terminal chambered types. The argument was advanced that false portals replaced true portals at the rear of the forecourt, possibly to distract tomb robbers.[70] This pattern cannot be supported by the evidence

Porthole entrance to the south chamber in the Windmill Tump long barrow, Rodmarton.

now available. Radiocarbon dates suggest that both types were being constructed in the early part of the third millennium BC and studies of the pottery found in the construction levels of the different types hints that laterally chambered examples were in fact the earliest.[71]

One point which emerges from existing knowledge of these tombs is that no single blue-print existed for their design. Rather, the variety of shapes, sizes, and chamber plans suggests that each community adopted a few components from a much wider repertoire of constructional devices according to their own preferences, ideas, and beliefs. This is particularly clear in the dispersal of chambers within the cairn and the degree of partitioning within each chamber. Indeed it has been suggested that the number of chambers present may in some general sense be a reflection of the organization of the communities themselves, perhaps the number of kinship units or family groups within the barrow-building community.[72]

Human bones are not only found in the chambers of long barrows, but also in the passageways, passage entrances, and, occasionally, in the forecourts. Inhumation was the usual burial rite, but some cremated bones has been found in most chambers which have been excavated carefully. With very few exceptions, burials are incomplete and disarticulated. The

Burials in the south chamber of the Hazleton North long barrow, Hazleton. The scale totals 300 mm. [Photograph: Alan Saville]

number of interments represented varies greatly: about 6 individuals at Bown Hill, between 27 and 30 at Hazleton North, about 38 at Belas Knap, and perhaps as many as 45 at Ascott-under-Wychwood (Oxfordshire).[73] However, unless total excavation and careful recovery have been achieved, the number of burials reported are probably gross underestimates of the number originally present. Evidence for differential burial according to age and sex[74] may be less real than is commonly thought, although on present evidence the number of infant burials represented is too low to account for the mortality rate usual in primitive societies. Overall, there are insufficient people represented by the burials in long barrows to account for the total middle Neolithic population of the region, but just what qualifications entitled a person to such burial are unknown.[75]

Careful studies of the human bones reveals something of the physical character of the tomb builders. In general they were well built, with an average height of about 1.6m, although it seems males were probably slightly taller than females. Skulls tend to be dolicephalic which means that the people were slightly long-headed.[76] Diseases such as arthritis and spina bifida have been recorded and dental disorders were common to judge from the condition of teeth and mandibles. One of the burials at Cow Common long barrow, Swell, suffered from severe clubfoot,[77] while a skull from a long barrow at Bisley has a circular trephination cut in it.[78]

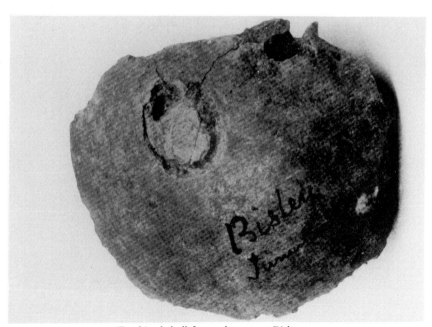

Trephined skull from a barrow at Bisley.

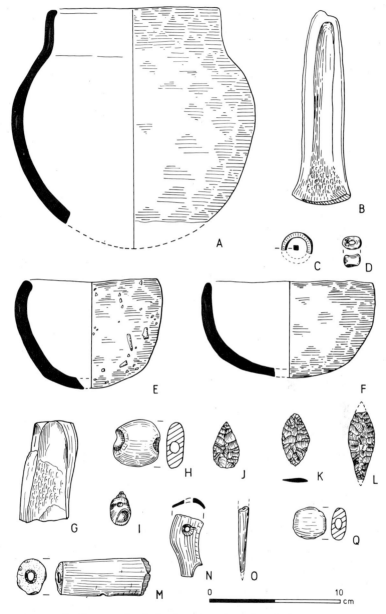

Potter, bone tools, flint arrowheads, beads and pendants deposited as grave goods in middle Neolithic long barrows in Gloucestershire. (A), (E) and (I) Nympsfield, Frocester; (B) Bown Hill, Woodchester; (C), (D), (H), (K) and (O) Notgrove; (E) Hazleton North; (F) and (G) Pole's Wood East, Swell; (L) and (M) Windmill Tump, Rodmarton; (N) Hetty Pegler's Tump, Uley; (Q) Eyford Hill, Upper Slaughter.

Grave goods are few, and mostly limited to personal items such as pottery cups, beads, pendants and other ornaments. Because of the generally mixed condition of the interments it is usually impossible to associate specific grave goods with individuals.[79] However, an exception was found in the entrance to the northern chamber complex at Hazleton North, where an extended male inhumation was accompanied by a large flint core under the right elbow and a quartzitic pebble hammerstone near the left hand.[80]

Ritual activity undoubtedly accompanied burial ceremonies, and possibly took place at other times too. The evidence for burial rites is slightly ambiguous, and it is often not even clear whether complete bodies, or only collections of bones, were placed in the chambers. One possibility which seems to fit the evidence recorded at a number of sites is that corpses were placed in the passageway until the flesh had decomposed, at which time parts or all of the skeleton was moved further into the tomb and eventually into the chamber proper. What is certain is that rituals involving the sorting of skeletal remains within the chambers and passages took place at most sites. Skulls and long bones, for example, are often found in piles against chamber walls. Bones were also selectively removed from the chambers, presumably for ceremonial use elsewhere. Here perhaps may be glimpsed a direct link between the use of the tombs and the rituals which took place at the causewayed enclosures.

The forecourts of long barrows, defined and partly enclosed by projecting horns on either side of the front of the mound, often provided the setting for rituals. Hearths and pits have been reported from a number of sites, including Nympsfield long barrow, and Windmill Tump, Rodmarton.[81] In some cases there are postholes in forecourts which may have held upright timbers or even supports for a structure. Excavations at the Notgrove long barrow, for example, provide vivid evidence of the rituals which took place outside the tomb. A stone lined trough was found in the centre of the forecourt and over it were unburnt human bones from at least two people. Around the trough were several burnt areas indicating the positions of fires and nearby was a series of stone-lined depressions containing dark soil and charcoal.[82] The general impression is that burning/cooking and perhaps feasting formed part of the rituals undertaken at long barrows, and in this context it is notable that pig bones are especially common in the forecourts of most tombs.

Radiocarbon dates from long barrows throughout Britain suggest that most were built between 3000 and 2600. This is such a short time within the prehistoric period that in some senses the long barrow tradition could be seen as little more than a fashion which swept the country. Detailed studies of the deposition of burials at Hazleton North suggests that this particular tomb, and by analogy others too, was build and used for a fairly short period within the duration of the long barrow tradition. The tomb was probably built about 2950 BC, the burials in the south passage and chamber giving a combined date of 2940 ± 30 BC while those in the north entrance

Excavations at the Nympsfield long barrow, Frocester, in 1974. The scales each total 2m.
[Photograph: Alan Saville]

gave a combined date of 2866 ± 36 BC. Overall, the deposition of burials at Hazleton North is unlikely to have taken place over a period of more than two or three centuries, perhaps rather less.[83]

Why middle Neolithic communities in Gloucestershire constructed such large monuments, with such small chambers, and at such great cost in terms of labour, is unknown. But one thing which does seem certain is that these monuments represented more than merely repositories in which to curate bones. Possibly they symbolized the identity of the community responsible for the construction of each, and at the same time provided a territorial marker indicating the ownership of land or resources.[84] If so, the presence of the ancestors may be seen as a way of giving these monuments special power through a cult of the dead. The barrows may have been perceived as the homes of ancestral spirits, the guardians of the land, and the source of fertility for crops, animals, and of course the human population too. In this the barrows may have been just as important for the living as for the dead.

Trade and exchange

Neolithic communities in Gloucestershire were not isolated groups. Common traditions of pottery manufacture and tomb design, for example, attest links with other groups, some of which lay far afield. Trackways undoubtedly facilitated communications, and formed both local and long-distance networks. The Jurassic Way following the higher ground of the Cotswolds is probably of considerable antiquity, and may even have been in use at this time.[85] Rivers would also have provided natural lines of communication between areas.

Direct evidence for interaction between communities is provided by the transportation and exchange of goods and raw materials. Mention has already been made of the use of flint for toolmaking at Crickley Hill and other sites, but since flint is not natural to Gloucestershire it must have been imported from Wessex, south-eastern England, East Anglia, or Yorkshire where it was mined from the chalk or collected from surface outcrops. Whether people from Gloucestershire travelled eastwards to collect flint from known sources, or whether nodules of raw flint were passed from group to group in a sort of chain of exchanges, is not known. However the flint was actually acquired, the result was that very large quantities, certainly many tons, were moved into the area during the Neolithic period.[86]

Alongside the exchange of raw flint there was also a trade in finished tools such as axes and adzes. These were manufactured not only in flint but also in fine igneous and metamorphic rocks such as outcrop in western and northern Britain.[87] Because Gloucestershire is nearer to flint-rich areas than stone-rich areas, the majority of axes, about 75%, were of flint. The remaining 25% comprise examples from a large number of more distant sources. The axe factories around Langdale in the Lake District were the largest single suppliers of stone axes to Gloucestershire, but Cornwall, North Wales, south-west Wales, and various other places contributed too. Some axes even came from overseas, as for example with a number of specimens made of porcellanite from Tievebulliagh in Northern Ireland which have been found near Andoversford. An axe from Bredon Hill (Hereford and Worcester) was of dolerite from Brittany, and a flint axe found at Colwall (Hereford and Worcester), came from Scandinavia.[88] Most impressive of all must be the jadeite axes which originated in northern Italy or Switzerland.[89] No jadeite axes have yet come to light in Gloucestershire, but a complete example is known from just over the county boundary at Conderton (Hereford and Worcester).[90]

The processes responsible for the distribution of flint and stone axes are as difficult to reconstruct as for the exchange of raw flint. Trade as we know it, with free enterprise, competition, and equivalence in transactions may have been totally alien to prehistoric societies. More likely is what may be called 'gift exchange'.[91] In this axes are passed from group to group in return for objects, services, or good will. The return, or reciprocal, exchange need not be immediate but could be delayed for weeks, months, or even years so that by building up the indebtedness of neighbouring communities a sort of primitive insurance system is developed for times of hardship when 'favours' can be called in. In this way axes and other goods may have remained in circulation for long periods of time and, through a succession of 'pass-ons', be moved great distances. Some items undoubtedly comman-

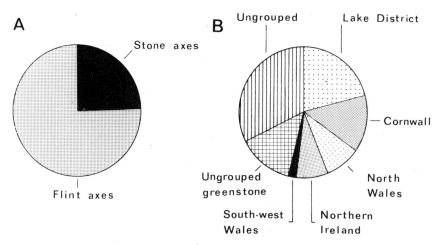

Pie charts showing: (A) the proportion of flint to stone axes found in Gloucestershire, and (B) the proportion of stone axes from the main identified source areas.

ded higher value through being prestige pieces, as perhaps with the jadeite axes which could not have been used for everyday woodworking without breaking. Bride wealth payments and other obligations could have been cemented by exchanges of prestige goods. A group of very large flint axes found at Crudwell (Wiltshire),[92] may represent a collection of prestige objects buried for some ritual purpose, or perhaps simply for safe-keeping in the course of their transportation westwards.

Other shortcomings in local resources were made good by exchange too. No suitable stone for querns is available on the Cotswolds and so it was obtained from elsewhere. Analysis of the specimen found in the Burn Ground long barrow, for example, showed that it came from the Bristol-Somerset coalfield.[93]

Personal ornaments were also acquired through long-distance travel or exchange. Shale beads, possibly of Kimmeridge shale from Dorset, are known from both the Notgrove long barrow and the Eyford Hill long barrow, Upper Slaughter,[94] and a shale pendant, again possibly of Kimmeridge shale, was found in a ditch within the enclosure at the Peak Camp. The dog-whelk pendant found at the Nympsfield long barrow must have been brought from the coast.[95]

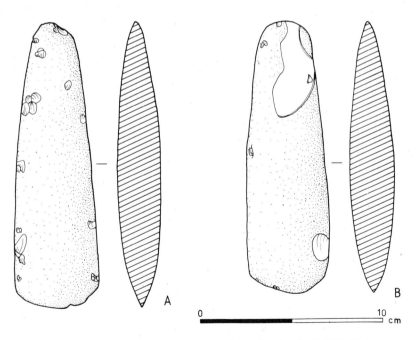

Two large flint axes from a possible hoard found at Crudwell (Wiltshire).

Community success

The middle Neolithic farming communities in Gloucestershire were very successful. According to the evidence available they maintained a relatively stable existence for about five centuries or so between 3000 and 2500 BC. They were effectively the first permanent residents in the area, and they certainly left their mark on the landscape through forest clearance and the construction of large monuments such as long barrows and causewayed camps which still survive as upstanding features to this day.

The organization of early farming societies was complicated. Much has still to be discovered about the structure of society and the nature of the activities undertaken at different types of site. But already an outline picture of the landscape at the time is beginning to emerge.

Clearances in the woodland were numerous enough to provide fields and grazing land to support a considerable population, although overall the countryside would have been very much more wooded than today. Settlements were probably fairly permanent, although whether every community had its own long barrow and enclosure, or whether several communities shared them is open to debate. It is notable, however, that The Crippets long barrow lies only 1.5km from the enclosure on Crickley Hill, while the West Tump long barrow lies only 2km south of Peak Camp. These two enclosures are intervisible with each other, but each is only intervisible with its nearest long barrow. Whether this was true of other barrows and settlements, is impossible to say with certainty as so much depends upon the extent of woodland clearance.

When looking at the evidence for middle Neolithic settlement it is always important to look for links between different types of site. Close ties between activities at barrows and enclosures have been evident for some time, but the existence of fields, grazing areas, and perhaps even seasonal pasture and manufacturing sites adds further dimensions to our comprehension of the organization of the landscape and the ways that individual communities exploited it.

Success is never endless, however, and for the farming groups of the middle Neolithic in Gloucestershire the boom period came to an end in the middle years of the third millennium BC. After about 2500 BC marked changes can be glimpsed in the archaeological evidence and this suggests fundamental, and apparently fairly rapid, changes to the settlement pattern, social organization, and lifestyles of communities in the area.

4

War and Peace (c 2500 – c 1600 BC)

The demise of the long barrow builders

During the later part of the third millennium BC, the late Neolithic period as it is traditionally known, new styles of decorated pottery (Peterborough ware) came into fashion and new types of ceremonial, ritual, and burial monuments began to be built. Underlying these changes new attitudes towards the dead can be detected, and for the first time there are traces of a hierarchy within society which can be glimpsed archaeologically by the fact that some individuals had access to fine and exotic objects while others did not.[1] In Gloucestershire, and indeed over much of southern England, these changes seem to be heralded by a break-down in the ways of life that characterized the middle Neolithic. This is most clearly seen in the abandonment of the causewayed enclosures and the ending of the long barrow tradition.

By 2500 BC, if not before, Crickley Hill had become nothing less than a small fortified village; a settlement surrounded by a deep rock-cut ditch and bounded by a high stone-faced rampart. How long it was occupied in this way is not known, but its end was sudden and violent. In the ditch, and along both sides of the rampart, the excavators found many leaf-shaped arrowheads; fire destroyed the gates, the houses, and the wooden fence topping the rampart. The site had been attacked and overrun,[2] but perhaps most importantly of all, the settlement was not rebuilt afterwards.

At the Peak Camp a similar, although less vivid, picture can be glimpsed. Arrowheads were strongly represented among the flint assemblage and two were found in the small area of rampart examined. As at Crickley Hill, the abandonment of the site took place before the introduction of Peterborough ware into the Gloucestershire area.[3]

Long barrows, which had seemingly been so important to middle Neolithic communities, were either abandoned or deliberately blocked up. At Nympsfield, stones and soil were piled into the forecourt to prevent further access to the chambers, and pottery intermixed with this blocking included early sub-styles of Peterborough ware known as Ebbsfleet and Mortlake wares.[4] Similar pottery was found in the fillings of the forecourts

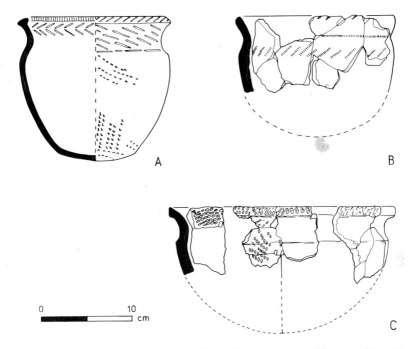

Peterborough style pottery from the blocking of long barrows in Gloucestershire. (A) Pole's Wood South, Swell; (B) Nympsfield, Frocester; (C) Burn Ground, Hampnett.

and chambers at other long barrows, for example Notgrove, Burn Ground, Bown Hill, Sale's Lot, and Poles Wood South.[5] At Windmill Tump, Rodmarton, the porthole entrance to the south chamber was neatly filled with dry-stone-walling. Blocking the chambers and forecourts was not, however, confined to the Cotswolds. Similar events can be seen at the West Kennet long barrow (Wiltshire), where over 70 cubic metres of soil and rubble were packed into all the chambers and the passage,[6] and also at Gwernvale (Powys), where large stones were used to fill the entrance passages.[7]

Some long barrows, such as Hazleton North, were not deliberately blocked in this manner, instead the outer walls, cairn, and chambers, seem to have slowly disintegrated and collapsed until the whole structure became a rounded stony mound much as we see today.[8]

The abandonment of the tombs and enclosures suggests deep rooted disenchantment with the traditional ways of life, and profound social change. But exactly what prompted such events is far from clear. One possibility is that there was increasing pressure on resources, especially the availability of good agricultural land, perhaps brought about by a rising

population.[9] Another closely related theory is that a reduction in soil
fertility, or a succession of bad harvests, led to food shortages and an
increase in warfare between communities.

The late Neolithic dark ages

The communities inhabiting Gloucestershire in the two or three centuries
following 2500 BC were pale reflections of their middle Neolithic forbears.
Sites of the period 2500–2200 BC can be recognized by the presence of
Peterborough ware, but they are few in number and restricted in their
distribution. Other than the finds from the blocking of long barrows, the
Cotswold uplands appear, on present evidence, to have been largely

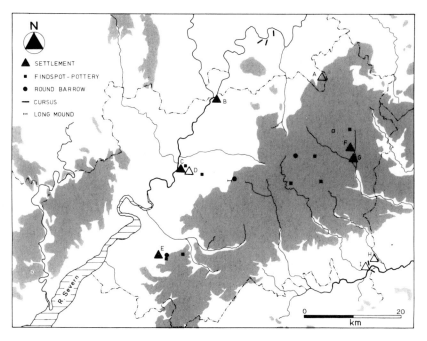

Map showing the recorded settlements, burials, and ceremonial sites dating to between
c 2500 and c 2000 BC. Filled triangles are settlement sites yielding Peterborough ware, open
triangles are settlements yielding grooved ware. A = Broadway (Hereford and Worcester);
B = Tewkesbury; C = Berkeley Street, Gloucester; D = Saintbridge, Gloucester; E =
Cam; F = Slaughter Bridge, Lower Slaughter; G = Salmonsbury, Bourton-on-the-Water;
H = Roughground Farm, Lechlade; I = The Loders, Lechlade. Only round barrows of
certain and probable late Neolithic date shown; for general distribution of round barrows
see page 95.

abandoned. By contrast, the main river valleys seem to have attracted attention and these may well have been the focus of settlement at this time.

Four occupation sites yielding Peterborough style pottery have been recognized in Gloucestershire. Perhaps the best known is at Cam, near Dursley, in the Severn Valley. Here, excavations in 1961 revealed two circular pits containing Mortlake and Fengate sub-styles of Peterborough ware, daub and a perforated macehead manufactured from local rock. Animal bones attest the presence of domesticated cattle (two breeds), sheep or goats, and pigs. Of these, pig bones were most numerous. Remains of red deer and wild boar were also present.[10]

At Gloucester, excavations in Berkeley Street yielded sherds of Mortlake ware, and these provide tantalizing evidence of a settlement near the River Severn.[11] The importance of the Gloucester area at this time is further emphasized by the fact that Peterborough pottery has come to light completely by chance at several sites around the city. At Barnwood, for example, a single piece of Mortlake ware and a large number of late Neolithic flint tools were recovered from gravel working,[12] while a small collection of what might also be late Neolithic pottery was found on a building site at Squire's Gate, Longlevens, in 1974.[13]

Further north, at Tewkesbury, excavations in 1972–3 in advance of the construction of a new cinema revealed a pit and other late Neolithic features containing a broken bowl of early Peterborough type (Ebbsfleet/Mortlake style). This bowl was decorated with twisted cord impressions.[14]

In eastern Gloucestershire the Windrush Valley provided a focus for settlement during this period. At Salmonsbury Camp, Bourton-on-the-Water, late Neolithic features were recorded in several of the areas excavated during the investigation of an Iron Age enclosure.[15] The features included a group of nine pits sealed beneath the Iron Age rampart. On another part of the site a number of ditch segments thought to be of late Neolithic date were excavated. Sherds of Peterborough ware and worked flints were found. Whether these remains represent a single occupation site, or parts of several, is uncertain.

North of Bourton-on-the-Water, near Slaughter Bridge, Lower Slaughter, gravel digging in the 1930s brought to light a pit containing a large sherd of late Peterborough ware (Fengate style) together with both human and animal bones.[16]

No late Neolithic settlements with Peterborough style pottery are known in the upper Thames Valley in Gloucestershire, but such sites are known in eastern Oxfordshire,[17] and at Home farm, Blunsdon St Andrew (Wiltshire), a pit containing sherds of Ebbsfleet style Peterborough ware and flint flakes was discovered in 1971 during the construction of a gas main between Cirencester and Swindon.[18]

From about 2200 BC Peterborough ware was replaced by new a style of

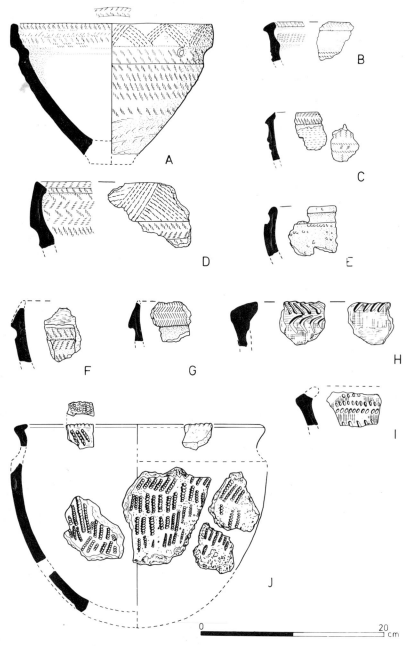

Selection of Peterborough style pottery from: (A)–(G) Cam, near Dursley; (H) and (I) Salmonsbury, Bourton-on-the-Water; (J) Cinema site, Tewkesbury.

pottery which is known as grooved ware because of its distinctive decoration. Apart from a possible sherd of grooved ware thought to have come from the Swell area, and the equally doubtful fragment found close to the Cow Common long barrow, also at Swell,[19] three sites in the county have yielded grooved ware from features which allow them to be regarded as settlements. All lie in river valleys and thus perpetuate the essentially lowland settlement pattern established by the users of Peterborough ware.

Around Lechlade, pits containing grooved ware were discovered at two sites in the course of rescue excavations and watching briefs during the early 1960s: The Loders and Roughground Farm.

At The Loders, at least two grooved ware vessels decorated in the Woodlands style, together with three broken flint tools – a knife, a point, and a scraper – were found in a pit which measured about 1m across and 0.9m deep. Animal bones were also present, including cattle, sheep, and pig. One bone, the sacrum of an ox showed traces of how the beast had been butchered, while another bone, a red deer metatarsus had been discarded only after the removal of several long thin slivers of dense bone, presumably for making pins or needles. The pit itself had probably once been a cooking place but was subsequently used as a convenient place to throw rubbish.[20]

At Roughground Farm, three pits and a posthole can be assigned to the grooved ware occupation of the site. The pits were between 0.9m and 1.4m in diameter, and could have been used for storing grain. Flint tools from the site included scrapers, a serrated flake, an arrowhead, and a variety of utilized flakes. Flintworking had clearly been carried out on the site as one of the pits contained a hammerstone, a core, and 15 flakes. Two bone points or awls were also found, together with the remains of at least six pots. More than half the animal bones were of pig, and a further quarter were of cattle. Several antlers from red deer were present, also a bone from a dog or wolf. Three radiocarbon dates from bone in the pits suggest that the site was occupied about 2000 BC.[21]

The third grooved ware site, at Saintbridge, Gloucester, is rather less impressive than the two at Lechlade, and must be interpreted as a settlement with some caution. The site was discovered by Patrick Garrod during rescue excavations in advance of a housing development. A hearth-pit and at least three postholes were recorded, the pit being loosely associated with a possible sherd of grooved ware.[22] Further excavations in the area in 1981 confirmed the presence of late Neolithic activity, but failed to locate any additional structural evidence.[23]

In the Avon Valley at Broadway (Hereford and Worcester), the remains of a small grooved ware settlement comprising scattered pits was discovered during gravel quarrying in the early 1930s.[24] Little is known about the site, but the pottery is decorated in altogether different styles to the vessels from Lechlade.

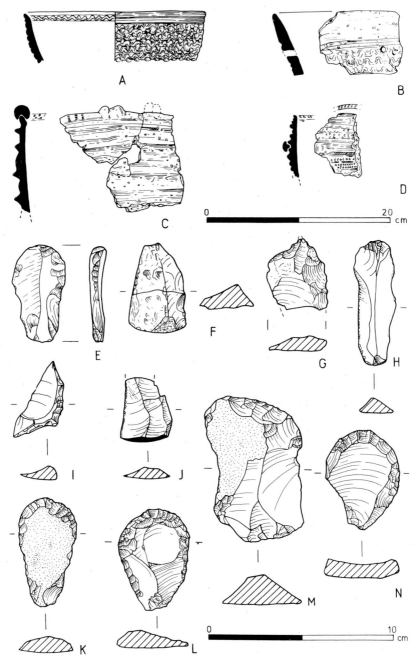

Grooved ware pottery and associated flintwork. (A), (B) and (H)–(L) from Roughground Farm, Lechlade; (C), (D) and (E)–(G) from The Loders, Lechlade.

What kind of houses were used by late Neolithic communities in the county is not known, but from the sites recorded to date it can be suggested that most settlements were small and possibly fairly short-lived. The animal bones show that pig was the most abundant species to judge from the number of bones found, although cattle, numerically in second place, may have contributed more to the everyday diet of the population through dairy produce as well as meat. No querns are known from late Neolithic contexts, but the presence of pits on nearly all the recorded settlements may indicate the production of cereals. Domestic crafts including flintworking and boneworking clearly took place at these late Neolithic settlements.

In general, late Neolithic Peterborough and grooved ware pottery tends to be poorly made in comparison with middle Neolithic wares. The range of forms was restricted, the vessel walls generally thick, and poorly crushed tempering agents were liberally used. Decoration was commonly applied to late Neolithic vessels, sometimes covering all or most of the outer surface.

Flintwork characteristic of the late Neolithic is generally more chunky, with less use of narrow blades and less intricate pressure flaking than during the middle Neolithic. New implement types were introduced during the late Neolithic, and among the most distinctive were the *petit tranchet* derivative arrowheads[25] which replaced the earlier leaf-shaped forms and which were possibly used for hunting. Unperforated stone and flint axes continued to be used.

Exchange networks broadly comparable with those operating in middle Neolithic times must have continued to provide flint and stone for tool-making. Pottery too may have been exchanged between groups. Ebbsfleet bowls from the blocking of the tombs at Nympsfield and Burn Ground were tempered with flint which contrasts strongly with locally made Peterborough pottery from settlement sites. Unless it is assumed that flintworking waste was crushed and added to local clays during the manufacture of these vessels, a source in north Wiltshire where flint and appropriate clay occur naturally in the same area is more likely.

Late Neolithic burials and ceremonial monuments

Burials which can confidently be assigned to the late Neolithic period in Gloucestershire are very scarce, although this may simply result from the fact that they are difficult to recognize because they lack distinctive grave goods.

At Slaughter Bridge, Upper Slaughter, a human cranium was found in a domestic pit containing Fengate style pottery,[26] although whether this can be regarded as a formal burial is open to debate.

Round barrows were probably the most common late Neolithic burial

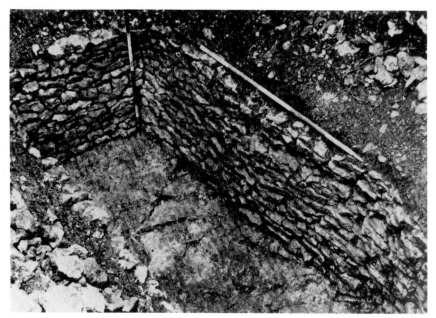

The boat-shaped cist in the centre of The Soldier's Grave, Frocester, during excavations in 1937. The scales are marked in 1 foot divisions.

monuments. They became the predominant barrow type about 2400 BC throughout the west of England, but sorting out those which were built in the third millennium from those of later date is far from easy.[27] Among the possible late Neolithic round barrows in Gloucestershire the most spectacular is The Soldier's Grave, Frocester. Perched on the escarpment edge overlooking the vale of Berkeley, this site comprised a round stone cairn some 17m in diameter and 2.1m high. Excavations in 1937 revealed a centrally placed burial cist shaped like a boat and lined with dry-stone-walling. In the cist were the remains of between 28 and 44 individuals together with a few animal bones and four pieces of undiagnostic coarse pottery.[28] Other possible round barrows of comparable date include The Waste, Hawling, and Barrow Piece, Coberley. Both contained cists constructed from dry-stone-walling within which were about seven inhumation burials.[29]

Round barrows were not, however, the only innovation during the late Neolithic. Although the long barrow tradition proper ended about 2500 BC, interest in long ceremonial monuments continued in the centuries that followed, and several new types of monument were developed.

One particularly widespread class of linear ceremonial monument is the cursus, and in Gloucestershire a fine example is known on the north bank of

Aerial view of the surviving part of the cursus at Lechlade, running from right to left above the modern road. The crop marks in the foreground belong to ring-ditches and later settlements. [Photograph: J.K.S. St Joseph; Crown Copyright reserved]

the River Thames at Lechlade.[30] The site was discovered through aerial photography and lies between the grooved ware settlement sites at The Loders and Roughground Farm. Like all cursus, it consists of an elongated rectangular-shaped enclosure defined by ditches which originally had internal banks. Its original length is unknown, but it is 50 metres wide, and the northern terminal is square in plan. Trial trenching in 1965[31] suggested that there was a line of postholes along the inner edge of the ditch, but excavations in 1985 demonstrated that these were of later date and not therefore connected with the cursus. An almost complete grooved ware pot was found about one-third of the way down the fill of the eastern ditch of the monument.[32]

Aerial photography has also led to the discovery of a cursus at Buscot (Oxfordshire), on the south side of the Thames just below Lechlade,[33] and at least three examples are known, again through aerial photography, beside the River Avon between Tewkesbury and Evesham (Hereford and Worcester).[34] Like the late Neolithic settlements, it is notable that all these cursus lie in major river valleys. Their function is far from clear, but they are presumed to have been ceremonial monuments. All are closely associated with rivers and streams and this may have been important to the rituals

Aerial view of the cursus and ring-ditches at Buscot (Oxfordshire). [Photograph: Jane Timby; Pilot: Ron Locke]

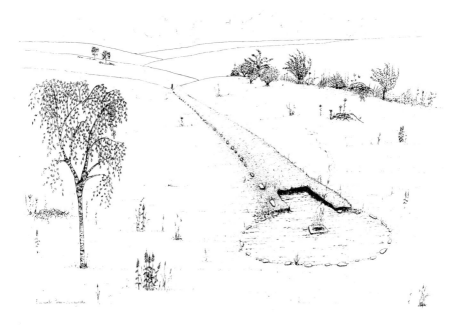

Reconstruction drawing of the long mound on Crickley Hill, Coberley. [Drawing: Liz Wilczynska]

enacted in or around them. Moreover, they seem to cluster together in little groups as if forming a series of ritual centres.

The most fully investigated linear monument which can tentatively be assigned to the late Neolithic period is the long mound on Crickley Hill. This structure was built in several stages, but when complete was nearly 100m long by 4m wide. The eastern end was built over the razed remains of the middle Neolithic enclosure, the whole long mound being made of soil which had possibly been brought to the site from elsewhere. When the soil was in place the builders laid limestone slabs at intervals along each side; under some slabs were deposits of animal bones. The eastern terminal was semicircular, its margin defined by a crescent of cobbling. In the middle of the cobbling was a large posthole, possibly the socket for a marker or totem. The western end was more complicated and comprised a circular paved area, in the centre of which was a large stone slab that may be interpreted as an altar of some sort.[35] How the monument was used is not totally clear.

Symbols of power

Within this later Neolithic society, new ways of symbolizing power and prestige developed. Bone pins, dress fittings, and ornaments were among the items adopted at this time, but among the most durable were new perforated stone tools.

Probably the earliest of these stone tools were the maceheads. Their function is unknown, but they do not seem to have been tools in the traditional sense because they show no traces of wear. The example from Cam was found associated with Mortlake and Fengate style pottery in a domestic context. Ovoid in shape, and made of local oolitic limestone, it was broken when discovered but new probably measured 64mm wide by 55mm thick by 86mm long. The central perforation had an 'hour glass' shaped profile because it had been made by drilling from both sides of the body probably with a wooden or bone drill and quantities of sharp sand.[36]

Three other maceheads have been found in Gloucestershire. Two come from near Rendcomb on the Cotswolds: one is of ovoid form made from olivine dolerite, the other, from Eycot Wood in the same parish, is made from greenstone imported from near Penzance in Cornwall.[37] The third

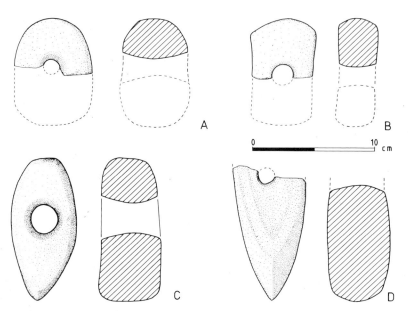

Maceheads and early style battle-axes from Gloucestershire. (A) Cam; (B) Eycot Wood, Rendcomb; (C) Roads Farm, St Briavels; (D) Gloucester.

macehead was found buried in undisturbed clay at 2 Grange Road, Gloucester, and is unusual because it is made of flint. The outline is rather irregular but the outer surface has been polished. A naturally formed hole has been exploited to provide the hafting arrangement.[38]

Soon after the appearance of maceheads, a variety of other objects including belt fittings and large arrowheads, seem to have acquired special significance which sometimes involved their deposition as grave goods. Perhaps the most notable type of object given this special treatment in the centuries following 2000 BC was beaker pottery. This is a well-made type of pottery, usually red or orange in colour, with thin walls and flat bases, and characteristically decorated with impressed or incised lines. Pottery of this type is not a development of native British Neolithic wares but owes its inspiration to late Neolithic wares in the Low Countries.[39]

It was once thought that beaker pottery, together with a range of other innovations, including new flintwork types, new technologies, metalworking, new burial rites, and new types of burial monuments, were introduced into this country by a group of invaders or immigrants. Admittedly, there may have been some folk movements at this time, but, in general, this interpretation can no longer be accepted for two reasons. Firstly, many of the features thought to have been introduced have now been shown to have a long ancestry in Britain. Single inhumation burial for example can be traced back to the end of the middle Neolithic period, as can the use of round barrows. Secondly, the new skills and technologies did not arrive all at once from a single source, rather they derived from many different sources and were adopted gradually, by local indigenous communities, over the whole beaker period.[40]

Beakers and innovation

Many schemes have been devised to classify beaker pottery, but at the most fundamental level three main styles can be recognized.[41] First, early styles which comprise all-over-corded beakers similar to those manufactured in the lower Rhine area. Second, middle styles characterized by so-called bell-beakers and short-necked varieties. Third, late styles characterized by long-necked types. Because of the ubiquity of beaker pottery the final stages of the late Neolithic, from about 1900 to 1600 BC are generally referred to as the beaker period.

In Gloucestershire, there are no complete beakers assignable to the early phase, although a large sherd of cord decorated beaker found beneath the rampart of the Iron Age hillfort on Crickley Hill may belong to this period.[42] Such a paucity of early finds is not unexpected since all-over-corded beakers are mostly confined to Wessex and parts of south-eastern

England. Middle and late beakers are, however, well represented in Gloucestershire, both on settlement sites and with burials.

As already indicated, the appearance of beaker pottery is but one element in a series of changes evident at this time, probably largely promoted by increased contact with mainland Europe and Ireland. Sometimes these changes involved the adoption of new types of artefact, on other occasions it was simply the quality of production that improved.

Flintworking was one traditional industry that underwent a great deal of change in the centuries following 2000 BC. Production was characterized by fine pressure flaking, extensive use of polishing, and a return to blade-based industries. New tools included barbed and tanged flint arrow-heads (which probably just pre-date the introduction of beakers), different types of small scrapers, and new knife forms.

The range of perforated stone implements also increased during the early second millennium BC to include battle-axes and axe-hammers alongside the more traditional maceheads. The earliest battle-axes have a simple outline with a rounded or slightly squared butt, the widest part of the body near the butt, and little or no splaying of the blade.[43] Two early examples are known from Gloucestershire. One, from Roads Farm, St Briavels in the Forest of Dean is made of quartz dolerite from the Whin Sill area of Northumberland; the second, recorded as having been found near Gloucester, is made of flint, but only the blade survives.[44] Axe-hammers are larger, and generally coarser versions of battle-axes, but none of early date are known in Gloucestershire. Other new stone objects such as the archer's wristguards and shale buttons, well known from Britain as a whole, have not be recorded in Gloucestershire to date.

Perhaps the most important development at this time was the introduction of metalworking. The working of copper and bronze may have been taking place on a small scale in the west of Britain during the late Neolithic, but the dating of early metalworking traditions is very difficult because so few types have been found on well-dated sites.[45] Axes were probably among the first metal objects made, and one of the earliest metal finds from Gloucestershire, and indeed from Britain as a whole, is the small copper axe from Hawling in the Cotswolds. This piece, which was a chance find, has a broad butt and slightly splayed blade.[46] It was cast in an open mould and hammered into shape. It may have been made in Britain, but could equally have been imported from Ireland.

Bronze, a mixture of copper and tin, soon replaced copper as the main type of metal used in the manufacture of tools and weapons. Again, early examples of bronze implements are known from Gloucestershire, including a pair of axes found during the construction of a house at Oddington[47] These represent the earliest known reliably provenanced group of axes from lowland Britain. Other early axes have been found at Bisley, Cleeve Hill,

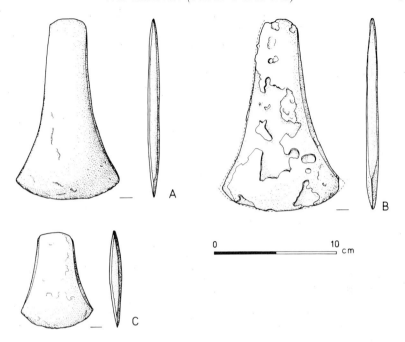

Early metal axeheads from Gloucestershire. (A) and (B) pair of bronze axes from Oddington; (C) copper axe from Hawling.

and Awre.[48] To these must be added the examples from just outside the county, for example those from Bredon Hill, Cropthorne, and Evesham (Hereford and Worcester), Monmouth (Gwent), and Oaksey (Wiltshire).[49]

No examples of the early tanged daggers or dagger/knives known from beaker contexts elsewhere have yet been recovered from Gloucestershire, and no sheet goldwork of the period has come to light. A small fragment of sheet bronze from a beaker burial at Sale's Lot, Withington, is the only metal object from this period which was not cast.[50]

Beaker settlement

Evidence for Beaker settlement in and around Gloucestershire suggests that although the low ground may have remained the focus of activity, there was by this time some expansion onto the higher ground. Four beaker settlement sites have been recognized in Gloucestershire, mostly of the middle beaker period.

At Barnwood, east of Gloucester in the Severn Valley, a trough-like

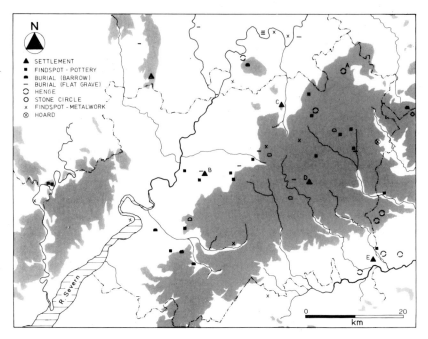

Map showing the recorded settlements, burial sites, and ceremonial monuments dating to between *c* 2000 and *c* 1600 BC. Round barrows with beaker pottery shown as filled symbols, those without shown open. A = Condicote Henge, Condicote; B = Barnwood; C = The Warren, Toddington; D = Oxpens Farm, Yanworth; E = Roughground Farm and Butler's Field, Lechlade.

feature was found in 1945 during the removal of topsoil prior to the commencement of gravel extraction. This trough was U-shaped in cross-section, 3.6m long, 2.1m wide, and 1.2m deep. The fill contained much burnt soil, together with a considerable amount of beaker pottery and flintwork.[51] The pottery represented several vessels of which the most complete was a fine beaker in short necked style with incised decoration consisting of parallel, herring-bone pattern, and zig-zag lines. Another vessel was represented by the rim and upper body portion from a very large pot-beaker which was probably some kind of storage container. As with most pots of this type it was decorated with incised fingernail impressions. Two further sherds from the trough came from other beakers of uncertain type. The flintwork includes scrapers, a knife, and a rod-shaped tool known as a fabricator. There were also two quartzite pebbles, battered at either end, which had clearly been used as hammerstones for flintworking.

The second beaker settlement is at Roughground Farm, Lechlade. Here, not far from the earlier focus of late Neolithic activity, were five pits

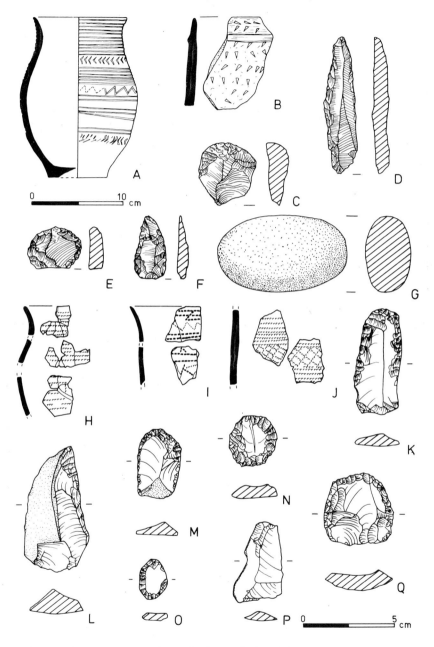

Selection of beaker pottery and associated stone tools and flintwork. (A)–(G) from Barnwood, Gloucester; (H)–(Q) from Roughground Farm, Lechlade. The upper scale relates to the pottery, the lower scale to the flint and stone objects.

containing a rich collection of beaker material. One of these pits yielded fragments of at least 23 pots, including several fine-ware vessels with comb impressed decoration, and portions of two large pot-beakers, one with impressed thumb-nail decoration. Flint tools from the pits included scrapers, knives, serrated flakes, and a fragment of a polished axe. In addition there was a considerable amount of flintworking debris. Fragments of sandstone querns and a few animal bones were also present. A radiocarbon date from the largest pit at Roughground Farm suggests that the site was occupied about 1750 BC.[52]

The remaining two beaker settlements in the county were discovered in 1985 during the construction of an oil-pipeline by the Esso Petroleum Company.[53] At The Warren, Toddington, two pits containing beaker pottery were revealed, while near Oxpens Farm, Yanworth, beaker pottery was found in a shallow ditch or hollow. Just outside the county, on Midsummer Hill, Eastnor (Hereford and Worcester), excavations by Dr Stan Stanford revealed a small collection of beaker sherds from hollows pre- dating the Iron Age hillfort. These suggest that a small hilltop beaker settlement may once have existed at the south end of the Malverns.[54]

Stray finds of beaker pottery from around the county hint at the existence of other settlements. At least two cave sites in the Wye Valley, Merlin's Cave and King Arthur's Cave, Whitchurch (Hereford and Worcester), have yielded beaker pottery suggesting that they may have been occupied, perhaps briefly, during this period.[55] At Shenberrow Camp, Stanton, one small sherd of decorated beaker was found sealed beneath the Iron Age rampart, together with a few pieces of flint including a broken scraper and a knife.[56] A piece of early beaker from a similar position at Crickley Hill has already been noted above,[57] and at Slaughter Bridge, Lower Slaughter, only a few metres from where the late Neolithic pits were found, a single sherd of beaker pottery came to light during trial excavations.[58] Other excavations which have turned up small quantities of beaker pottery include those at Saintbridge, Gloucester, Berkeley Street, Gloucester, The Buckles, Frocester, Temple Guiting 3 round barrow, and Langford Downs, Langford (Oxfordshire).[59] A small sherd from the 1925 excavation at Leckhampton hillfort, for long held to be a beaker sherd[60] may in fact be a piece of middle Iron Age pottery decorated with incised lozenge patterns.

None of the settlement sites known from the county are large, and none preserve traces of the houses and buildings used by beaker period communities. Evidence of their farming and subsistence activities is also poor, but there is enough to suggest that most were mixed farmers.

Beaker burials

The classic beaker burial comprises a single crouched inhumation in a rock-cut or slab-lined cist or grave, sometimes below a round barrow but more often without a mound, either singly or within a small cemetery.

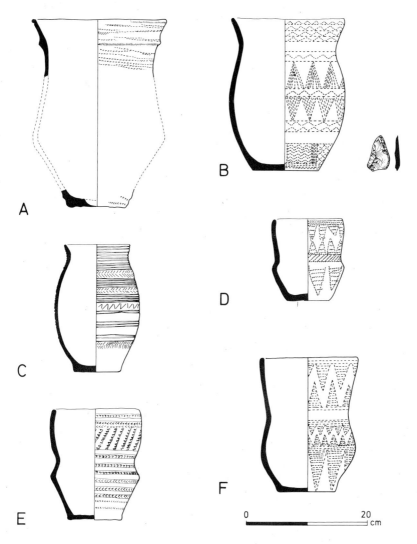

Selection of grave goods from beaker burials in Gloucestershire. (A) Sale's Lot, Withington; (B) Barnwood, Gloucester; (C) Prestbury; (D) Slaughter Bridge, Lower Slaughter; (E) Hall Road, Leckhampton; (F) Ivy Lodge Farm, King's Stanley.

Some graves contain beakers, and, on occasions other objects, but because many contained no grave goods at all they can be difficult to date with certainty.

At Sale's Lot, Withington, a beaker grave was dug into the top of the long barrow, which had by that time been out of use for perhaps four or five centuries. The burial was that of an adult male of about 40 years of age. The accompanying pot was of middle beaker style, decorated with notched-comb impressed lines. A tiny piece of sheet bronze from the burial may be the remains of an ear-ring, a type of personal ornament introduced during the beaker period but relatively rare in Britain as a whole.[61]

At Barnwood, Gloucester, a beaker grave was found very near to the settlement site already described. The burial was that of an adult male, and, in addition to a fine beaker pot, a flint knife had also been placed in the grave.[62] Similar evidence was found at Slaughter Bridge, Lower Slaughter, where again a beaker burial was found very near to the site of a late Neolithic and beaker settlement. It is difficult to determine whether or not a barrow was originally present at this site, but the burial itself was that of an adult female aged about 40. The body had been placed on a roughly north-south axis in a contracted position with the head to the south and the arms flexed so that the hands were close to the shoulders. The beaker, which was of the long necked variety, lay on its side over the bones of the left arm with its mouth facing towards the body.[63]

Another certain beaker burial was found in a gravel pit at Prestbury to the north of Cheltenham. The pot was of middle beaker type, rather similar in its form and decoration to one from the settlement at Barnwood. The inhumation which it accompanied was that of an adult male.[64] Other beaker graves may be indicated by the complete beaker found at Hall Road, Leckhampton, during the construction of a housing estate in the early 1960s,[65] and by the base of a small beaker found during gravel extraction at Shurdington in 1935.[66] However, in neither case were any human bones reported so it is possible that these finds indicate settlement sites.

No beaker cemeteries have been found in Gloucestershire, but just outside the county in the Avon Valley at Lower Moor, Hill and Moor (Hereford and Worcester), a group of three graves, all containing beakers, were found during gravel digging.[67]

Three round barrows of beaker date are known in Gloucestershire. At Ivy Lodge Farm, Kings Stanley, a beaker burial was found when a barrow was being dug into in search of stone for road repairs. In the centre of the barrow was a slab lined cist in which was a crouched inhumation, accompanied by a fine long-necked beaker. The age and sex of the individual was not determined.[68] Four sherds of beaker pottery are known from the primary burial in a barrow at Lechmore, Horsley, which appears to have been a cremation burial contained in a small pit.[69] Excavations by

Professor Richard Atkinson at Frampton on Severn in 1948 apparently found a primary burial associated with beaker pottery within a round barrow that survived only as a ring–ditch. A secondary burial in the ditch itself may also have been associated with a beaker.[70]

Just outside the county, on Bredon Hill (Hereford and Worcestershire), excavations by Nicholas Thomas in 1963 uncovered a remarkable beaker burial in a central pit under a small round barrow. In the pit were the bodies of two people, an adult male aged about 50 and an adult female aged about 30. They were accompanied by two middle period beakers together with four barbed and tanged flint arrowheads, a flint knife, and a bone spatula of a type possibly used in leatherworking.[71]

In addition to these certain examples, there are a number of burials from the county which probably date to the same period, but because no pottery was included in the graves exact dating is very difficult. On the west side of the Severn, a slab lined cist containing the crouched inhumation of a male youth was found at Beachley, Tidenham, during the construction of a bungalow in 1964. There were no grave goods and no traces of a barrow.[72] East of the Severn, a flat grave, probably of beaker date, was found at Tewkesbury during redevelopment work in the town,[73] while at Ched-

General view of the stone cist discovered at Beachley, Tidenham. Scale totals 6 feet. [Photograph: C. Barnett]

worth on the Cotswolds a round barrow excavated by Professor W.F.Grimes during the last World War contained a central cist measuring 1.3m by 1m within which were two crouched inhumations; an adult male and an adult female.[74] Other round barrows of this same period include the Northfield Barrow, Charlton Kings[75] and the Swell 1 barrow at the west end of Cow Common, Swell, which contained a slab-lined grave in which were the crouched remains of an adult male with the head to the north-east.[76] Finally, mention may be made of the Broadbarrow Green barrow, Haresfield, which contained a partially cremated body accompanied by a fine flint knife of plano-convex type.[77]

New monuments

Beaker communities maintained some interest in the long monuments of middle and late Neolithic date. Long barrows seem to have still been recognized as sacred sites because, in addition to the beaker grave inserted into the Sale's Lot long barrow, Withington, small quantities of beaker pottery have been found in secondary contexts at four other long barrows: Eyford Hill, Notgrove, Westcote Heath, and Randwick.[78] In all cases, however, the exact nature of the activities leading to the deposition of this pottery is not known.

A new type of linear monument which appears during the beaker period is the stone row. These are especially common in the south-west of England, and while there are no known examples in Gloucestershire itself the one at Trelleck (Gwent), lies only just outside the county boundary. This row, known locally as Harold's Stones, comprises three uprights set on a slight arc.[79] Its purpose is unknown.

Apart from the construction of stone rows, however, the passion for long sinuous monuments gave way to a preoccupation with round monuments during the early second millennium BC. Round burial monuments have already been mentioned, but alongside these a variety of new classes of circular monuments appeared, of which the best known are henges and stone circles.

Henges are circular enclosures formed by a large ditch with an external bank. They are found throughout Britain, the largest being massive earthworks like that at Avebury (Wiltshire).[80]

Condicote henge is the only definite example of a henge monument known in Gloucestershire to date. The site comprises two nearly circular ditches with a single bank between them. The internal diameter of the bank is about 112m, and the area enclosed totals about 0.9ha. Ploughing has reduced the size of the bank greatly over the past 100 years of so, but the outline of the site can still be discerned at ground level, and details of the

Harold's Stones, Trelleck (Gwent). [Photograph: Author]

ditches and banks can be still more clearly seen from the air. The antiquary G.B Witts recorded that in the 19th century the banks were so steep 'that it is difficult to climb to the top'.[81] Typologically, Condicote henge is rather unusual and is classed as a Group Ia type because of its double ditch, single bank, and, according to present evidence, only one entrance. Watching briefs in the late 1950s and an excavation in 1977[82] have provided a certain amount of information about the site. The inner ditch was cut some 2.0m down into solid bedrock and was about 4.2m wide. Little remained of the banks, but charcoal from the fill of the ditch provided radiocarbon dates demonstrating that the monument was built before the 18th century BC. Investigation of a substantial area of the interior of the site failed to reveal any features which were certainly contemporary with the use of the site, although one possible socket for a standing stone was recorded. Studies of the snail-shells from the ditch suggest that the monument was situated in a small woodland clearance rather than open county. A beaker presence at Condicote henge is indicated by the remains of least two coarse finger-nail ornamented vessels in the fill of the inner enclosure ditch. Associated with the pottery was a small collection of flintwork including tools and waste debris, and also a number of animal bones including cattle, sheep and pig. Remains of a dog were also represented. The excavator suggested that this deposit was deliberately dumped in the ditch from the direction of the

Aerial view of Condicote Henge. [Photograph: W.A. Baker]

interior of the henge and may either indicate occupation of some kind, or perhaps the debris from ceremonies which took place within the monument.

A possible henge at Cutsdean has been identified from aerial photographs,[83] but nothing is now visible on the ground and further work is required before it can be cited as a definite example. Outside Gloucestershire, henges are known on the Cotswolds at Westwell and perhaps also Langford, both in Oxfordshire.[84]

Very small henges, usually called *hengi-form* monuments, have been recorded by aerial photography on the Thames gravels between Kempsford and Lechlade,[85] and in the Avon Valley at Nafford (Hereford and Worcester).[86]

A second class of circular monument constructed from beaker times onwards is the stone circle. Over 1000 of these are known in Britain, mostly in the north and west.[87] The only example on the central Cotswolds is at Rollright (Oxfordshire). This site has recently been the subject of a detailed study by the Oxford Archaeological Unit.[88] The stones are set in a nearly perfect circle, about 31.6m in diameter, and are known as The King's Men because of associated legends. Originally there were about 20 stones, but in the 1880s others were added to make the monument appear more impressive. The exact date of the site is not known, but it is generally regarded as being an early example of its type. The portal dolmen known as the

General view of the cutting through the inner ditch of Condicote Henge during excavation in 1977. The scale in the bottom of the ditch totals 2m. [Photograph: Alan Saville]

Whispering Knights, and a standing stone known as the King Stone, lie near the stone circle, but are in fact quite separate monuments and of different dates.

Both henges and stone circles have been ascribed mystical functions connected with astronomy and ritual. Much has been made of supposed alignments with celestial bodies and the care which is evident in their setting-out and construction. Some may have been used as primitive calendars for documenting the seasons or perhaps eclipses, but many of the claims made for these monuments simply do not find support in the evidence. More prosaic functions might indeed be suggested, among them the definition of neutral ground where groups from different areas could meet for ceremonies, or perhaps the exchange of goods, information and women.

Society, land-use, and population

Taking the evidence for settlement, burial, and ceremonial monuments of the beaker period as a whole, three conclusions may be drawn. First, the settlement areas favoured in late Neolithic times, namely the main river valleys, remained important focal areas through the period 2000–1600 BC.

Second, during the beaker period there was an expansion of settlement which resulted in the recolonization of upland areas, particularly the Cotswolds. Third, that certain areas, such as around Condicote on the Cotswolds, Lechlade in the upper Thames Valley, and Evesham in the Avon Valley emerge as ritual centres wherein there were marked concentrations of burial and ceremonial sites.

Small scattered farmsteads were probably the usual form of settlements, and it is therefore rather interesting that in two cases, Barnwood, Gloucester, and Slaughter Bridge, Lower Slaughter, burials and settlements of about the same period have been found within a few metres of each other. This may suggest that settlements were close to their burial grounds, both presumably being set within a cluster of fields and grazing areas.

Environmental evidence suggests that woodland was still widespread during the beaker period. Condicote henge appears to have been surrounded by open woodland and tall grass for some time after its construction.[89] The pollen sequence from Ashmoor Common (Hereford and Worcester), studied in detail by Dr Tony Brown, shows that the levels of lime pollen decreased during the late Neolithic and beaker period and that after an estimated date of approximately 1750 BC there was the first appearance of cereal pollen.[90] This evidence corresponds nicely with the archaeological indications of a gradual expansion of settlement during the same period.

The ritual centres of the Cotswolds, the upper Thames Valley, and lower Avon Valley were not as large as similar groups of cursus, henges, and *hengi-form* monuments elsewhere in Britain, for example around

Aerial view of the Rollright stone circle, Rollright (Oxfordshire). [Photograph: B. Durham]

Stonehenge (Wiltshire) or Dorchester-on-Thames (Oxfordshire),[91] but they are nonetheless impressive, and were presumably of considerable local and regional importance. To what extent these 'ritual landscapes' interfered with normal agricultural activities is not clear, although the evidence from the Lechlade area suggests that here at least settlement and ritual were undertaken in the same general area.

Compared with other parts of southern England, beaker burials from Gloucestershire are rather poor. The only finely crafted objects placed in the graves were the beaker pots themselves and occasional flint tools; items such as shale buttons, necklaces, and metal tools and weapons are all absent according to present evidence. However, not everyone was buried with a beaker, and this alone implies limited access to fine objects and in turn suggests a rudimentary hierarchy within society – ranking or class distinctions of some kind. In the centuries following 1600 BC this question of social ranking, and the development of elites within the communities living in Gloucestershire comes still further to the fore as the area lost its status as a social backwater and became drawn into the mainstream of events taking place in Wessex and central southern England.

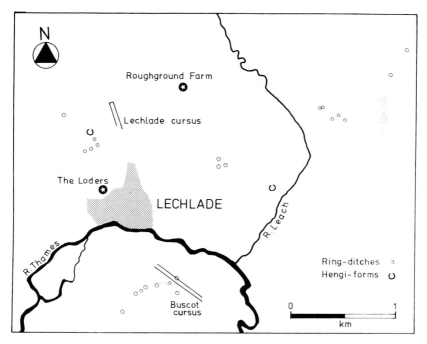

Map of the Lechlade area showing late Neolithic, beaker period, and early Bronze Age settlements, burials and ceremonial sites.

5

The Green and Pleasant Land (c 1600 – c 700 BC)

Maintaining the elites

Many of the traditions established in the early second millennium BC carried through into the centuries between 1600 and 700 BC, the Bronze Age.[1] Familiar monuments such as stone circles, stone rows, and round barrows continued to be constructed and used, and the period as a whole witnessed relatively few major changes.

One factor underlying the success of most communities during the Bronze Age was undoubtedly the fact that a climatic improvement during the early Bronze Age brought warmer and drier conditions, with a growing season several weeks longer than today.[2] This allowed the colonization of large tracts of upland such as Dartmoor and the Cambrian Mountains, and even though the population was probably rising at the time, the expansion of settlement into these new areas effectively reduced competition for agricultural land.

Distinctions between those who had access to fine objects and those who did not were emphasized more than ever before by the manner in which people were buried. Communal burials like those of the Neolithic and beaker period were very scarce in the Bronze Age. The focus of burial ritual shifted towards the individual, whether male or female, and there is so much variety in the range of grave goods placed with the dead that it is tempting to believe that society was ordered with rather greater complexity than the basic extremes of rich and poor, powerful or subservient. Some graves contain weapons, others special pots or certain types of tools (eg. razors), and yet others only dress fittings such as pins or buttons. Whether these can be directly interpreted as the graves of warriors, leaders, priests, craftsmen, or traders, is open to question, but it is clear that in all cases the production of prestigious objects was central to the maintenance and display of status.[3] Styles of pottery, metalwork, and dress fittings underwent constant modification, partly because of the innovative flare of the craftsmen and partly perhaps in response to the demand for new and novel ways of displaying status, power, prestige, and importance through material possessions.

Much of the evidence available for the Bronze Age period in Gloucestershire derives from burials, and it is therefore appropriate to look in detail at these first. Traces of settlements are scarce, possibly because they have rarely been looked for in a systematic way, but stray finds of the period allow some insights into the nature and extent of domestic and ceremonial activities.

Round barrows, cemeteries and burials

Round barrows were the most widespread type of burial monument used during the Bronze Age, and of the 300 or so currently known in the county the majority probably belong to this period. It must always be borne in mind, however, that round barrows were constructed from Neolithic time onwards and that a good number must therefore be of pre-Bronze Age date.[4]

On the Cotswolds, many round barrows survive as circular mounds,

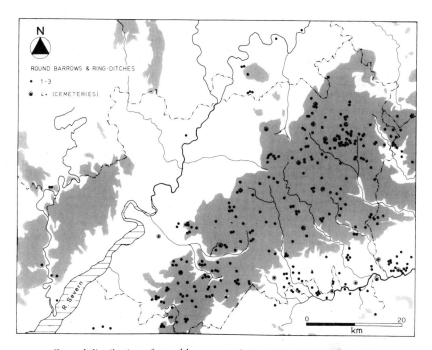

General distribution of round barrows and ring-ditches in Gloucestershire.

Bronze Age round barrow known as Nan Tow's Tump, Didmarton. [Photograph: Author]

'tumuli' as they are sometimes known. Among the largest are the Beech Pike Barrow, Elkstone, and Nan Tow's Tump, Didmarton, each of which measures over 30m across and 3m high. At the other end of the size-spectrum are numerous small barrows which are less than 10m across and originally perhaps only 1m high. These smaller barrows are particularly vulnerable to damage or obliteration through ploughing and stone clearance.

Many different types of round barrow can be identified on the basis of their shape and form,[5] but the majority of round barrows on the Cotswolds belong to the bowl barrow type – so-called because in profile they resembles an up-turned bowl. Other types, including bell barrows and disc barrows are present, but they can be hard to recognize without excavation.

Barrows were constructed in a variety of ways. Some comprise little more than heaps of rubble over a central grave, but the more elaborate examples were carefully built with a kerb or retaining wall around the outside to give the mound greater stability. Some barrows were surrounded by a circular ditch which not only delimited the sacred area of the barrow but also served as a quarry from which to obtain rubble for the mound. Where barrows have been severely reduced by ploughing the encircling ditch, or ring-ditch as it is then known, may be all that survives. How many

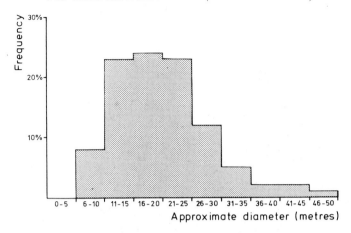

Graph showing the diameter of round barrows and ring-ditches in Gloucestershire.

barrows have been lost in this way is an open question, but aerial photography has brought to light many ring-ditches which no longer retain surface traces of a mound,[6] and it seems likely that a significant number of barrows on the Cotswolds have disappeared since prehistoric times.

In the Severn Valley and the upper Thames Valley very few upstanding round barrows remain. This is partly because the barrows in these areas were built of earth and gravel which degrades very easily, and partly because these areas have been heavily cultivated since prehistoric times and almost no pre-Roman earthworks of any sort survive. However, scores of ring-ditches have been discovered by aerial photography in the main river valleys during the last 30 years or so.[7]

A few round barrows have been identified west of the Severn in the Forest of Dean, but many more undoubtedly await discovery.

Overall, the distribution of known round barrows and ring-ditches in the county is very uneven. There are distinct concentrations of barrows and ring-ditches around Condicote in the north Cotswolds, Lechlade in the upper Thames Valley, and to a lesser extent in the lower Avon Valley. These were all centres of ritual and ceremonial activity in the late Neolithic and beaker periods, and it is perhaps a reflection of their importance that they retained some sort of significance through into the Bronze Age.

Another feature of the distribution of round barrows and ring-ditches is that they sometimes cluster together to form small cemeteries. Pairs of barrows are fairly common, as indeed are groups of three, but the sign of a real cemetery is when there are four or more barrows or ring-ditches in a small group. At least a dozen barrow cemeteries are known in and around Gloucestershire, mostly on the Cotswolds, but also in the major river valleys.[8] It is noticeable that, generally speaking, they are evenly spread, at

Aerial photograph of a ring-ditch at Black Bourton, Carterton and Black Bourton (Oxfordshire). [Photograph: Author; Pilot: Ron Locke]

Excavation of an early Bronze Age ring-ditch cut through by a late Bronze Age pit alignment at Butler's Field, Lechlade. The scales each total 2m. [Photograph: David Miles]

intervals of about 10km, although in the Condicote area they are more closely packed. Among the most impressive cemeteries are those at Hull Plantation, Longborough which contains at least nine barrows, and Cow Common, Swell, which contains at least ten barrows. Characteristically, barrow cemeteries either contain, or lie adjacent to, a middle Neolithic long barrow. Quite why this should be is hard to explain, but two possibilities may be considered. On the one hand is the argument that there was continuity in the use of a site for barrow building because of its special significance as a sacred area. On the other hand is the purely practical point that barrows are a hindrance to agriculture and that in order to minimize the loss of productive land it was convenient to site a new cemetery in an area already occupied by burial mounds.

Although round barrows display a number of superficial similarities in their form and construction, the burials found within them vary greatly in terms of content and the rituals that accompanied their deposition. To some extent these differences represent changing fashions in burial rite, and this is most clearly seen in the swing from inhumation to cremation during the early and middle Bronze Age, so that by about 1200 BC inhumation was the exception rather than the rule. Altogether, five main types of burial have been recorded under round barrows in Gloucestershire, and these are considered separately in the following sections.

Dagger graves

One particularly distinctive series of early and middle Bronze Age burials are dagger graves, which as the name suggests are graves in which the deceased is accompanied by one or more daggers or knives. Many examples have been recorded in Wessex where, during the early Bronze Age, they represent one component of a series of particularly well-appointed graves sometimes known as Wessex Culture graves.[9] In Gloucestershire no less than seven such burials may be identified with more or less certainty.[10]

The most celebrated dagger grave in Gloucestershire is at Snowshill on the north Cotswolds. Excavated before 1877 by an unknown antiquary, the evidence was later published by Canon Greenwell.[11] From this account it is clear that the round barrow was a large one, originally perhaps over 25m in diameter and 2.5m high, and that it was built of limestone rubble. The primary grave was a slab lined cist that had probably been partly sunk into the natural ground surface. In the grave was the inhumation of an adult (probably male) accompanied by a bronze dagger, a bronze spearhead, a bronze crutch-headed pin and a polished stone battle-axe. The dagger, which has an ogival-shaped blade and three rivet-holes for attaching the haft, has come to be regarded as exemplary of its type and lends its name to the Camerton-Snowshill dagger series.[12] The spearhead is of an early form,

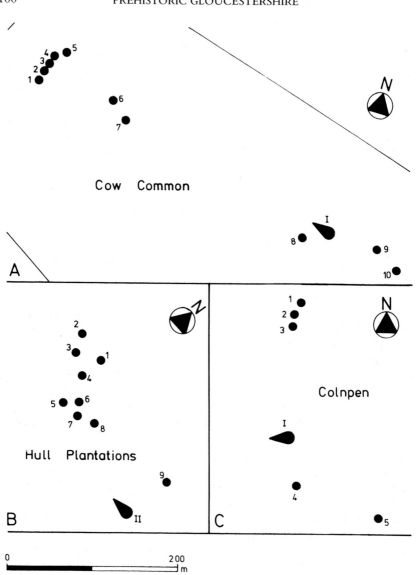

Round barrow cemeteries in Gloucestershire: (A) Cow Common, Swell; (B) Hull Plantations, Longborough; (C) Colnpen, Coln St Dennis.

little more than a dagger provided with a socket and a small tang to enable it to be mounted on a long shaft. The crutch-headed pin is of continental type and shows the extent of long-distance communications operative at this time. The battle-axe, manufactured from Hyssington picrite which outcrops at Cwm Mawr on the Powys/Shropshire border, is a developed form of an implement whose ancestry can be traced back to late beaker times.

At Naunton, also on the north Cotswolds, another burial accompanied by à knife-dagger was found in the late 19th century during the construction of the railway through the parish.[13] The site was excavated by the Reverend David Royce on 10th September 1876, and under a mound of earth and stone he found a slab-lined cist, about 1.3m square, containing the cremated remains of a woman and a child accompanied by a small knife- dagger with two rivet holes. Small knife-daggers of this sort, probably knives in fact, typically accompany females.

The Soldier's Tump on Tiddenham Chase in the Forest of Dean, was excavated by Dr Scott Garrett in 1951–2 and contained a very similar burial to that at Naunton.[14] The barrow was 24.3m in diameter and comprised a central cairn enclosed within a retaining circle of stone rubble. Under the centre of the mound was a slab-lined cist cut into the original ground surface and covered by a large flat stone slab. Inside the cist were the cremated remains of two individuals: an adult female and a very young child. The accompanying grave goods comprised a bronze knife-dagger with two rivet-holes, a bronze awl with a flattened tang, three fossil encrinoid beads (two long tubes and a disc) and a shale pendant. About 2.3m to the east of the main cist was another, rather smaller cist, again cut into the natural bedrock, and in this instance containing only the cremated remains of an adult. Unfortunately it was impossible to establish whether this interment was male or female because the bone had been very heavily burnt.

It seems likely that some or all of the bodies in this barrow at Tiddenham had been cremated next to where they were buried because the ground was noticeably reddened around about, and there were fragments of burnt bone scattered over the old ground surface beneath the mound. There is also evidence that the burials were deposited late in the year after harvest because analysis of the charcoal revealed portions of the fruit of white charlock which grows amongst corn.[15]

The remaining four dagger graves in the county are less well documented. A dagger with an ogival-shaped blade in the Ashmolean Museum, Oxford, is recorded as having come from a barrow near Cirencester,[16] and another, of so-called Plymstock-Totland type, is known to have come from a small barrow at Ablington, Bibury, although no details of the burials are known.[17] A recent surface find of a Camerton-Snowshill type dagger blade on the Swell 7 round barrow in the Cow Common barrow cemetery,

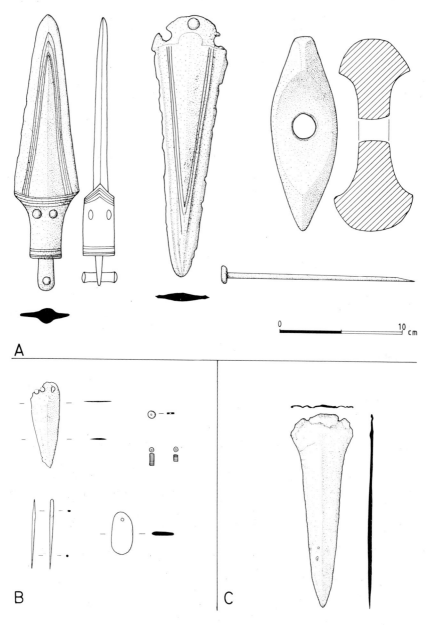

Grave goods from early Bronze Age dagger graves. (A) Snowshill; (B) Soldier's Tump, Tidenham; (C) Colesbourne Park, Colesbourne.

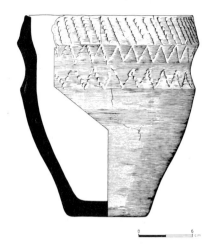

Collared urn from Cirencester.

Swell, probably represents another such burial disturbed by ploughing,[18] and finally a six-rivet Camerton-Snowshill type dagger from Colesbourne Park, Colesbourne,[19] is in such fine condition that again a disturbed burial is the most likely source.

To the south of the county, St Oswald's Tump, in the barrow cemetery at Marshfield (Avon) is a further local example. Here, a complete dagger with two rivet-holes, and the tip of a second dagger, were found accompanying a cremation in a stone cist at the centre of the barrow.[20]

Collared urn burials

Among the most familiar forms of Bronze Age burial rite is the deposition of cremations in collared urns. These distinctive ceramic vessels, usually heavily decorated, probably developed from late Neolithic Peterborough and grooved ware style pottery, perhaps with some influence from beaker wares.[21] The pots themselves were simply domestic vessels, of which the largest and most elaborate were selected for use as burial urns. Both male and female interments are known from collared urn burials, although with cremated remains it is often difficult to determine the age and sex of an individual with certainty.

At least nine burials in collared urns are known from the county, including examples from upstanding barrows and ring-ditches.

At Bourton-on-the-Water, between Slaughter Bridge and Stow Bridge, a group of three ring ditches was revealed during gravel quarrying in the 1920s and 1930s.[22] The largest had a diameter of about 30m and the ditch, which had a V-shaped profile, was up to 2m wide and 1.5m deep. What type of burial was contained within this ring-ditch is not known, but in an adjacent ditch was the grave of a young woman whose cremated remains had been placed inside a collared urn decorated with cord impressed lines arranged in herringbone style. Within the third ring-ditch was the burial of another young female whose cremated remains were contained in a plain collared urn.

At Burn Ground, Hampnett, near Northleach, excavations in advance of the construction of a Second World War airstrip revealed a cemetery of six round barrows clustered around the end of a long barrow.[23] Barrow 1 was about 10m in diameter, built of stone, with a kerb delimiting the mound. The primary burial was a cremation, probably an adult male, but a secondary cremation, cut into the mound, included a collared urn. In barrow 2, which was about the same size and constructed in a similar way, the primary burial comprised only two pieces of bone, but nearby was a small bronze awl with an oblong sectioned tang. Cut into the mound were two secondary burials, a cremation with a few fragments of collared urn, and, in a slab covered pit, a complete collared urn together with a flint knife. Curiously, there was no sign of any cremated bone with this last mentioned deposit.

Other burials accompanied by collared urns are represented by the remains of an urn and a piece of bronze recovered during quarrying at Camp Farm, Farmington,[24] a fragmentary urn from near Nailsworth,[25] and a complete urn from a barrow near Cirencester.[26] One further collared urn, now in Gloucester City Museum, is thought to come from a barrow in Gloucestershire, but which one is not known.[27]

Instead of urns, some early Bronze Age burials were accompanied by small ceramic funerary vessels known as accessory cups. One such vessel is known from Gloucestershire, and it is of a type rather fancifully known as an incense cup. It had two holes in the side and stood 40mm high and 65mm in diameter. It is said to have come from a barrow near Cheltenham, but its exact origin and present whereabouts is not known.[28]

Cremation pits

Over half of the round barrows that have been investigated in Gloucestershire prove to cover nothing more than a cremation burial in a simple pit or hollow cut in the original ground surface. This may indeed have been the normal burial rite for the majority of people.

The simplicity of these burials should not, however, be taken to imply simplicity of ritual, for excavated sites show that burial beneath a round barrow in the mid second millennium often involved several stages of activity. The picture is well illustrated by the evidence from the Bevan's

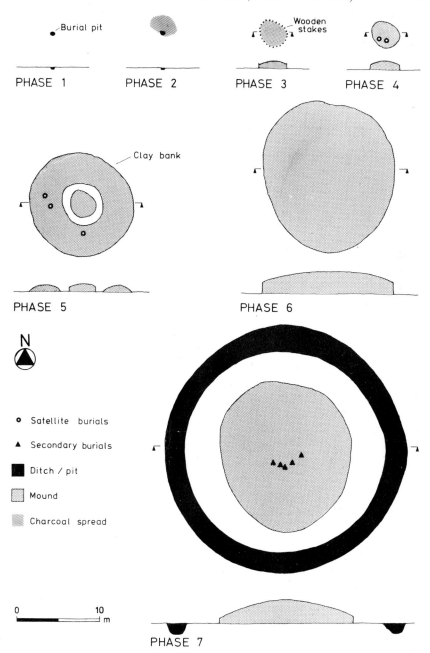

Plans and sections illustrating the main phases in the development of the Bevan's Quarry round barrow, Temple Guiting.

Quarry round barrow, Temple Guiting, excavated by Helen O'Neil in 1964.[29] The site is one of a small cemetery of four or more barrows. The primary burial, a cremation without grave goods, was placed in a small hole dug into the original ground surface. A fire was then lit either over or beside the burial and this resulted in a spread of ash and burnt soil around and over the grave. When these rituals had been completed, a mound of turves was built over the burial and the remains of the fires, the mound being edged with wooden stakes driven into the ground at intervals of about 0.4m. The turf mound was then capped with small overlapping stones, and two further cremation burials were added at this time by simply digging a pair of holes into the top of the mound. In the fifth stage the mound was enlarged by the addition of a wide clay bank, standing free of the turf mound and making the whole monument some 13m in diameter. Another three cremations were added after the construction of the bank. In stage six the outer face of the clay bank was revetted with a loosely built dry-stone-wall, and the whole area of the barrow was built-up with stone rubble to form a cairn measuring 15m in diameter. Finally, an area up to 4m wide around the barrow was cleared of topsoil, and beyond this a ditch 2.5–3m wide and 1.3m deep was excavated right round the barrow. The whole thing must have been an impressive feature. In its final form the barrow probably stood some 1.5–2.0m high and, when new, would have appeared creamy-white because of the exposed rock.

Other barrows were probably less pretentious. Swell 8, the round barrow nearest to the Neolithic long barrow in the Cow Common cemetery, was excavated by Alan Saville in 1974–5 and proved to have been little more than 10m in diameter when new.[30] The central burial was a cremation, and, as at Bevan's Quarry, a fire had been lit over or beside the burial pit after the ashes of the deceased (probably an adolescent) had been interred. Samples of charcoal from the burnt timbers under Swell 8 gave radiocarbon dates in the mid 15th century BC, but they were massive pieces of oak from mature trees and the actual burial may in fact have been rather later.

Whether bodies were cremated on the site of the barrow, or brought for burial after cremation elsewhere, is not always clear. In some cases, for example at Cold Ashton barrows 1 and 2 (Avon), and Avening barrows 6b and 6c, the cremated remains of an individual were found buried under one barrow and the funeral pyre under a neighbouring mound.[31] In contrast, at Swell 3, another of the Cow Common cemetery group, the body appears to have been cremated where the burial was made. In this case a bone pin, which may have been a dress fastener or perhaps of shroud pin, was burnt with the body and became incorporated with the burial deposit.[32] At Swell 5, in the same group of barrows, the primary cremation was probably that of an adult male whose ashes had been buried in a pit cut through the pyre on which the body had been burnt. In this case an unburnt bone pin was found on top of the burnt bones so it may have fastened a cloth in which the bones had been wrapped.[33]

Many of these burials contain only a proportion of the ashes that would result from cremating a body, and it must be assumed that either they were token deposits and the remainder were disposed of elsewhere, or that those carrying out the burial rites simply did not bother to gather up all the ashes.

Biconical urn burials

In addition to collared urns, a variety of other pottery vessels were used to contain cremations. Among the more elaborate vessels were the Wessex biconical urns and barrel urns, of which one example of each is known from Gloucestershire.

The Wessex biconical urn was found in the Swell 1 barrow within the Cow Common cemetery.[34] The urn itself is heavily decorated with applied cordons, cord impressed triangular motifs, and, most distinctive, four applied horseshoe-like decorations which look like handles. It had been set

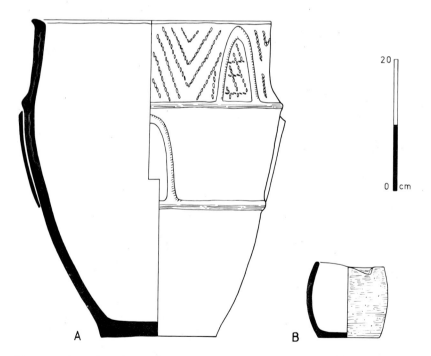

(A) Biconical urn from the Swell 1 round barrow, Swell; (B) small barrel urn from Burn Ground round barrow 6, Hampnett.

in an inverted position and contained the cremated remains of an adult along with a bronze razor which had passed through the pyre. This burial had been inserted into the mound of a late Neolithic round barrow as a secondary deposit.

The barrel urn was found in barrow 6 within the Burn Ground cemetery, Hampnett.[35] It is small and roughly made, but appears to have accompanied the primary burial in the barrow, of which only a few scraps of cremated bone survived.

Animal burials

The burials placed under round barrows were not always of humans. At Bourton-on-the-Water, a ring-ditch 29.2m in diameter which had been revealed during the construction of a new car park in 1972 proved to contain only a single burial pit within which were the remains of two dogs.[36]

The end of the round barrow tradition

From about 1200 BC the tradition of round barrow building began to decline. The reuse of earlier barrows by inserting secondary cremations increased, and in common with middle Bronze Age practices elsewhere in southern England, flat cremation cemeteries became common.

Middle Bronze Age cremation cemeteries are characterized by the use of distinctive types of urns which in central southern England are known as Deverel-Rimbury type urns after a collection recovered from two barrows in Dorset. These urns are large bucket-shaped pots, often rather coarse, with only slight decoration which is usually restricted to lines of fingernail impressions. The largest Deverel-Rimbury style cemetery in Gloucestershire is at the Bevan's Quarry round barrow, Temple Guiting.[37] Here, five burials were dug into the top the earlier barrow, perhaps several centuries after its initial construction. Most were confined to the south-east quadrant of the mound, presumably because some special significance attached to that orientation. Some burial deposits contained more than one individual, and altogether a minimum of six adults (including males and females) and one child were represented. The cemetery may have extended beyond the Bevan's Quarry barrow itself, and may even have spread as far as the nearby site of Temple Guiting 3 which also apparently contained a scatter of secondary urns.[38] All the urns from the Bevan's Quarry cemetery are limestone tempered and probably of local manufacture. Indeed, Deverel-Rimbury cemeteries are typically situated close to settlements.[39]

Single finds of Deverel-Rimbury type urns have been reported from two other sites. At Lower Swell a biconical urn with two plain, applied cordons

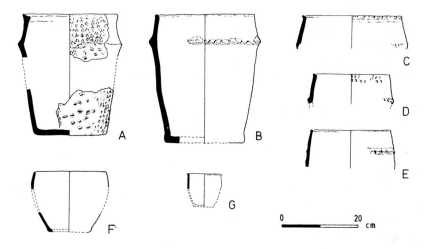

Deverel-Rimbury style urns from Bevan's Quarry round barrow, Temple Guiting.

was found in 1935, together with the cremated remains a young adult, possibly female, in a previously unrecorded barrow.[40] Nearby, on Cow Common, Swell, a Deverel-Rimbury style urn with a simple horizontal line of finger-tip impressed decoration on the shoulder was found stratified above the Wessex biconical urn already referred to from Swell 1.[41]

Burials which can be dated to the late Bronze Age (1000–700 BC) are very scarce in Gloucestershire. Some of the cremation cemeteries may have continued in use down to perhaps 800 BC, but on ceramic grounds it is unlikely that any were used much later. Among the latest cremation burials made in round barrows must be the example from Chedworth Woods, excavated before 1872, and comprising a bipartite urn together with burnt bones, possibly of a female.[42] One interesting exception to the cremation tradition of the late Bronze Age is a crouched inhumation found at Roughground Farm, Lechlade, which has a radiocarbon date of about 900 BC.[43] If nothing else, this find raises the question of how many other unaccompanied inhumations in fact belong to this period.

Standing stones

In some parts of Britain, small cemeteries of the middle and late second millennium BC were marked by standing stones.[44] A number of such stones can be recognized in the Gloucestershire area, although they have sometimes been interpreted as the remains of Neolithic long barrows.

Standing stones. (Left) The Long Stone, Minchinhampton. (Right) The Queen Stone, Goodrich (Hereford and Worcester). The scale in the right-hand picture totals 2m. [Photographs: Author]

There are two reasons for rejecting such an interpretation in most cases. Firstly, few long barrows incorporate upright stones of very large size, and secondly, some of these standing stones are found so near to authentic long barrows that they prompt the question: why would one long barrow has been so extensively robbed that only a single upright is left standing while similar mounds nearby were left untouched ?

One of the most impressive standing stones on the Cotswolds is the Long Stone, Minchinhampton.[45] This giant slab of local limestone stands over 2.3m high and is set in an elevated position on generally flat ground. Nearby is another standing stone, The Tinglestone, Avening, which sits uncomfortably on top of a long barrow, and to the south there are further standing stones at Boxwell Lodge, Boxwell with Leighterton, and The Grickstone, Horton (Avon).

In the north Cotswolds the most notable standing stone is The King Stone, Rollright (Oxfordshire/Warwickshire border). Recent excavations have shown that here the standing stone lies among a group of small Bronze Age burial monuments which variously date to the middle centuries of the second millennium BC.[46]

West of the River Severn three standing stones have been recorded to date. Nothing is known of the Long Stone, beside the Staunton to Coleford road, but in the 1870s when a standing stone on Closeturf Farm, St Briavels, was destroyed bones were said to have been found.[47] Digging in the vicinity of the Queen Stone on the Huntsham peninsula, Goodrich (Hereford and Worcester), also turned up bones and pottery.[48] In contrast to the other standing stones in the area, this last mentioned example is situated on low ground.

Settlement

Early Bronze Age

No early Bronze Age settlements are known in the county, although occasional stray finds like the large piece of cord-decorated pottery found during a watching brief at Oldbury Road, Tewkesbury,[49] and the sherds of Bronze Age pottery from Lechlade[50] perhaps hint at where they might be found. Some of the many flint scatters known both on the Cotswolds and in

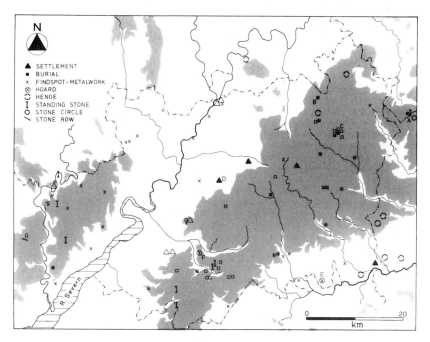

Map showing the distribution of recorded sites dating to between *c* 1600 and *c* 1000 BC. Open triangles indicate doubtful settlement sites. Filled squares indicate dagger/knife graves, half filled squares indicate urn burials, open squares indicate other burials. A = Rollright (Oxfordshire); B = Snowshill; C = Cow Common, Swell; D = Hucclecote Villa Gloucester; E = Down Ampney hoard; F = Rodborough hoard; G = Trelleck (Gwent).

the Severn Valley may also betray the existence of such sites, but at present insufficient analysis has been undertaken to make identification certain.

Despite this paucity of occupation sites, stray finds and burials of the period 1600–1400 BC suggest that settlement was widespread in the county. The distribution of barrows includes major concentrations on the high ground and in river valleys. Stray finds of perforated stone implements such as the axe-hammer of Hyssington picrite from Cromhall (Avon),[51] and the sandstone adzes from Cutsdean and Hucclecote[52] are also widely scattered, and bronze implements of this period are equally well dispersed.

Middle Bronze Age

The spread of burial sites and stray finds of metalwork, which by this time included new types of axes known as palstaves alongside the traditional range of tools and weapons, suggests that the same basic distribution of settlement was maintained through the middle Bronze Age. The only notable change is an increase in the number of finds of this period known from the Forest of Dean and the area west of the Severn. However, beside this rather general evidence for the extent of settlement there are a number of sites which have yielded traces of middle Bronze Age occupation.

At Slade Barn, Hawling, a small Deverel-Rimbury style pot was found in a ditch or pit in the course of quarrying.[53] No further exploration of the site was undertaken, and some doubt as to whether this find should be interpreted as a burial or settlement debris must remain. Recently, however, fieldwalking in the area has revealed that the quarry is on the edge of a major flint-scatter that includes much material of Bronze Age date.[54] This, coupled with the fact that a barrow cemetery lies only 300m away, suggests that here was the site of a small settlement replete with burial ground.

The Severn Valley seems to have been an important area for settlement in middle Bronze Age times. At Hucclecote, a ditch containing the remains of at least three Deverel-Rimbury style pots, together with worked flints and two pebbles, was found beneath the Roman Villa during excavations in 1933.[55] From the published description, it sounds as if this ditch might have been a gully encircling a round house, and if correct this would be entirely typical of settlements of the period.

At Frocester, the systematic excavation by Eddie Price of a large Iron Age farmstead and Roman villa, has also brought to light traces of earlier occupation.[56] A large pit or shaft 3.0m deep is the earliest feature, and in the bottom was a stout oak post radiocarbon dated to about 1200 BC. Many pieces of struck flint were found in the fill of this shaft, but whether it was a well or served some ritual purpose is uncertain.

In the northern part of the Severn Valley, middle Bronze Age settlement has also been encountered at Holm Castle on the outskirts of Tewkesbury.[57] Here, excavations by Alan Hannan in the early 1970s revealed a ditch 42m long with an entrance gap about 3m wide at its mid-point. Nearby was a pit of Bronze Age date.

Just outside the county at Beckford (Hereford and Worcester) a substantial boundary ditch up to 2.5m deep and containing charcoal which yielded a radiocarbon date of about 1400 BC was discovered during excavations in 1972–3.[58]

At Roughground Farm, Lechlade, middle Bronze Age occupation dating to about 1000 BC includes a selection of fingernail-impressed pottery of Deverel-Rimbury style from pits and ditches, together with lines of postholes and fences. A collection of animal remains from one of the pits was dominated by sheep bones, but whether this is representative of middle Bronze Age settlements throughout the county is impossible to say at present.[59]

A rather different type of occupation site is known at Sandy Lane, Leckhampton.[60] Here, excavations by Dr Christopher Young revealed a mound of burnt limestone situated beside a small stream. In addition to pottery and flintwork there was part of a clay mould for casting a bronze socketed spearhead. Perhaps rather similar, although at the time of writing strictly undated, is the stream-side cooking pit discovered beneath a thick deposit of hill-wash and alluvium at The Buckles, Frocester.[61] At this site there was no burnt mound, but the cooking pit had been used on several occasions and as a result a layer of charcoal and ash up to 80mm thick had accumulated over the bank of the stream.

Cave sites continued to be used during the Bronze Age, for burials and for temporary shelter, and a bronze razor was recovered from Merlin's Cave, Whitchurch (Hereford and Worcester) in 1924.[62]

No certain enclosures of middle Bronze Age date, such as are known elsewhere in southern England, have been identified in Gloucestershire, although they might be expected. One possible site of this type that would merit investigation is a rhomboid cropmark enclosure high on the limestone plateau at Scotsquarr Hill, Harescombe.[63] Near the enclosure are at least three round barrows, and a bronze razor has been reported as a stray find from the area.[64]

Late Bronze Age

Late Bronze Age occupation sites are few in number, but since they occur in much the same areas as middle Bronze Age sites it can be suggested that settlement remained well dispersed during the early first millennium.

In the Severn Valley at Frocester, occupation continued into the late Bronze Age, and at some time in the 7th or 8th century BC a series of

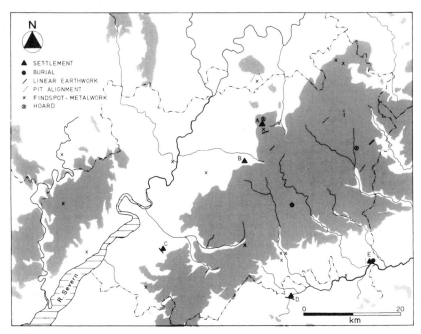

Map showing the distribution of recorded sites dating to between *c* 1000 and *c* 700 BC.
A = Nottingham Hill, Gotherington; B = Sandy Lane, Leckhampton; C = Frocester
Court, Frocester; D = Ashton Keynes (Wiltshire); E = Roughground Farm and Butler's
Field, Lechlade.

The large late Bronze Age ditch at Frocester. The scale totals 6 feet. [Photograph: Author]

boundary ditches was laid out.[65] Excavation of the largest of these shows that it was fairly consistently 1.3m deep and about 4.3m wide; no causeways or crossing points have been found in the portion examined. The site lies on a low gravel ridge, and since the ditch runs roughly along the centre of the ridge it may be supposed that its purpose was to divide the area of slightly raised ground into two roughly equal parts.

In the upper Thames Valley a linear boundary ditch of rather similar form to the one at Frocester has been recognized from aerial photographs at Ashton Keynes (Wiltshire).[66] Although strictly speaking undated, this boundary also bisects a spread of gravel, and is particularly interesting because a sub-rectangular enclosure is joined to it. Within this enclosure are traces of at least one circular house.

Other possible occupation sites of the late Bronze Age include Roughground Farm, Lechlade,[67] Sandy Lane, Leckhampton,[68] and Nottingham Hill, Gotherington.[69] This last mentioned site is particularly interesting as the evidence of late Bronze Age occupation first came to light when a hoard of bronze objects, including swords, a knife, a palstave, and a variety of tools and fittings, was brought to the surface in the course of ploughing. Subsequent excavations revealed pits and a trackway, although it was not possible to demonstrate the relationship between the hoard and the supposedly Iron Age ramparts that defend the hilltop (see p.126 below).

Metalworking

Throughout the Bronze Age, the skills of metalworkers in Britain developed apace, and an ever greater range of objects were produced. Bronze and gold were the main metals used, and by the early first millennium BC most of the techniques of metalworking that are familiar today – casting, hammering, annealing, riveting, alloying, and soldering – had been developed and were widely used. Other technical changes during the period included the introduction of lead bronze to facilitate casting, and the manufacture of hollow moulds in which to cast intricate tools, weapons and ornaments. Together, these various technological changes allow the identification of a series of industrial phases, each characterized by specific types of product and manufacturing techniques. The later part of the early Bronze Age is represented by the Arreton Down industry, followed by the Acton Park and the Taunton industries of the middle Bronze Age, and then the Penard, Wilburton, and Ewart Park industries of the late Bronze Age.[70]

Metalworking certainly took place within the county, as shown by the mould fragments from the stream-side settlement at Sandy Lane, Leckhampton.[71] Indeed it is surprising that there is not more evidence of metalworking in the area because the upper Severn Valley was certainly a

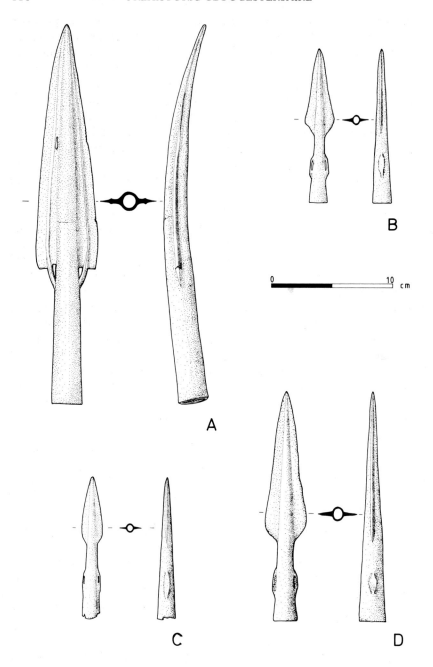

Middle Bronze Age spearheads. (A) Dudgrove Farm, Fairford; (B) Fosse Road, Cirencester; (C) and (D) Down Ampney hoard.

focus for early Bronze Age industries, and the river would have provided people living in the Gloucestershire area with direct and easy access to the main ore-bearing areas such as north Wales and the south-west peninsula.

Most of the Arreton tradition metalwork of the early Bronze Age in Gloucestershire comes from the dagger graves, but stray finds include a fine tanged spearhead from Brackenbury Ditches, North Nibley,[72] a pair of kite-shaped spearheads from Rodborough Common,[73] and flanged axes from: Staunton, High Nash, Viney Hill, Whittington, and Kilcot Wood, Newent.[74] The last mentioned axe is decorated with incised lines arranged in a chevron design. The hoard of bronzes from Westbury-on-Trym (Avon), is also of Arreton tradition,[75] and comprises three decorated flanged axes and a chisel or tracer which was probably a metalworker's tool.

By the middle Bronze Age the organization of metalworking had become fairly complicated, and it has been suggested that production took place at two distinct levels.[76] Firstly there was the localized manufacture of tools and ornaments, perhaps by a community craftsman or a locally based part-time metalworker, and secondly there was regional production of fine weapons, probably by specialist craftsmen. With this distinction in mind it is notable that the 20 or so axes and palstaves from Gloucestershire that can be dated to the middle Bronze Age are widely scattered throughout the county. Most are of fairly standard types, although the axe from Weston-sub-Edge is rather unusual as it was a craftsman's tool dating to about 1300 BC.[77] In contrast, the 13 or so middle Bronze Age spearheads cluster in the east of the county; only four examples having been found west of the Cotswold escarpment. One possible explanation for this pattern is that the distribution is influenced by the strongly regional weapon-producing workshops in the middle and lower Thames Valley.[78]

Although caches or hoards of metalwork, possibly deposited during times of unrest, are a well known feature of the middle Bronze Age, the only example from Gloucestershire is the pair of side-looped spearheads from Down Ampney[79] which came to light during the routine ploughing of an arable field. No middle Bronze Age ornaments of the Taunton industrial phase are known from Gloucestershire despite its proximity to the heartland of the ornament distributions in north Somerset.

In the later Bronze Age the two distinct levels of production common in earlier centuries apparently merged and both everyday items and fine weapons were made by local smiths. Few late Bronze tools and weapons are known from Gloucestershire, but they do seem to be scattered widely around the county. Stray finds of socketed axes include examples of two regional styles (Sompting types and Llanarth types), while a winged axe from Sudeley belongs to the Penard phase.[80] Spearheads, all of socketed type with a peg-hole to secure the shaft, are known, from Kempsford, Cirencester, Abbeydale, and Coughton Marsh (Hereford and Worcester).[81]

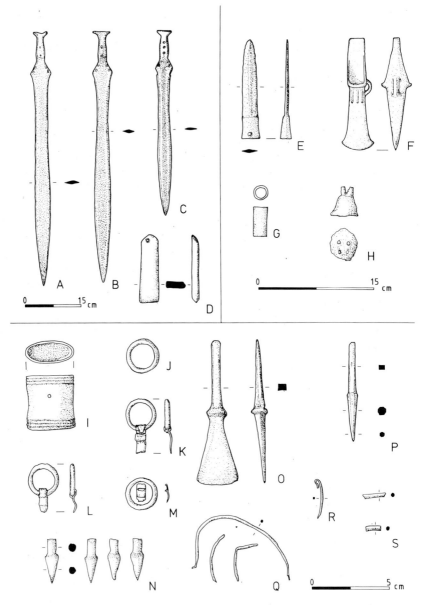

Hoard of Ewart Park tradition bronze weapons, tools, and ornaments from Nottingham Hill, Gotherington.

More unusual finds include a bronze knife with a square sectioned tang from Cleeve Hill, Southam,[82] and the bronze saw, possibly of Penard phase, from Brackenbury Ditches, North Nibley.[83] A bronze barbed and tanged arrowhead is known from just over the county boundary at Beckford (Hereford and Worcester).[84]

Perhaps the most important finds of late Bronze Age metalwork from the county are represented by two hoards. The first came to light in 1907 during ploughing near Bourton-on-the-Water.[85] It appears that the pieces lay under a large stone about 0.3m below the ground surface. The hoard comprised eight socketed axes which belong to the Ewart Park industrial phase, broadly 8–9th century BC in date. Stylistically, all the pieces are of Stogursey, or South Wales, type and it is notable that no two had come from the same mould.

The second hoard was found on Nottingham Hill, Gotherington in 1972, again during routine ploughing.[86] A small excavation followed the initial discovery of the first two pieces, and eventually the hoard was found to contain a total of 25 objects. As a result of the excavation it was discovered that the pieces had been buried together in a wooden box, and that weapons, tools, and ornaments were mixed up together. The most spectacular pieces were three complete bronze swords, of Ewart Park phase, all with broad leaf-shaped blades and cast tangs. In addition there was a whetstone, possibly for sharpening the swords, a side looped palstave, a socketed knife, a bronze ferrule, a casting jet, a scabbard chape, four conical head rivets, four cast bronze rings with strapwork, three pieces of bronze wire, a bronze pin of roughly rectangular section, a tanged chisel with centre stop, a tanged awl, and two rivets.

Whether these two hoards were connected with settlements is not known, but taken together they suggest that during the last centuries of the late Bronze Age conditions in the area prompted the hiding of valuable objects which were not subsequently recovered by their owners.

Ceremonial and ritual sites

Barrows and standing stones were important features of the middle Bronze Age, and some stone rows and stone circles may have been maintained down to about 1100 BC. By the turn of the first millennia, however, the construction and use of these monuments had all but ceased and new types of ceremonial activity seem to have been favoured, of which the most widespread was a preoccupation with rivers, bogs and wet places.

Interest in watery places may of course have had much earlier roots, shown perhaps in the location of cursus monuments beside rivers, but from about 1000 BC onwards much of the fine metalwork that had formerly been deposited in graves was instead deposited in rivers or wet places. The River Thames has yielded many late Bronze Age weapons,[87] and there are numerous large collections of similar items from bogs and old river beds in the upper Severn Valley in Hereford and Worcester, and Shropshire.[88] It is therefore slightly surprising that only three or four pieces of Bronze Age metalwork from Gloucestershire are known to have come from rivers or bogs. These include the middle Bronze Age basal looped spearhead from Batsford Park, Moreton-in-Marsh, which was found in a stream,[89] a middle Bronze Age palstave from the River Severn at Wainlode,[90] a basal-looped spearhead found on Dudgrove Farm, Fairford, which probably came from the River Thames,[91] and, the most recent find in this group, a late Bronze Age socketed spearhead from Abbeydale, near Gloucester, which came to light in a layer of peat or waterlogged alluvium and when found still had a portion of its wooden shaft projecting from the socket.[92] From just outside the county, a late Bronze Age peg-hole spearhead from Coughton Marsh, Walford (Hereford and Worcester),[93] may also be a wetland find. It is, however, notable that the two largest spearheads from the area, those from Croughton Marsh and Dudgrove Farm are both, from wet places.

Why fine metalwork was deposited in wet places is not clear. One possibility is that the objects were sacrificial offerings to water gods, another that they result from battles being fought nearby. A more likely explanation is that these objects were grave goods and that they were deposited with either complete bodies or cremated remains.[94] Such an explanation would certainly provide a mechanism for the disposal of the dead after round barrows and flat cremation ceremonies ceased to be fashionable, and there would also be a neat element of continuity in the disposal of tools and weapons with the dead which goes back to late Neolithic times. However, until further research has been undertaken, and some of the human remains from rivers properly dated, these possibilities must remain highly speculative.

Society and land-use

The expansion of settlement that began in the beaker period, if not earlier, seems to have continued though the Bronze Age, probably prompted by a growing population. By the end of the middle Bronze Age there is good evidence from occupation sites, stray finds, and burials that most of Gloucestershire was settled, with perhaps as many as 60 to 100 communities at any one time. It cannot, however, be assumed that land-use was consistent over the whole the county, or indeed remained the same throughout the Bronze Age. The Cotswolds in particular pose a problem, because although the settlements of late Neolithic, beaker period, and Bronze Age date clearly concentrated in the valleys and on lower ground, many barrows have been recorded on the uplands, and people clearly visited these areas regularly even if they did not live there all the time.

One possibility, suggested for the Cotswolds, is that parts of the uplands were open areas available for hunting and grazing by pastoralists based on the lower ground in the upper Thames Valley and the Severn Valley.[95] Another possibility, is that because a much greater density of Bronze Age arrowheads has been recorded on the Cotswolds than for earlier periods or in the area around about, the uplands may have been a waring zone at this time.[96]

Whatever the true pattern for the early and middle Bronze Age there is already good evidence that things were changing more rapidly during the last centuries of the late Bronze Age.

The construction of linear ditches such as those known at Frocester, Beckford (Hereford and Worcester), and Ashton Keynes (Wiltshire) marks the beginning of a new concern for the partitioning of the landscape, a concern that can be seen at other sites too. At Butler's Field, Lechlade, for example, excavations in 1985[97] revealed that a major land boundary represented by a line a large pits each nearly 2m deep and 2m across was constructed in the late Bronze Age across the centre of a gravel terrace. Other, very similar, pit alignments are known from aerial photographs at Condicote, Temple Guiting, and Great Rissington,[98] and while none of these have strictly speaking been dated, they can provisionally be assigned to the same period as the Lechlade alignment on the basis of their form. Elsewhere on the Cotswolds, linear boundaries can still be seen as earthworks, as for example on Icomb Hill near Stow on the Wold, Cleeve Common, and Freezing Hill, Doynton (Avon). In all these cases the boundaries comprise a bank and ditch which runs for hundreds of metres across the landscape.[99]

To this archaeological evidence must be added the environmental evidence which documents the opening-up of the landscape in the early first millennium BC. At Ripple Brook, Ripple (Hereford and Worcester), the pollen sequence clearly shows that between about 900 BC and 400 BC the vegetational character of the area changed from being heavily wooded, perhaps with some pastoral activity, to a landscape almost totally cleared of trees and intensively farmed.[100] It was during this same period that substantial deposits of alluvium began to build up in the Severn and Avon Valleys,[101] and probably also in the Windrush Valley.[102] The most likely source of detritus for the formation of this alluvium is soil washed from cultivated fields. Together, all this evidence suggests an intensification of agricultural production starting in the late Bronze Age.

New land-use patterns and agricultural intensification are not, however,

Pit alignment at Butler's Field, Lechlade, during excavation. [Photograph: David Miles]

the only changes that can be discerned at this time. From about 1000 BC there is an obvious increase in the quantity and sophistication of weaponry available in the area – the first arms race. By the end of the late Bronze Age slashing swords such as those in the Nottingham Hill hoard were widely available alongside the more traditional spears. Moreover, the presence of sword chapes and harness fittings in Ewart Park phase hoards suggests that by this time horses were being used in battle.

Whether all Bronze Age weapons were used in earnest, or whether some were simply for display and ceremony is not clear. A few pieces look too fine to have been of much use on the battlefield and these may have been prestige weapons, but the smaller less elaborate pieces are usually found broken or bent and these were undoubtedly used in battle. Direct evidence for Bronze Age warfare was found at West Littleton Down, Tormarton (Avon) when the skeletons of two young adult males in a pit or ditch came to light during the construction of a pipeline in 1968.[103] Both bodies had apparently been buried without ceremony and they both displayed the marks of mortal wounds inflicted by spears tipped with bronze spearheads. Each had a hole through the pelvis where a spear had penetrated the bone, and one of them still had a spearhead lodged in his spine when the excavators uncovered the skeleton. A radiocarbon date from this body places the incident in the 10th century BC.

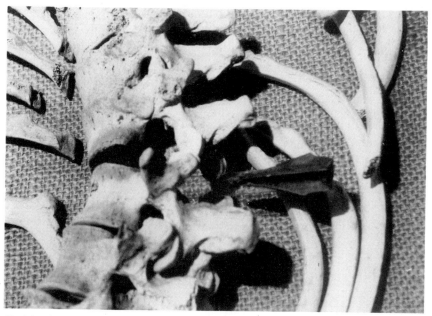

Burial II from West Littleton Down, Tormarton (Avon), with bronze spearhead adjacent to where it was found lodged in the spine. [Photograph: Author]

Taking all the available evidence together, the picture that begins to emerge is one of increasing unrest among the communities living in the area during the early first millennium BC. Agricultural intensification may be glimpsed, perhaps as the availability of good agricultural land came under pressure from a rising population and a halt on any further expansion of settlement. The demarcation of land units implies that greater emphasis was being placed upon the ownership of specific areas. In consequence, warfare may have become rife, and there might even have been raiding or battles between neighbouring communities.

6

The Age of the Hillforts (c 700 – c 100 BC)

Social unrest and new materials

The division between the Bronze Age and the Iron Age at about 700 BC is traditionally defined in terms of technical developments in the art of metalworking, particularly the replacement of bronze by iron as the main metal for manufacturing tools and weapons. That this change took place is certain, but it must not be allowed to overshaddow the far more fundamental transformations taking place within society at about the same time.

The indications of unrest which could be glimpsed in the late Bronze Age accelerated during the 7th and 6th centuries BC. Fortified villages, hillforts as they are often known, began to be built again in the west of England for the first time in over a thousand years.[1] Agricultural intensification seemingly continued apace, and greater quantities of weapons were produced than ever before.

Quite why these changes should occur over a relatively short period, and with such impact, in the mid-west of England is not entirely clear, but they may have been indirectly related to a deterioration in the climate.[2] Between about 1000 BC and 600 BC the climate became colder and wetter, to the extent that by about 800 BC the shorter growing season and the effects of soil exhaustion forced many upland communities to abandon their farms in the hills.[3] As a result of this exodus, resources in the areas surrounding the uplands came under great pressure from an increased population trying to live off less land. It is therefore hardly surprising that areas like the Cotswolds and Welsh Marches show the first signs of unrest and the earliest hillforts.

The introduction of ironworking may also have been part of this general pattern of social change rather than the result of a technological breakthrough as so often believed.[4] The skills to work iron had probably been available to metalworkers in northern Europe since the beginning of the first millennium BC, but bronze was convenient and there was no reason to change. Supplies of copper, tin, and lead were easily obtained through exchange networks that had been operating for centuries, despite the fact that iron ore was more easily and more widely available. However, when supplies of raw materials for making bronze were disrupted by unrest among the communities living in the ore-bearing areas of western Britain, the situation changed. Locally available supplies of iron ore suddenly came into their own and it would have been quite natural for craftsmen to change over to iron for making tools and weapons.

One lasting effect of the construction of defended villages in the early and middle Iron Age is that settlements have survived in large numbers, to the extent that the archaeology of the period is dominated by studies of occupation sites.

Early Iron Age hillforts

Within Gloucestershire there are about 35 hillforts, mostly along the Cotswold escarpment and on the high ground in the east of the county.

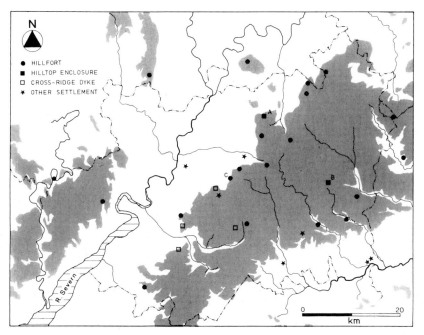

Map showing the distribution of recorded sites dating to between *c* 700 and *c* 300 BC. A = Nottingham Hill, Gotherington; B = Norbury Camp, Northleach with Eastington; C = Crickley Hill, Coberley.

Only five hillforts are known to the west of the Severn on the Forest of Dean uplands.[5] Beyond the county boundary there are two examples each on Bredon Hill and the Malvern Hills (Hereford and Worcester), and of course others on the Cotswolds to the north-east in Oxfordshire and to the south-west in Avon. To the west of the River Wye there are numerous small hillforts in Gwent, and Hereford and Worcester.[6]

The hillforts of Gloucestershire are not, however, all of the same date or purpose; different types were built at different times, and during the course of the Iron Age the function and role of hillforts changed. This makes discussion of the evidence rather difficult, especially when dealing with sites which have not been excavated. It is, therefore, necessary to draw upon evidence from a much wider area in order to understand the evidence from the county.[7] Pottery provides one of the main ways of dating hillforts, and in the early Iron Age two types predominate: distinctive fine angular profile bowls (sometimes decorated with incised lines or coated with haematite slip) and large jars with elaborated rims and fingertip decoration.[8]

The earliest Iron Age hillforts that can be recognized in the Gloucester-shire area fall into two distinct types: large hilltop enclosures and small heavily defended settlements.

Hilltop enclosures

Two large hilltop enclosures are known in Gloucestershire: Nottingham Hill, Gotherington, and Norbury Camp, Northleach with Eastington.

Nottingham Hill occupies a spur of the main Cotswold escarpment that projects westwards into the Severn Vale.[9] Two parallel ramparts cut off the promontory and enclose an area of about 49ha. The interior of the enclosure is fairly flat; the steep slopes providing natural defences on the north, south, and west sides. Little is known of the nature or extent of occupation within the enclosure, although small-scale excavations in 1972 suggest at least two phases of activity.[10] The earliest was represented by a markedly worn track running down the long axis of the enclosure, the second by a hearth in the middle of the track and five sub-circular soil-filled depressions scattered on either side. These depressions may be storage pits, but they were not excavated. A collection of late Bronze Age (Ewart Park phase) metalwork was recovered from the interior and suggests an early origin for the use of this hilltop, although not necessarily for the construction of the defences.

Norbury Camp lies on the crown of the Cotswold dip slope.[11] The defences consist of a single bank and probably a ditch on the east and west sides, an embankment and scarping along the north side, and a steep natural slope along the south side. The area enclosed is about 32ha. In 1977 an excavation under the direction of Alan Saville in the centre of the enclosure revealed the presence of three structures.[12] Each consisted of four postholes

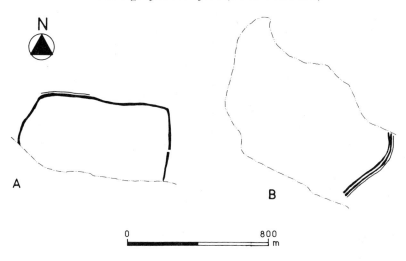

Hilltop enclosures at (A) Nottingham Hill, Gotherington, and (B) Norbury Camp, Northleach with Eastington.

arranged in a square with sides 2m-3m in length. These structures, known as 4-posters, are highly distinctive of the Iron Age period in southern England, and are thought to have been above-ground granaries.[13]

Interpreting the evidence from Norbury Camp and Nottingham Hill is not easy in view of the limited amount of excavation that has taken place, but both display features which may tentatively be connected with the storage of agricultural produce, and following the arguments used for similar sites elsewhere, these enclosures may be seen as defended food stores which may also have been used as stock enclosures, perhaps with limited occupation.[14]

In the central Cotswolds around Stroud there is a group of sites which are broadly similar to the large hilltop enclosures which may have served the same purpose. These are all simply large flat, steep-sided, promontories which are defended by a cross-ridge dyke comprising a bank and ditch set across the neck of land where the promontory joins the main hill. The best examples are: Cooper's Hill, Brockworth; Pen Hill, Kings Stanley; and Randwick Wood, Randwick. Another possible example is at Juniper Hill, Edgeworth, although the area of hilltop enclosed here is very small.[15]

Defended settlements

The second class of early Iron Age hilltop site is the defended settlement. These are small, typically less than 4ha, and they are almost always situated

Cross-ridge dyke in Randwick Woods, Randwick. [Photograph: Author]

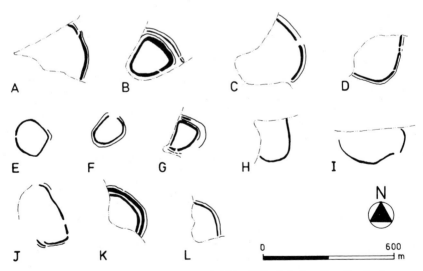

Early type hillforts on the Cotswolds. A = Crickley Hill, Coberley; B = Brackenbury Ditches, North Nibley; C = Hinton Hill, Dyrham and Hinton (Avon); D = Leckhampton Hill; E = Windrush Camp, Windrush; F = Roel Camp, Sudeley; G = Shenberrow Camp, Stanton; H = Beckbury, Temple Guiting; I = Ablington Camp, Bibury; J = Norbury, Colesbourne; K = Cleeve Cloud Camp, Southam; L = The Castles, Horton (Avon).

in strategic and highly defensible positions. They are heavily defended, usually with a single massive rampart, although occasionally with a pair of ramparts, and particular attention is often given to the entranceways which, as weak points in the defences, were frequently provided with outworks or long entrance tunnels leading to heavy wooden gates.

The most completely known early hillfort in Gloucestershire, and indeed in the whole of southern England, is on Crickley Hill. Here, annual excavations since 1969 under the direction of Dr Philip Dixon have revealed much detail about the interior of the settlement and its history. Full appraisal of the site must await the completion of the excavations, but some preliminary results have already been published.[16]

Crickley Hill is a triangular-shaped promontory projecting westwards from the main Cotswold escarpment. A single massive rampart cuts off the spur, and lesser ramparts have been traced round the north and west sides. The enclosed area is about 3.8ha, and radiocarbon dates suggest that the first Iron Age age defences were built before about 650 BC.

The earliest rampart was built of dry-stone-walling which was laced together with a complex framework of timbers, and fronted by a flat-bottomed ditch cut down about 3m into the solid limestone bedrock. A single gateway provided the only way into the fort from the north-east. Inside, the remains of six large rectangular houses have been found, the largest over 24m in length and between 7m and 8m wide. The main houses

Crickley Hill, Coberley, from the air. [Photograph: Harold Wingham]

Crickley Hill, Coberley. Reconstruction of the round-house period of occupation.
[Drawing: Philip Dixon]

were arranged either side of a road that continued the line of the entrance
passage, although more houses and at least 27 other structures, many of
them 4-posters, have been found scattered over the remainder of the
enclosed area. The rampart provided a formidable defence, and in a small
pit nearby was a quantity of sling stones ready to hand for times of trouble.

Strong as they were, the defences of this early hillfort ultimately proved
inadequate because archaeological evidence shows that the settlement was
captured, the buildings thrown down, and the timber-laced rampart burnt.

After a lapse of some time, possibly decades, the site was reoccupied. A
new entrance comprising massive stone bastions either side of the main
inner gate, and a hornwork with its own outer gate, was constructed,
while, at the same time, the rampart was remodelled on a grand scale.
Inside, the inhabitants lived in round houses rather than long houses. The
largest house was over 15m in diameter and it dominated the settlement just
inside the entrance. The cobbled roadway leading into the fort skirted
round this large house and passed a row of smaller round houses, each one
about 8m in diameter. Clusters of 4-posters were set at a slight distance
from the houses.

This second hillfort at Crickley fared no better than the first, as it was in its turn attacked and overrun. This time the site was not rebuilt and the hilltop was apparently abandoned until Roman times. The successive forts at Crickley, with their distinctive house plans and the abrupt changes in rampart design are thought to represent occupations by different populations, perhaps even different groups of people.[17]

Approximately contemporary with the use of Crickley Hill was the occupation of the nearby hillfort on Leckhampton Hill above Cheltenham. Although badly disfigured by quarrying, the single rampart at Leckhampton can be seen to enclose about 2.8ha on the escarpment edge. Excavations in 1925 and 1969[18] revealed that the rampart had been burnt, but that originally it was about 6m wide and consisted of a stone core revetted with dry-stone-walling tied together with timber lacing. A ditch was cut in front of the rampart, separated by a berm about 1m wide. The entrance to this fort was defended by a pair of semicircular guard chambers, one set into the terminal of the rampart on either side of the gate. Nothing is known of the occupation in the interior of this site.

Another early Iron Age hillfort on the Cotswolds was Shenberrow Camp, Stanton.[19] This site is D-shaped in plan, and is defended on three sides by a double line of ramparts but on the fourth side by only a single line. Excavations in 1935[20] showed that the inner rampart had a dry-stone revetment wall on its inner face and a ditch nearly 3.3m deep. Pottery from the site comprised typical early Iron Age types, including *situla* jars with rounded shoulders and flat-topped rims decorated with finger-tip impressions. No definite buildings were discovered in the small areas of the interior examined, but in a cutting near the centre of the site was a large storage pit 3m in diameter and 2.6m deep. When excavated, this pit proved to contain abundant quantities of domestic refuse including broken pottery, animal bones, charcoal, and a fragment of human skull.[21]

Other early Iron Age hillforts on the Cotswolds include Cleeve Cloud Camp, Southam, with a double line of ramparts,[22] and Burhill Camp, Buckland, which has been partly levelled by cultivation in recent centuries.[23] The hillfort at Brackenbury Ditches, North Nibley may also belong to the early group of forts in view of its position and the arrangement of its defences.[24] Just outside the county the hillforts at Lyneham (Oxfordshire), and Chastleton (Oxfordshire), were also occupied in early Iron Age times.[25]

In west Gloucestershire some of the hillforts in the Forest of Dean may belong to the early Iron Age, but in the absence of firm dating evidence it is impossible to be certain. Just outside the county, however, Midsummer Hill, Eastnor (Hereford and Worcester), began life in the early Iron Age,[26] as did Bredon Hill Camp, Kemerton (Hereford and Worcester). Excavations at this last mentioned site between 1935 and 1937[27] revealed several phases of construction which began with a typical early Iron Age stone-

Aerial view of Cleeve Cloud Camp, Southam. [Photograph: Harold Wingham]

faced rampart and external U-shaped ditch.[28] Like Crickley Hill, the fort on
Bredon Hill was certainly attacked and razed at least once. Among the
debris which fell into the entrance passage after one such attack were six
human skulls which may originally have been set on a shelf or gantry above
the entrance, perhaps as trophies of war.[29]

Early Iron Age non-hillfort settlements

Hillforts and hilltop enclosures were not the only settlements of the early
Iron Age period in Gloucestershire. In both the Severn Valley and the upper
Thames Valley, and on the high ground of the Cotswolds there were small
enclosures and unenclosed sites which were probably occupied at the same
time as the hillforts. Most of these are only known through stray finds of
distinctive early Iron Age type pottery, as for example at: Sandy Lane,
Leckhampton; Crypt Grammar School, Gloucester; Barnsley park; and
Siddington.[30]

Two early Iron Age sites at Lechlade, The Loders and Roughground
Farm, are known in more detail thorough excavation. At The Loders, the
early Iron Age occupation was represented by a cluster of eight pits cut into

the natural gravel subsoil. These had probably been storage pits when first dug, but when they were no longer needed for that purpose they were filled with domestic rubbish. Finds included pottery, much of it fine quality ware, animal bones indicating the presence of cattle and sheep, and clay loom weights suggesting that weaving took place on the site.[31] Nearby, at Roughground Farm, traces of a circular house about 6m in diameter together with numerous pits, and a few gullies, were located in advance of gravel quarrying between 1958 and 1965. More recently, a circular post-built house was found overlying the late Neolithic cursus in an excavation just south of Roughground Farm.[32]

Middle Iron Age hillforts

About 400 BC, many of the small heavily defended early hillforts went out of use. Crickley Hill, for example, was not reoccupied after being razed for the second time, and the same story is told by the evidence from

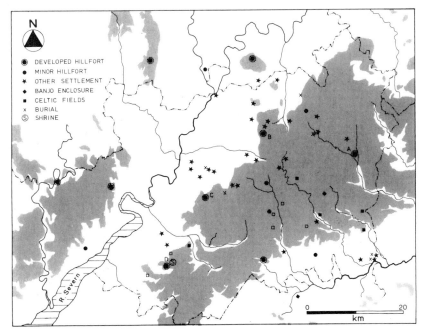

Map showing the distribution of recorded sites dating to between *c* 300 and *c* 100 BC. Open square symbols indicate doubtful areas of celtic fields. A = Salmonsbury, Bourton-on-the-Water; B = Cleeve Cloud Camp, Southam; C = Kimsbury, Painswick; D = Uley Bury, Uley.

Shenberrow Camp, and Leckhampton Hill.[33] In their place new types of hillforts and large enclosures emerged, and these can be most easily recognized through their distinctive construction and the presence of various new styles of pottery which developed at about the same time. This pottery includes barrel-shaped jars, plain burnished bowls with round shoulders, and bead-rimmed bowls, often in dark fabrics. Decoration included linear tooling, stamped or impressed motifs, and curvilinear decoration in the continental La Tène art styles.[34]

Developed hillforts

The most impressive hillforts of the middle Iron Age in Gloucestershire fall into what Professor Barry Cunliffe has called the developed hillfort tradition.[35] These contrast with the earlier sites in being generally much larger and by being defended by several lines of ramparts. The defences were not constructed with timber lacing and a revetment of dry-stone-walling as was common in the early Iron Age, rather they were built of earth and rubble piled up in what is called the 'glacis style'.[36]

There was probably an overall reduction in the number of hillforts occupied during the middle Iron Age, although because each site was larger this does not imply a decrease in population.

Best known among the developed hillforts in Gloucestershire is Uley Bury, Uley, a large, roughly rectangular fort, situated on a promontory projecting from the main Cotswold escarpment south of Stroud.[37] The area enclosed totals about 13ha. The defensive earthworks mostly represent the artificial enhancement of the naturally steep slope surrounding the prom-ontory by terracing and embankment. For most of the perimeter three lines of defences were constructed, an inner bank, an upper terrace with skirting bank, and a lower terrace. Entrances can be identified at the south, east, and north corners, of which the last mentioned, with inturned ramparts, may have been the most important.

Rescue excavations at the site in 1976 under the direction of Alan Saville and Dr Ann Ellison provide a few details of the ramparts along the east side, and the eastern entrance.[38] From this work it is clear that the defences were constructed by cutting back into the natural hill-slope to create more or less level platforms and then, using the quarried material and perhaps additional spoil, the platforms were widened by dumping. This had the effect of increasing the angle of slope between the two terraces. The final task was the addition of ramparts along the edge of the upper terrace, and perhaps on the lower one too. A radiocarbon date from carbonized cereal grains sealed in the construction of the upper terrace suggests that the hillfort as we see it today was built about 300 BC.

In the eastern entrance the excavations revealed a cobbled roadway leading into the fort. No investigations have taken place within the interior,

Aerial view of Uley Bury hillfort, Uley. [Photograph: Royal Commission on the Historical Monuments of England]

although Iron Age pottery has been picked up from the surface of the ploughed fields and aerial photography during the dry summer of 1975 revealed numerous cropmarks indicating the presence of internal compounds, boundary ditches, and circular structures, probably houses.[39]

Equally impressive is Kimsbury hillfort, Painswick Beacon. Here, an area of about 2.8ha is enclosed by a triple line of ramparts along the east, west, and south sides, but with only a single line along the north side.[40] The main entrance is at the south-east corner and the inner bank is here inturned to form an elongated entrance passage thus providing greater control over who entered the fort. The interior of the site is badly damaged by quarrying, and is now used as a golf course. Near the centre of the site is a circular hollow about 6m in diameter and about 2.5m deep. It is surrounded by a low bank and may conceivably have been a well.

Both Uley Bury and Kimsbury rely greatly on topography for their visual impact, but at Salmonsbury Camp, Bourton-on-the-Water, a developed hillfort which is rather larger than Uley Bury was built on a gravel platform between the River Dikler and the River Windrush. The defences comprise two close-set ramparts, each with an external ditch, enclosing a total area of about 22.6ha. There are entrances in the north-west and south-east sides. An annex of perhaps 6ha is defined by two ditches on the south-east side, but its date is not known. An intermittent stream flows through the site, although where it ran in Iron Age times is not known.[41] Excavations by Dr Gerald Dunning between 1931 and 1934 have revealed evidence of the design of the ramparts and the nature of occupation in the interior.[42] In cutting I through the rampart on the south-east side of the site, the inner bank was found to be 18.2m wide, and the ditch 10.9m wide and

Aerial view of Kimsbury hillfort, Painswick. [Photograph: Harold Wingham]

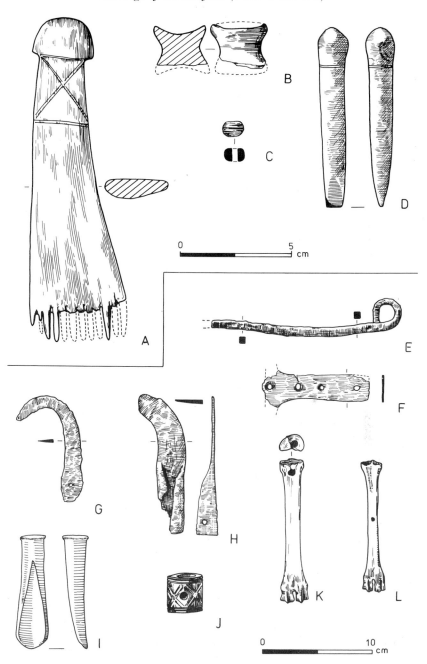

Selection of everyday items from Period I levels at Salmonsbury, Bourton-on-the-Water.

3.6m deep. The outer rampart was about the same size, but the outer ditch was slightly smaller at 5.4m wide and 3.3m deep. Both ramparts were of glacis construction.

In the interior, excavations revealed storage pits and at least two round houses. These houses were each about 6.7m in diameter, and were defined by rings of postholes which had formed the walls, and a central posthole that gave additional support to the roof. Both houses were surrounded by drainage gullies to carry away water from the roof.

Some of the hillforts in the Forest of Dean may also be considered as part of the developed hillfort tradition. Welshbury Camp, Blaisdon, for example, although small at only 1.7ha, is an impressive fort with three lines of ramparts on the south and west sides and a single line along the other two sides.[43]

To the south of the county the site of Sodbury Camp (Avon), is another fine example of a developed hillfort, with a double line of ramparts around the north, south and east sides, but only a single line of defences along the

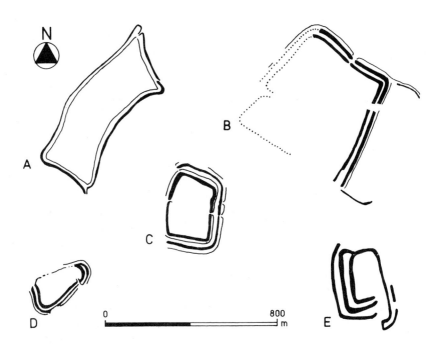

Developed hillforts in Gloucestershire and north Avon. A = Uley Bury, Uley; B = Salmonsbury, Bourton-on-the-Water; C = Sodbury Camp (Avon); D = Kimsbury, Painswick; E = Welshbury, Blaisdon.

western side.[44] To the north of the county lies the well-known developed hillfort on the Herefordshire Beacon (Hereford and Worcester).

As a group, the developed hillforts seen to show less concern for defence than their early Iron Age predecessor. The situation of Salmonsbury Camp, for example, can hardly be regarded as strategic, while at Kimsbury and several other forts the ramparts are massive on two or three sides, but very weak elsewhere. The conclusion which must therefore be drawn is that these hillforts performed rather different roles to the defended settlements of the early Iron Age, with the emphasis on the construction of impressive and imposing monuments rather than defence. It may also be noted that none of the developed hillforts in the area show signs of warfare such as can be seen in the early forts. Indeed, it has been suggested that by middle Iron Age times warfare had became highly formalized, with individual champions fighting for the honour of a community rather than open warfare between groups.[45]

Other hillforts and defended enclosures

Alongside the large developed hillforts were rather smaller and less imposing hillforts and defended enclosures. In some cases early hillforts were remodelled during middle Iron Age times by the addition of extra lines of ramparts. Without excavation such changes are hard to demonstrate, but from irregularities in their ground plans such developments may be suspected at Cleeve Cloud Camp, Brackenbury Ditches, and perhaps also some of the sites in the Forest of Dean like Symond's Yat, English Bicknor, and Spital Meend, Tidenham.[46] More secure evidence is available from Midsummer Hill (Hereford and Worcester),[47] and Bredon Hill Camp (Hereford and Worcester), where the ramparts were probably refurbished in the glacis style during the middle Iron Age.[48]

New hillforts other than the developed hillforts were also certainly built during this period, among them the example in Lydney Park. This site was investigated by Sir Mortimer Wheeler in 1928–9 during his excavation of a Roman temple dedicated to the god Nodens which has been built inside the hillfort long after it had fallen out of use.[49]

Wheeler's excavations revealed that the hillfort was a promontory camp with the neck of the promontory cut off from the rising ground to the north by a double system of ramparts and ditches. The inner of the two ramparts was continued along the eastern side, but whether there was ever a corresponding defensive earthwork along the western side is uncertain. The ramparts were constructed in the glacis style; the area being 1.8ha. Pottery from the site includes classic middle Iron Age bead-rimmed jars and some stamped and incised wares. Little is known of the occupation in the interior, although areas of paving and several postholes were located beneath Roman occupation layers.

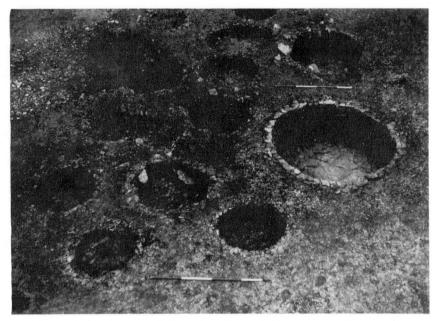

Middle Iron Age settlement at Guiting Manor Farm, Guiting Power, under excavation in 1974. Scales each total 2m. [Photograph: Alan Saville]

Non-hillfort middle Iron Age settlements

As in the early Iron Age, many of the settlements in the county consisted of small enclosures and farmsteads. About 30 such sites are currently known with some certainty, and they are roughly evenly spread throughout the area except for the Forest of Dean. Most can be assigned to the middle Iron Age by their pottery. Some of the very large number of sites recognized only as cropmarks, must also belong to this period. However, without excavation, their dating is often uncertain.[50]

On the Cotswolds the most completely investigated non-hillfort site is at Guiting Manor Farm, Guiting Power.[51] Here, excavations directed by Alan Saville in 1974 uncovered a cluster of 18 rock cut pits, probably storage pits. Most were fairly small, ranging from 1m to 1.8m in diameter and less than 1m deep. One exception, pit 6, was about 2.5m in diameter, about 1m deep and was lined with fine dry-stone-walling. Some of the pits were surrounded by stakeholes suggesting that perhaps a structure of some kind stood over them. Exactly what was stored within most of these pits is uncertain, although the larger examples could well have been grain silos. Such pits are typical of middle Iron Age sites throughout southern England and are

Aerial photograph of banjo enclosures at Ashton Keynes (Wiltshire). [Photograph: Author; Pilot: Ron Locke]

demonstrably very effective for storing grain.[52] No houses were found on the site, perhaps because relatively recent ploughing had removed any traces of postholes, but a geophysical survey revealed the presence of a rectangular enclosure just south of the excavated area, and this may have been where the inhabitants of the site actually lived. Occupation debris thrown into the pits after they ceased to be used for storage included broken pottery, animal bones, an iron knife, and a bronze awl.

A second, rather similar, site is at Wood House, Guiting Power.[53] Investigations here revealed a pit containing middle Iron Age pottery together with animal bones, burnt stones, charcoal, and two lumps of iron slag which suggest that iron working had taken place in the vicinity.

In 1985, during the construction of the Esso Midline through the county, a previously unrecorded middle Iron Age settlement came to light at Winson, near Cirencester.[54] This site proved to be an enclosed settlement, and, in addition to the boundary ditch, postholes and pits were discovered. Among the finds were pottery, animal bones, a bone weaving comb, an bronze brooch of La Tène I style, fragments of salt containers from the Droitwich area, and carbonized grain of wheat and barley.

Elsewhere on the Cotswolds traces of similar settlements have been found at about a dozen other sites,[55] but most result from chance finds, and it is often far from clear whether the site is that of an enclosure or an open settlement.

One distinctive type of enclosure found on the eastern slopes of the Cotswolds is the 'banjo enclosure', so-called because its plan resembles the shape of a banjo in that it has a circular occupation area approached by way of a long narrow trackway flanked by a ditch on either side. One banjo enclosure is known near Northleach,[56] and others have been found near Ashton Keynes (Wiltshire) from aerial photographs.[57] Once it was thought that banjo enclosures were simply stock corrals, but recent excavations suggest that some at least were high status sites, perhaps the homes of important people.[58]

In the Severn Valley, middle Iron Age settlements have been located at over a dozen sites, but as with the Cotswold examples, most are only known through chance finds and partial excavations. One exception to this is the site at Frocester Court, where excavations by Eddie Price have revealed the plan of a single large settlement, comprising a ditched enclosure within which were up to six round houses, not all necessarily occupied at the same time, but most probably of 2nd century BC date.[59]

Provisional reconstruction of the middle-late Iron Age enclosed settlement at Frocester Court, Frocester. [Drawing: Philip Moss]

Work is still continuing, but present evidence suggests that this was not a farmstead as such but rather a nucleated settlement rather similar to what we might nowadays call a hamlet. Bronzeworking and ironworking took place within the settlement. Other enclosures, such as the one at Long Brook Camp, Churcham[60] which measures some 320m by 200m suggest that similar settlements may exist elsewhere in the lower Severn Valley, and that they may even have been the principal form of settlement site in this part of Gloucestershire.

Another extensive middle Iron Age settlement is known just outside the county in the Avon Valley at Beckford (Hereford and Worcester). Here, a settlement covering more than 4ha was excavated between 1972 and 1979 in advance of gravel quarrying. The site comprised a series of large ditched enclosures or compounds, remodelled several times, and each containing round houses, clusters of pits, and smaller internal compounds. Each compound was probably a nucleus for an individual family group; the whole cluster being something like a small village.[61] At Broadway, also in Hereford and Worcester, a rather smaller middle Iron Age settlement is known, perhaps a single farmstead.[62]

The middle Iron Age settlements in the upper Thames Valley contrast markedly with those already described in the Severn Valley and Cotswolds. Enclosures are scarce, and even those that are known tend to be small and contained within larger areas of unenclosed occupation.

The most thoroughly investigated middle Iron Age settlement in the upper Thames Valley is at Claydon Pike, Lechlade.[63] Here, excavations by the Oxford Archaeological Unit under the direction of David Miles and Simon Palmer have brought to light a series of occupation sites situated on gravel islands surrounded by marshy areas. On the middle island, investigated in 1981, at least ten round houses and a 4-poster were found, although as a group these represented several phases of occupation and there were probably only four or five structures in use at any one time. The standard house was about 8m in diameter, surrounded by a circular drainage gully, and in some cases set within its own penannular enclosure. The doorway of most houses opened to the south-west, and inside there was usually a clay lined pit full of burnt stones, possibly a cooking pit.

Similar collections of houses were found on the other two islands investigated, and around them fields defined by ditches have been traced over an area of about 3ha.[64]

Other middle Iron Age sites are known through aerial photography all along the Thames in eastern Gloucestershire and west Oxfordshire.[65] The sheer number of sites known as cropmarks suggests that the upper Thames Valley was one of the most densely occupied parts of the west of Britain at this time.[66]

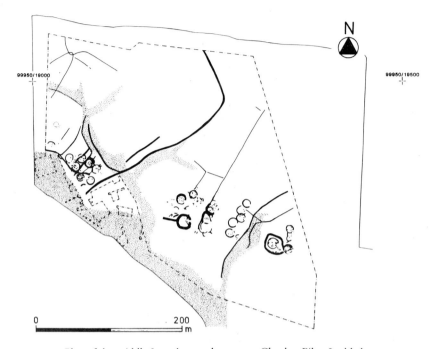

Plan of the middle Iron Age settlements at Claydon Pike, Lechlade.

Middle Iron Age round house under excavation at Claydon Pike, Lechlade. The scales each total 2m. [Photograph: David Miles]

Farming and subsistence

Early and middle Iron Age communities in Gloucestershire practised a mixed farming economy, although at present there is insufficient evidence to identify any variations in the relative importance of animal husbandry as against cultivation in different parts of the county.

At Guiting Manor Farm, the bones of cattle, sheep, and pig were represented in the debris found in the pits. The assemblage was small, but 64% of those identified were sheep, 27% cattle, 5% horse, 2% pig, and other mammals including dog made up the remainder.[67] Sheep were also well represented at The Loders, Lechlade,[68] and at Salmonsbury Camp.[69] At Shenberrow Camp, cattle and sheep were represented in about equal proportions,[70] while at Uley Bury pig predominated in the early levels but declined in importance later.[71]

Cultivation is attested by carbonized grain from beneath the rampart at Uley Bury,[72] from the burnt remains of two 4-posters on Crickley Hill,[73] and from the non-hillfort site at Winson.[74] From these samples it is clear that both wheat and barley were grown on the Cotswolds. At Claydon Pike a rather different picture can be glimpsed because such small quantities of grain (spelt and barley) were recovered from middle Iron Age features that it seems the communities who lived on the site were consumers of cereals

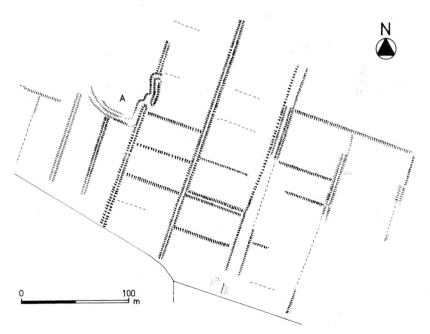

N

0   100
m

Plan of the celtic fields at Aldsworth. A = Possible enclosure.

rather than large-scale producers. This is supported by environmental evidence from the site which indicates a generally open landscape dominated by grassland.[75]

Excavations at hillforts and open sites in the county have revealed the widespread presence of storage pits and 4-posters, while quern-stones for milling grain into flour have been found on many sites.

Direct evidence for farming comes from the fields and paddocks surrounding the settlements at Claydon Pike and Frocester Court,[76] and suggests that, in some areas at least, the countryside was quite orderly with land-parcels enclosed by ditches and perhaps hedges near to settlements. Mention may also be made of the so-called 'celtic fields' recorded at Aldsworth, Eastleach, Kings Stanley, Casey Compton, and elsewhere.[77] These comprise square or rectangular fields visible now as lynchets which formed as a result of soil moving down-slope and accumulating against field boundaries. Dating is of course difficult, but in many parts of southern England such fieldsystems have been shown to be Iron Age or earlier in date. Today, celtic fields only survive on hillslopes that have remained inaccessible for cultivation in recent centuries, but at one time they were probably rather more extensive.

Possible Iron Age ard-marks were recorded at Lodge Farm, Alveston (Avon), during the construction of the M5 though the south of the county.[78] These ard-marks appeared as a criss-cross pattern of V-shaped scratches in the natural bedrock surface. Their importance lies in fact that they show the cultivation of heavy clayey soils in the Severn Valley in pre-Roman times.

Environmental evidence for farming in the early and middle Iron Age shows a continuation of the pattern established in the late Bronze Age. Substantial areas of woodland had been cleared by the middle of the first millennium BC, and this is borne out by the archaeological evidence for a predominance of sheep at several Cotswold sites because sheep require abundant pasture. In the upper Thames Valley, investigations of waterlogged material from claydon Pike, confirm that grassland predominated in the east of the county.[79]

In the Severn Valley detailed evidence for vegetational changes are shown by the pollen sequence from Ripple Brook (Hereford and Worcester).[80] Here, tree pollen levels fell sharply between 620 BC and 420 BC, while levels of cereal pollen rose suggesting that in this part of the valley, as at Alveston, arable cultivation was a very significant part of the farming regime. The Ripple Brook pollen sequence is all the more interesting for the Iron Age period because the peat from which it was obtained lies only 150m west of Towbury hillfort, Twyning. This particular hillfort, which lies between the River Severn and the River Avon, has not been excavated and so is difficult to date, but on the basis of its form and size it could well be an early Iron Age site. If so, then the clearances identified in the pollen sequence presumably reflect the activities of the inhabitants of the fort.

Production and exchange

Throughout the Iron Age period trade and exchange on a local, regional, and sometimes international level was considerable. Domestic crafts were undertaken at most settlements.

Textile production, represented archaeologically by loom weights and weaving combs, is relatively common throughout the area, and it may be suggested that the high levels of sheep bones on some settlement sites reflect the value of this animal as a source of wool.

Pottery production undoubtedly took place locally, and traces of it may be represented by finds from Kings Beeches, Southam.[81] Much of the fine pottery used on the Cotswolds was, however, imported from west of the Severn where regional production centres have been identified around the Malvern Hills and in the Wye Valley.[82] Analysis of the pottery fabrics from Iron Age sites in Gloucestershire shows that anything from 1% to over 40% of wares were imported from west of the Severn. As might be expected, however, there is a general decrease in the frequency of imported wares the further eastwards one travels across the county.[83] Regional styles of decoration are also evident at this time, perhaps reflecting cultural areas of some kind.[84] In a few cases pottery of exceptional quality was transported very considerable distances, and a vessel in the Glastonbury style which was found by Patrick Garrod on a settlement site at Abbeydale on the outskirts of Gloucester came originally from Cornwall.[85]

Everyday items, such as querns and whetstones, that could not be obtained locally were traded from areas where suitable rock outcrops naturally, such as in the Forest of Dean and the Bristol region. Ornaments such as glass beads and shale bracelets were also regularly traded.

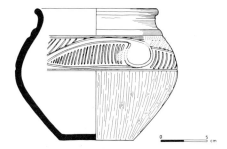

Glastonbury style pot found at Abbeydale, Gloucester, by Patrick Garrod. The vessel was manufactured in Cornwall.

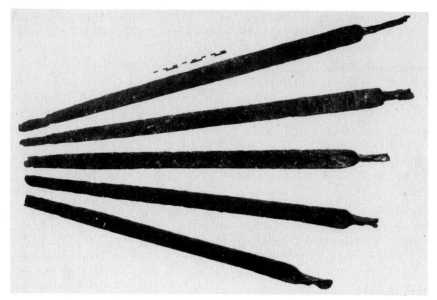

Selection of currency bars from Salmonsbury Camp, Bourton-on-the-Water. [Photograph: Gloucester City Museum]

Another product which was probably highly prized was salt as, among other things, it was presumably widely used for curing meat. During the Iron Age most salt was produced on the coast and around saline springs such as those at Droitwich (Hereford and Worcester), and then transported to where it was needed in ceramic containers manufactured in a coarse fabric known as briquetage. Briquetage vessels from the Droitwich area are known from the hillforts at Salmonsbury Camp, Shenberrow Camp, Crickley Hill, Lydney Park, and Uley Bury, and from non–hillfort sites at The Knolls, Guiting Manor Farm, Winson, and Claydon Pike.[86]

Metalworking was a domestic craft during the Iron Age, and is attested at a number of sites in and around the county. At Frocester, for example, both bronzeworking and ironworking appear to have been taking place within the settlement enclosure, while at Wood House, Guiting Power, only ironworking is attested.[87]

Iron ore would have been available to craftsmen in Gloucestershire from the Forest of Dean and the Bristol coalfield region, although no conclusive archaeological traces of ore extraction of pre-Roman date have been found in either area.

Three sites in Gloucestershire have produced what are called iron 'currency bars', but which in fact appear to have been iron ingots conveniently standardized for transportation and exchange. The largest group in the county, if not in the whole of Britain, was found in 1860 at

Salmonsbury Camp.[88] This collection of bars, about 147 in all, were of the sword-shaped variety. Subsequently, more such bars have been found at the site.[89] Another hoard, this time of seven spit-shaped bars was found in the fill of the ditch of the enclosure at The Ditches, North Cerney, in 1984,[90] while two more spit-shaped bars were found in the ditch at Uley Bury, during rescue excavations in 1976.[91] At present no currency bars have been found on non-hillfort sites on the Cotswolds, and this may suggest that supplies of iron were redistributed from the hillforts to craftsmen working elsewhere. A hoard of ten currency bars were, however, recovered from a pit at Beckford (Hereford and Worcester) where they are associated with a radiocarbon date of 160±120 BC (Birm – 432).[92]

For much of the middle Iron Age period, exchange between Britain and the continent of Europe was at a low ebb compared with earlier times, although some goods and ideas were imported. Among these were new types of dress fasteners in the form of brooches based on the safety pin principle. Early examples have been found in the county at Crickley Hill, among other sites, and they were made in both iron and bronze. Continental styles of art, the La Tène styles, were also adopted in Britain, and found outlets in the way pottery and fine ornaments were decorated.

There is some evidence from Britain as a whole that trade links with the Mediterranean world developed during the middle Iron Age,[93] and it must be recorded that two possible Mediterranean imports have been found in Gloucestershire. The earliest is a south Italian ceramic column-krater of 5th century BC date which was found in 1901 by workmen building houses in

Bronze strap-link with enamel inlay from Sudeley. The object measures 79mm across. [Photograph: British Museum]

Sandhurst Lane, Gloucester.[94] No details of its provenance or the circumstances in which it was found are known. The second piece is a 4th century BC bronze jug of Etruscan manufacture apparently found at Tewkesbury, although again the exact circumstances of recovery are not known.[95] Both these pieces may of course be recent imports and of no consequence, but, if genuine, they suggest that the Severn estuary was a port of call for ships engaged in foreign trade during the Iron Age.

Burial and ritual

Evidence for burial in the early and middle Iron Age is very sparse, and it is generally thought that whatever practices pertained in the later Bronze Age continued through into the Iron Age. Nonetheless a few burials are known from Gloucestershire.

Scattered inhumations in pits which were used for the disposal of domestic rubbish are not unusual in the Iron Age.[96] Human bones were found in the single pit investigated at Wood House, Guiting Power, and the pit in cutting C at Shenberrow Camp, while at Salmonsbury Camp, two skeletons were found in pits on site IV, and three skeletons in pits on site III.[97] Two further skeletons of unknown date were discovered near the

South Italian ceramic column-krater of 5th century BC date found in 1901 in Sandhurst Lane, Gloucester. An Iron Age import or a recent collectors item? [Photograph: Gloucester City Museum]

south-western ramparts at Salmonsbury in 1983 during the construction of a pipeline.[98]

Slightly more formal burials are also known, although in most cases uncertainty surrounds the circumstances of their deposition. At The Loders, Lechlade, for example, the crouched inhumation of a young man aged between 20 and 25 was found amid a cluster of early Iron Age pits, but the dating of the grave is problematic.[99] Similarly, at Norbury Camp a single inhumation was found in a rock cut grave adjacent to the 4-posters; again there were no grave goods and while the body was found lying on its left side with the head to the north in appropriately Iron Age style, dating is far from certain.[100] At Roughground Farm, Lechlade, crouched inhumations were found cutting late Bronze Age features, and one was radiocarbon dated to the 2nd or 3rd century BC.[101] At Barnwood near Gloucester the inhumation burial of a young woman aged about 16 or 17 was found accompanied by a complete barrel-shaped, hand-made pottery vessel of middle Iron Age type.[102] A possible cremation burial in an early Iron Age type pot and accompanied by a stone pounder is known from Ebworth. Cranham, although the exact circumstances of the find are not known.[103] known.[103]

Stone-lined grave at Ireley Farm, Stanway, after excavation.

The most elaborate middle Iron Age burial from the county comes from Ireley Farm, Stanway.[104] Here, rescue excavations revealed two stone-lined graves, perhaps part or all of a small cemetery. The first grave, 2.1m in length, contained the remains of a tall robust adult male placed in fully extended posture. In the grave there were also three sherds of middle Iron Age pottery, grains of carbonized wheat, sheep bones, a flint flake, charcoal, and a piece of ferruginous limestone which had been placed on his breast. Whether these were all grave goods or accidental intrusions during burial is uncertain. The second grave was that of a small female, also fully extended, and with potsherds, a flint flake, and animal bones in the grave.

Outside the entrance to the hillfort on Leckhampton Hill, is a square-shaped enclosure around a small mound. This has often been regarded as an Iron Age burial monument because of similarities with burial structures in Yorkshire and Humberside. However, excavations at the Leckhampton barrow in 1925 revealed no sign of a burial,[105] and Leslie Grinsell inclines to the view that the site is a post-medieval tree-clump enclosure.[106]

Ritual sites of the Iron Age period are as scarce as burials in Gloucestershire, although some hillforts may have contained sacred enclosures or shrines. In addition, some Roman temples probably overlie late prehistoric sacred sites of various sorts, and certainly this was the case at West Hill, Uley. Here, excavations under the direction of Dr Ann Ellison, revealed a series of prehistoric ritual and ceremonial monuments pre-dating a Roman temple dedicated to Mercury.[107] During the middle Iron Age a square-shaped enclosure was constructed. It was about 20m across, and was bounded on at least three sides by a ditch. Traces of external banks were located on the east and west sides. Inside were several pits.

Society and land-use

The old idea that during the Iron Age everyone lived in small farmsteads and congregated at the hillforts to defend themselves during times of trouble no longer fits the available evidence. Most of the hillforts that have been excavated seem to have been occupation by substantial communities for long periods. Moreover, by the middle Iron Age there were clearly several different types of hillforts and enclosures being built, and considerable variation in the size and form of non-hillfort settlements constructed in different parts of the county.

On the Cotswolds a crude hierarchy of settlement types can be discerned. The people living in, or responsible for, the developed hillforts in the middle Iron Age seem to have been able to command considerable resources. This is clearly seen in their ability to mobilize and organize the massive labour forces needed to construct large hillforts like Uley Bury, or

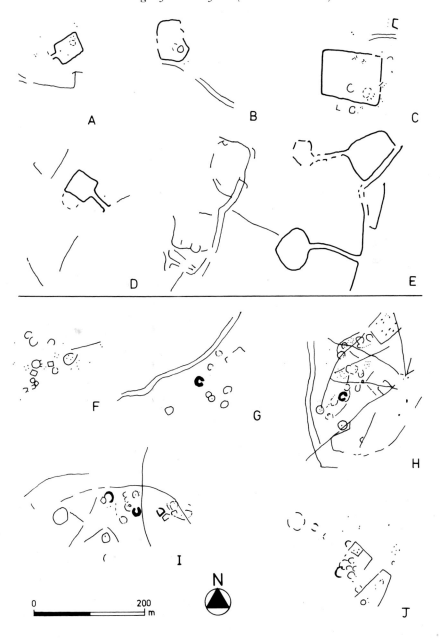

Plans of cropmarks showing (A)–(E) middle Iron Age enclosed settlements on the Cotswold uplands in eastern Gloucestershire and west Oxfordshire, and (F)–(J) middle Iron Age open settlements in the upper Thames Valley in eastern Gloucestershire and west Oxfordshire.

Salmonsbury Camp, and also in terms of their access to raw materials such as iron currency bars. Professor Barry Cunliffe has suggested that, as the social unrest which gave rise to the need for the early hillforts died down, so one fort within each block of land emerged as the focus of the settlement pattern while the other hillforts declined and fell out of use.[108] In this sense the major hillforts became central places for dispersed communities, perhaps providing specialist ritual, ceremonial, cultural, and educational services. They could also have become storage and redistribution places for foodstuffs and raw materials, and possibly even the seat of government, or centres for the judiciary. The wide spacing of developed hillforts may lend weight to the argument that they served fairly large areas, although whether they should necessarily be seen as the residences of chiefs or leaders cannot be determined from present archaeological evidence.

Below the developed hillforts in the settlement hierarchy there seems to be a tier of minor hillforts and larger enclosures, and below this small enclosures and perhaps a few open sites. Understanding these is difficult because few have been excavated, but it does seem that most are isolated from one another, that there is no evidence for trackways between, and that there are few traces of associated fieldsystems except around the edges of the Cotswolds. The overall impression is one of a series of territories, each controlled by a single community. Several such groups may have been tied to a major hillforts through patronage or kinship, so reducing their isolation.

In the upper Thames Valley quite a different picture can be glimpsed. There are no major hillforts of the kind found on the Cotswolds, and the settlements here are mostly unenclosed groups of houses and compounds. Linking settlements together are trackways and fields. In an important piece of research on the differences between settlements on the Oxfordshire Cotswolds and those in upper Thames Valley, Dr Richard Hingley suggests that the patterns which can be seen among sites on the low ground may be related to the communal control of land and the development of communalistic societies.[109] The sharing of access to land and resources in this way would remove the need for central places and defined territories. At another level the communities in these areas may have had an altogether different outlook on life and different ideologies as a result of their circumstances.

How the Iron Age settlements in west Gloucestershire relate to these patterns is not at present clear. In the Severn Valley nucleated settlements, both enclosed and unenclosed, seem to be common and may, therefore, represent a third pattern of land-use and social organization.

Taken together, the evidence of settlement patterns, the extend of land clearance, and what little is known of farming regimes, it becomes clear that there was considerable diversity in the way land was used during the middle Iron Age, even within a small area like Gloucestershire.

7
The Kingdom of the Dobunni
(c 100 BC – c AD50)

New contacts and new friends

Events in Gloucestershire during the century and a half or so before the Roman invasion of Britain, the late Iron Age period, are closely bound up with changes in internal and external relations over southern Britain as a whole. Before looking at the Gloucestershire area in detail, something of these general changes needs to be outlined.

From about 100 BC, southern Britain was drawn into close contact with the continent of Europe through trade and exchange. To what extent this was brought about by the increased production of raw materials and finished goods in Britain and Gaul it is impossible to say, but there can be little doubt that the Roman advance through France, coupled with Germanic pressures from the north, forced the communities of northern and north-western Gaul to look to their British neighbours for support, and perhaps new markets for their goods.

The main focus of this trade was the south coast, and a number of trading settlements developed, for example Mount Baden in Plymouth Sound (Devon), and Hengistbury Head in Christchurch Harbour (Dorset).[1] Among the goods imported were fine pottery, including wheel-turned vessels, amphorae containing wine from Italy, and metalwork such as brooches and ornaments.[2] It was also at this time that coins were introduced into Britain, mostly Armorican issues that had been circulating in northern France for some decades.[3]

By the middle of the 1st century BC, Gaul had been conquered by the Romans and cross-channel trade dried up for a while, before redeveloping between south-eastern England and Roman Gaul. This shift in the axis of trade brought Hampshire, Sussex, Kent, and Essex into the vanguard of developments and left Dorset and the south-west of England with only limited access to continental markets.[4] The range of goods imported into south-eastern Britain followed traditional patterns however, focusing on wine, fine table wares, and luxury status items. From about 10 BC through to the Roman conquest the intensity of this trade accelerated. The use of coins increased, and some parts of the south-east, particularly Essex, Hertfordshire, Sussex, and north-east Hampshire, developed semi-urbanized lowland settlements which are usually called *oppida*[5].

One important spin-off from having the Roman world as a close neighbour from the mid 1st century BC onwards, is that there are occasional references to life in Britain in the writings of the classical authors.[6] Caesar made sorties to Britain in 55 and 54 BC and so had first-hand experience of British late Iron Age society. Among the gleanings possible from his writings, and those of others, is that the British were preoccupied with warfare, that the people wore their hair long and many (?men) had unshaven upper lips, and that it was customary for some people to die their bodies blue with woad. To what extent these observations were representative, or even true, cannot be determined, for such questions are incapable of solution using only archaeological evidence. Much effort has, however, been expended in trying to make use of Caesar's statement that people from Belgium (the Belgae) crossed to Britain to invade and loot, after which they stayed to till the fields.[7] Attempts were made to match distributions of pottery, coins, and burial practices with the spread of these Belgic people, and elaborate schemes of folk movements within Britain were proposed. It is now realized, however, that archaeological evidence and historic narrative such as this cannot be married easily.[8] Many of the features previously regarded as distinctive of Belgic invasions can now be better explained as evidence of exchange and trade between Britain and Gaul.

Core and periphery – Gloucestershire in the late Iron Age

For geographical reasons, southern and eastern England were the areas most effected by increased trade with Gaul and the changes to the axis of trade in the 1st century BC. Indeed, by the early 1st century AD the area south-east of a line roughly between the Solent and the Wash had started to experience the development of urbanized communities and the adoption of customs derived from the classical world.[9] Beyond this core zone was a periphery zone covering a crescent-shaped area stretching from Dorset in the far south, through Somerset, Gloucestershire, the east Midlands, and on to Yorkshire in the north. While this region hardly enjoyed the full effects of continental contacts, it did at least profit from the closer links with the Roman world. Gloucestershire lay firmly within this periphery zone.[10]

The emergence of a core zone and a periphery zone probably owed much to the economics of trade and exchange during the period. Luxury items such as those already mentioned flowed out from the classical world in return for goods and raw materials. As with most expanding empires, the

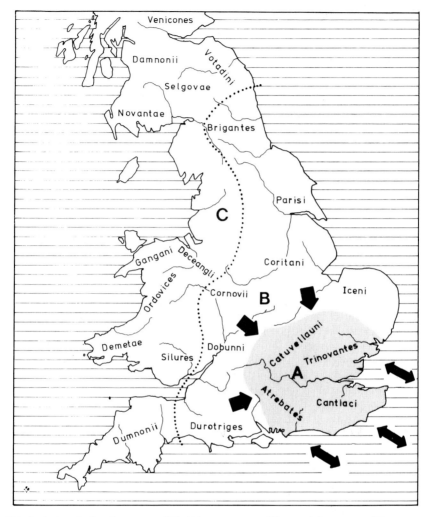

Britain during the late 1st century BC. (A) = core zone; (B) = periphery zone; (C) = outer zone.

Roman world lacked essential raw materials and labour at its heart and rectified this by pursuing a policy of expansion and foreign trade. Strabo, writing in the 1st century BC/AD provides a list of the goods imported by the Roman world from Britain, namely: slaves, grain, cattle, gold, silver, iron, and hunting dogs.[11] Not all of these things could have easily been obtained from within south-eastern England, and the conclusion must be drawn that some were acquired from the neighbouring hinterland (the periphery zone) and indeed perhaps further afield. Dr Colin Haselgrove has

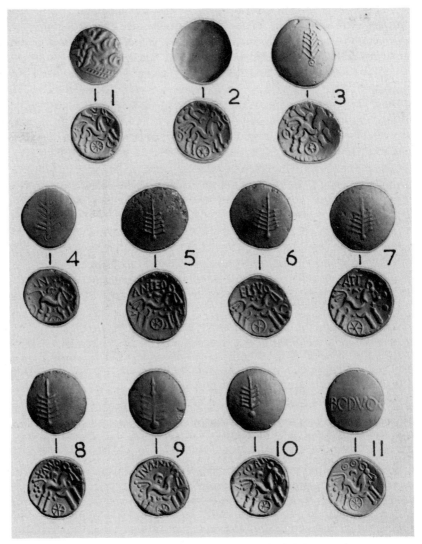

Selection of gold Dobunnic staters from southern England. [Photograph: Corinium Museum]

suggested that the Cotswolds may have served as a source of cattle in this system.[12]

Coins from Gloucestershire dating to the late 1st or early 2nd century BC are the earliest signs that the area was being drawn into trade with the core zone to the south, and ultimately continental Europe. Armorican coins have been found at Frampton Mansell near Chalford, and at Bream in the Forest of Dean, while other Gaulish coins from the area include examples from Cirencester and Dymock.[13] These early coins include gold and silver pieces, but exactly how they were used is not clear. It is unlikely that they served as modern coins do in everyday transactions, rather they were probably tokens of some kind which could be used to convert wealth from one form to another.[14]

In the later 1st century BC, the arrival of Gallo-Belgic coins, coupled with the existing knowledge of earlier coins, prompted the local production of gold and silver coins, and also so-called forgeries which had a copper core beneath a silver or gold wash. These coins show regional distributions and Gloucestershire lies at the heart of one such group which can be used to roughly define the tribal area of the Dobunni.[15] The coins appear to have been issued by a single authority, and so this area may be loosely referred to as the kingdom as the Dobunni.

The earliest Dobunnic coins are uninscribed.[16] The gold examples, staters, carry a branched ornament on the obverse and a triple tailed horse motif on the reverse. On the silver series there is a head surrounded by other motifs on the obverse and the triple tailed horse on the reverse. Later, the designs on both gold and silver coins became more stylized, especially the head and the horse, and a name, presumably the issuing authority, was frequently added. Seven such names are known: *Anted, Eisu, Catti, Comux, Inam, Corio,* and *Bodvoc.*[17] These may be abbreviated rather than complete names, but they represent the earliest names we have for the leaders of communities living in the county.

The presence within Gloucestershire of coins from other areas of Britain, for example Durotrigian coins from Dorset, and Catuvellaunian coins from Essex, serves to underline the fact that inter-regional exchange networks extended over wide areas during the late Iron Age. Other than the coins, however, there is little evidence that much imported material found its way to Gloucestershire until the last few decades before the Roman conquest when cross-channel trade reach its peak.

Settlement

Against this backdrop of changing social and economic relations, the basic settlement pattern and economy of late Iron Age communities in Gloucestershire shows remarkable continuity from earlier centuries. This is seen not only in the continuity of occupation at individual sites, but also in the fact that the diversity of settlement across the area was maintenance. Pottery studies are not, at present, sufficiently far advanced to allow a detailed chronology for the late Iron Age in this area, but enough is known to sketch the outline.

Farms and villages

In the Severn Valley at Frocester Court, the middle Iron Age ditched enclosure underwent minor remodelling in the 1st century BC/AD.[18] Some new ditches were constructed, others simply cleared out, and to the east at least three small enclosures were added, perhaps gardens in which spade cultivation took place. No firm traces of any houses of this phase have been found, although there is some evidence for a rectangular structure outlined by postholes which might have served as a dwelling. It was, however, a wealthy settlement around the time of the Roman conquest to judge from the fact that two Dobunnic coins, a Roman coin of Claudius (AD 37–54), and a few sherds of *terra nigra* pottery from northern Gaul have been found on the site.

At Claydon Pike in the upper Thames Valley an extensive late Iron Age settlement covering 2ha or more lies a few hundred metres south-west of its middle Iron Age predecessor.[19] Again the occupation area was unenclosed, although within the overall spread of activity there were various small compounds. Round houses about 8m in diameter lay within these

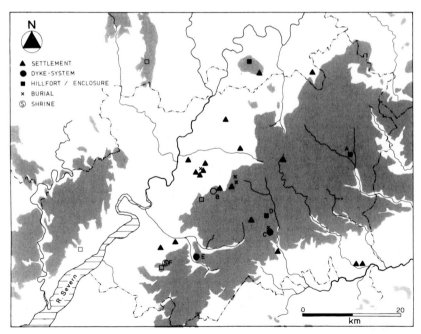

Map showing the distribution of recorded sites dating to between *c* 100 BC and *c* AD 50. A = Salmonsbury, Bourton-on-the-Water; B = High Brotheridge; C = Bagendon; D = The Ditches, North Cerney; E = The Bulwarks, Minchinhampton; F = West Hill, Uley. Open symbols indicate doubtful sites.

compounds, together with smaller features, usually about 4m in diameter, of uncertain function. Analysis of the finds is not complete at the time of writing, but among the more unusual pieces is a base silver Dobunnic coin, and a silver coin minted in Rome in 152 BC. The concentration of settlement evidence at Claydon Pike suggests a small nucleated village, and on the basis of evidence from cropmarks along the Upper Thames gravels such sites were probably fairly numerous.[20]

Elsewhere, open settlements of the period are more difficult to identify with certainty in the absence of extensive excavations. At Andoversford, the Roman town of Wycomb partly or completely covers a late Iron Age settlement.[21] At least three Dobunnic coins have been found on the site, one inscribed *Eisu* as well as several late Iron Age brooches and part of a La Tène III horse-bit. Excavations by Wilfred Cox to the west of the main settlement revealed late Iron Age occupation in the form of pits and ditches. A fragment of a stone mould, such as might have been used to cast blanks from which to make coins, was found during this excavation. Aerial photographs of Wycomb show several circular ditched enclosures beside the stream along the west side of the site; at least one is probably a house.[22]

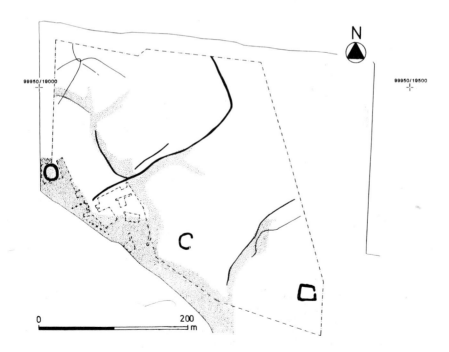

Late Iron Age settlements at Claydon Pike, Lechlade.

In the Severn Valley at Witcombe Roman villa, ditches were found beneath the Roman structures and these probably relate to a late Iron Age settlement on the site.[23] In Gloucester slight traces of a late Iron Age or conquest period settlement have recently come to light on the northern outskirts of the city at Kingsholm.[24] Among the finds are a number of Dobunnic coins, and pits and ditches containing 'native ware' pottery have also been recorded in the vicinity. Rather more ephemeral traces of late Iron Age occupation have been recorded from Barnwood on the east side of Gloucester[25] and at Duntisbourne Abbots.[26]

Nothing is known of the nature and extent of occupation in the Forest of Dean during the late Iron Age beyond the very limited inferences that can be drawn from occasional stray finds. The presence of an Armorican coin in a scoul (open iron mine) at Bream suggests that iron-ore was being extracted in the vicinity.[27] Studies of iron-ore fragments found at Bagendon (see below p.166) suggested that it derived from the Forest of Dean.[28]

Hillforts and large enclosures
Assessing the use of hillforts in Gloucestershire during the late Iron Age is difficult because relatively few have been investigated. The abandonment of hillforts in favour of valley-bottom settlements such as can be detected in

Fragment of possible coin mould from Syreford Mill, Wycomb, Whittington. [Photograph: Author]

south-eastern England[29] is probably not a marked feature of settlement in Gloucestershire at the time.

The enclosure at The Ditches, North Cerney, which was probably fortified with a single defensive rampart bounding an area of about 4.3ha in the later part of the middle Iron Age, certainly continued to be occupied through the late Iron Age period, and has indeed produced the richest collection of late Iron Age luxury imports known from the county.[30] Excavations by Stephen Trow have revealed that during the late Iron Age a second ditch was apparently dug immediately inside the existing rampart. The fill of this ditch contained considerable quantities of fine table wares imported from Gallia Belgica (*terra nigra* and *terra rubra*), together with imported central Gaulish wares and amphorae. There was evidence for the manufacture of coins in the form of mould fragments, and Dobunnic coins are also known from the site. An intaglio stone from a ring was found on the ploughed surface of a field within the enclosure. This stone depicts a youth walking on the tips of his toes, his right arm outstretched behind and his left arm flexed. A herm is shown in profile and there is a low table of some kind in front. Close dating of this piece is difficult, but it is probably of the Augustian period – the late 1st century BC. The date of its loss cannot, however, be determined.[31]

Another hillfort occupied continuously from middle Iron Age times through into the late Iron Age was Salmonsbury Camp.[32] This site has attracted considerable attention because of its size and uncharacteristic location, and was classified by Professor Barry Cunliffe as an enclosed

Excavation of the entranceway at The Ditches, North Cerney. [Photograph: Stephen Trow]

oppidum comparable with examples in south-eastern England.[33] In fact, there is nothing among the range of finds from Salmonsbury Camp, or in the form of the structural evidence recorded, to set it apart from other hillforts occupied during the late Iron Age in the periphery zone. Excavations between 1931 and 1934 by Dr Gerald Dunning revealed two main phases of occupation, the earliest (Period I) belonging to the middle Iron Age and the later (Period II) belonging to the late Iron Age.[34] No great time-lag separated the two periods of occupation, and indeed some of the linear decorated pottery forms of the earlier period continued in use during Period II, suggesting continuity of settlement. The same applies to the defences; once established during the middle Iron Age they were not refurbished until the Roman period or later.

Within the earthworks at Salmonsbury traces of late Iron Age occupation were mostly confined to the western part of the site. In area III a small palisaded enclosure had been constructed within the defences but it did not remain in use for very long and within the late Iron Age period its ditch was back-filled and paved over. One, or possibly two, round houses were associated with the late Iron Age phase of occupation. In area IV stone paving was also found but, although a stone hearth was located, no traces of a building were discovered. The finds from the late Iron Age occupation included a range of wheel-turned pottery, probably locally made, together with two Dobunnic silver coins, one inscribed *Anted*, quern-stones, knives, a crucible fragment, spindle whorls, tools, and a few ornaments including a shale bracelet and beads. Imports to the site were rather less numerous than at The Ditches, but included some La Tène III style brooches[35]. A rather unusual pedestal-based pottery vessel with a long neck and fluted globular body was thought by Dr Kevin Greene[36] to be an import from the Lower Rhineland or Gallia Belgica, but this is by no means certain.[37]

To what extent The Ditches and Salmonsbury may be regarded as representative of the hillforts in the county is not clear because evidence from other sites is scant. Uley Bury, a site where late Iron Age occupation might be expected, has yielded little or no appropriate evidence[38] although it may be noted that cropmarks recorded within the ramparts suggest the presence of internal palisaded enclosures like those at Salmonsbury.[39]

Dyke-system enclosures

Two sites in Gloucestershire, Bagendon and Minchinhampton, stand apart from other late Iron Age monuments because of their size, and the fact that they are bounded by a series of discontinuous dykes.[40] Of the two, Bagendon is by far the most fully investigated, but even here the sample known through excavation is only a tiny fraction of the interior and is not necessarily representative of the complete site. Bagendon has often been included among the so-called territorial *oppida* of south-eastern England,

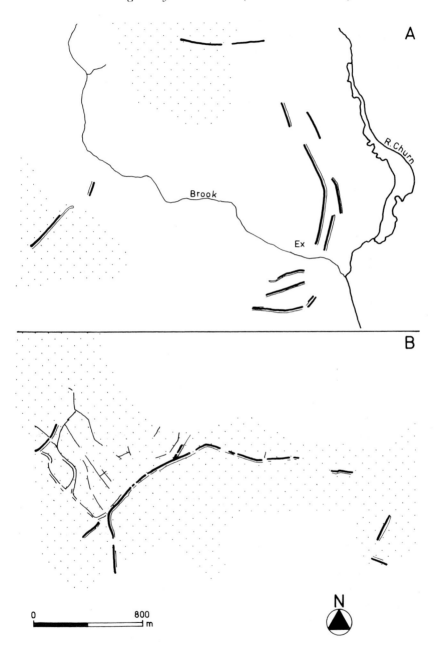

Late Iron Age dyke-system enclosures at (A) Bagendon, and (B) Minchinhampton. Land over 190m OD stippled. Ex = position of archaeological excavations at Bagendon.

such as Camulodunum (Colchester, Essex), or Silchester (Hampshire)[41], but Bagendon only shows a few features of the *oppida* tradition and hardly deserves that appelation.

Bagendon lies about 4.5km north of Cirencester in a small valley leading westwards off the main Coln Valley. A series of dykes loosely define a rectangular area of about 200ha in the valley bottom and across the slopes on either side. Large gaps exist in the circuit on the south and west sides, as they are preserved today, while along the east and south sides there is some duplication of dykes perhaps suggesting that a pair of parallel earthworks once defined this part of the enclosure. Early accounts[42] suggest that the dykes were formerly rather more complete than today, although it is still unlikely that a complete circuit ever existed.

Excavations at Bagendon took place between 1954 and 1956 under the direction of Elsie Clifford, and, more recently, in 1980–1 under the direction of Dr Richard Reece and Stephen Trow. The deposits revealed on these occasions indicate a complicated succession of occupation that divides into four broad phases.[43] In the first phase evidence of metalworking was abundant in the areas examined. Clay lined ditches, some perhaps to hold water, were revealed, together with paved areas. In the second phase metalworking again predominated but the earlier ditches had been filled and sealed by stone paving, while new and apparently rather similar ditches were dug nearby. An iron-smelting furnace and possible blowing pits were

Dyke beside Cutham Lane, Bagendon. [Photograph: Author]

found, and one or more houses may have been present. Nearby was an area given over to the production of Dobunnic coins, and from here came a number of finished coins and pieces of moulds in which coin blanks were probably cast before being hammered. In phase III both the metalworking area and the mint area were paved over and several round houses constructed. A similar arrangement was present in phase IV.

The excavations also investigated the dykes on the east side of the enclosure, and revealed them to be substantial ramparts with an outer rock-cut ditch some 3.5m wide and about 2m deep. The bank was of dump construction.

Occupation debris included quantities of wheel turned pottery, bone points, rubbing stones, grinders, daub, various bronze and iron tools, and ornaments. Imported goods included *terra nigra*, *terra rubra*, samian ware, glass, and brooches. Amphorae sherds were also recovered, including Spanish and Italian types[44] from phase I onwards.

Dating the construction and occupation of Bagendon is not easy. Traditionally, the settlement was thought to span the period AD 20 through to the Roman conquest or a little later,[45] but various reconsiderations of the finds have suggested a later starting date, perhaps AD 25 or 30.[46]

The Minchinhampton enclosure is rather less well documented than Bagendon, and its setting is altogether different because it lies at about 200m above sea-level on a high plateau. Surviving earthworks, known locally as the Bulwarks, define a roughly oval area of perhaps 120ha centred on the

Stone floor over a ditch revealed during excavations at Bagendon in 1955. The scale is marked in 1 foot divisions.

The Bulwarks, Minchinhampton Common. [Photograph: Author]

present village, but, as at Bagendon, they appear to be discontinuous.[47] Their relationship with other earthworks preserved on Minchinhampton Common is uncertain, and it is also notable that the ditch lies inside the bank.

Excavations through the Bulwarks by Elsie Clifford in 1937 demonstrated that the ditch was rock-cut, about 7m wide, some 2.2m deep, and with a flat bottom about 1.55m wide. The adjacent bank was separated from the ditch by a berm 2.7m wide. The bank was well constructed with an internal revetment wall facing the ditch.[48] However, finds from the excavation provide little useful evidence for dating the construction of these dykes, although they must have been raised after the middle Iron Age because sherds of middle Iron Age pottery were incorporated in the bank.

Interpreting the evidence from Bagendon and Minchinhampton is far from easy. However, it seems that, by the time of the Roman conquest in the mid 1st century AD, Bagendon had emerged as a focal point in the settlement system of the area, probably rightly regarded as *Corinion* which is referred to by the writer Ptolemy.[49] The form of the settlement in the last decades before the Roman invasion may have been little more than an extended farmstead or small village, perhaps the seat of the petty kings whose names are recorded on the coins. The dykes could have enclosed fields and grazing areas as well as domestic accommodation, and perhaps this is the reason they are so extensive and discontinuous. A prosaic function may also underlie the construction of the Minchinhampton enclosure. Internally ditched enclosures are relatively common among the

Excavation through the Bulwarks, Minchinhampton, in 1936. The scales are marked in 1 foot divisions.

prehistoric earthworks of Wessex and were probably used as stock enclosures to corral animals in rather than to keep people or animals out. It is tempting to interpret the Minchinhampton enclosure in the same way and to link it to the trade in animals with communities living in the core zone to the south-east. However, such speculation requires substantiation before it can be accepted.

Farming and food production

Until the analysis of finds from Frocester Court, Claydon Pike, and The Ditches has been completed, any assessment of farming in Gloucestershire during the late Iron Age must be provisional.

Animal remains from Bagendon suggest that cattle provided the main source of meat (representing about 50% of the bones present) and that most of the animals were slaughtered when they were about 2 to 2.5 years old.[50] Sheep and pig were also represented, but in small quantities, as too was domestic fowl. The horse bones present indicate the use of small animals up to about 12 hands high, rather like present-day New Forest ponies. No cereals were found, although grindstones and rubbers attest the processing of grain. The diet of the inhabitants at Bagendon was supplemented at least occasionally by oysters which must have been transported from the coast.

Preliminary assessments of the animal bones from The Ditches, suggests that here too cattle and sheep were the main species of animals kept, with pig present in rather lesser numbers. Roe deer bones suggest that hunting may have helped supplement the diet here.[51]

Animal bones from Salmonsbury Camp included the remains of cattle, sheep, pig and goat,[52] and, in addition to the finds of querns and rubbers, an iron sickle and an ox-goad were recovered.[53]

Crafts and industry

The presence of extensive metalworking areas with abundant waste material at Bagendon suggests that specialist craftsmen were working at this site.[54] In addition to the production of iron tools and everyday items, coins and brooches were manufactured in bronze, lead and silver. Iron nails were also made. Similar craft specialization may also be discerned in the production of pottery during the immediate pre-conquest period as this was the time that wheel-turned wares were first introduced.

Domestic crafts continued at most settlements, and evidence for textile manufacture in the form of triangular clay loom weights and bone weaving combs are common finds on late Iron Age and early Roman occupation sites.

Throughout the late Iron Age, fine objects, especially finely decorated objects, were highly prized. A carved stone cone from Barnwood[55] is covered in curvilinear decoration, and a superficially similar object was found as a stray find at Salmonsbury.[56] This last object may, however, be a weight. A bronze bowl with three attached bull's heads from Lydney Park, also belongs to this period,[57] as do the very fine embossed bronze bands from Rodborough Common.[58]

Death, burial and ritual

During the late Iron Age, formal burial rites appear again in the archae-ological record after a virtual absence for nearly a millennium. Great variety in burial tradition is represented by the few examples known.

Cremation burials have been recorded at two sites, Barnwood and Bagendon. Both have evidence for late Iron Age occupation in the vicinity suggesting that cemeteries were sited near settlements. At Barnwood nine burials were found in two distinct clusters; one containing four burials, the other five.[59] In every case the bodies had been thoroughly burnt and the ashes placed in urns. Such urns are common in south-eastern England in the

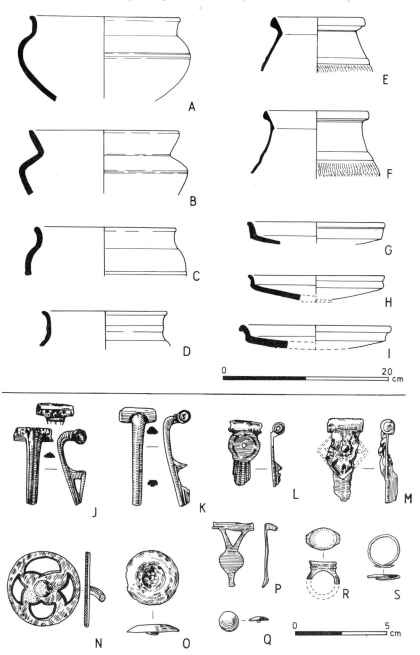

Selection of late Iron Age pottery, brooches, and domestic items from Bagendon.

late Iron Age and continued as a native tradition in the ceramic industries of the early Roman period. Because of this it is difficult to date the Barnwood urns precisely, but they may well belong to the decade immediately before the Roman conquest. Another cremation burial in a similar urn, and in this instance associated with a bronze bead, was found at Barnwood in 1934 in the vicinity of the earlier finds.[60]

The cremation cemetery at Bagendon was discovered in 1861 near the Rectory, but it was poorly recorded.[61] All that can be said is that six urns were found; there is no reference to the presence of bones or grave goods.

Burials at hillfort and enclosure sites probably continued, and human skeletal remains have been found at Bagendon[62] and Salmonsbury Camp.[63] However, the suggestion that some of the human bones found in late Iron Age deposits at Salmonsbury were the results of cannibalism cannot be substantiated.

Inhumation burials are represented by two finds on the Cotswold escarpment near Birdlip. The first, and by far the richest late Iron Age cemetery known in the west of England, was found in 1879 during quarrying for roadstone.[64] The exact position of the site is not known, but it lies somewhere between Birdlip village and the Air Balloon public house in the area called Barrow Wake. Full details of the arrangement of the burials were not recorded, but from the various surviving accounts it seems likely that at least four individual graves were discovered.

Three graves were found together, although whether as separate cists or a single cist is not clear; probably the former. Of these the two outer burials were males, the middle one female. All had their heads to the east and were seemingly fully extended inhumations buried at a depth of about 1.5m. The graves were lined and covered with slabs of local limestone. No grave goods accompanied the two male burials, but the female was associated with a rich array of very fine objects. A large bronze bowl covered her face and around about was a bronze mirror, a silver brooch, a bronze expanding bangle, a bronze animal-head pattern knife handle, a small bronze bowl, a drop handle, a finial loop, tweezers, bronze rings and a collection of beads possibly from a necklace. These objects may represent wealth accumulated over a period of time. The mirror is particularly splendid, with incised curvilinear designs on the back and enamel inlay on the handle. The latest object in the assemblage is the silver brooch which stylistically belongs to the Almgren series 2 brooches of La Tène III date, possibly manufactured about AD 40 or a little later. Its deposition in this grave must therefore have been on the very eve of the Roman conquest if not just after.

Several days after the finding of the first three burials, a fourth grave came to light about 6m to the north.[65] It seems that this grave was not lined with stone slabs as the others had been. It contained the extended inhumation of an adult male, and, like the rich female already described, the

Grave goods from the late Iron Age cemetery at Birdlip. The two semicircular bronze bucket mounts (bottom right) probably derive from a male grave, the remaining objects were found with an adult female during quarrying in 1879. [Photograph: Gloucester City Museum]

face was covered, this time with a metal rimmed vessel, presumably a wooden or a leather bucket of which only the mounts survived. The finding of a piece of twisted gold wire apparently from the vicinity of the cemetery may also be significant and may perhaps indicate the presence of other unrecorded burials in the same group.

It is likely that a late Iron Age settlement existed nearby at Birdlip, as finds of early Roman pottery have been found during fieldsurvey, a Dobunnic coin of *Bodvoc* is known from the village, and small-scale excavations in advance of the construction of the Birdlip bypass revealed the drainage gully and entrance of a probable late Iron Age round house.[66]

One final burial site which should be mentioned is the inhumation grave found on Crickley Hill before 1883.[67] No details of the burial itself or its position are recorded, but a collection of four iron objects preserved in Gloucester City Museum probably accompanied the interment. The interpretation of the objects is more difficult; one is perhaps a bracelet, but the others are of uncertain purpose.[68]

The middle Iron Age ritual enclosure at West Hill, Uley, continued in use during the late Iron Age.[69] One, or possibly two, small timber buildings

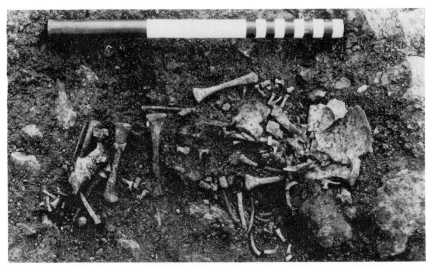

Burial of an infant aged 9–12 months found under a post forming part of the wall of a late Iron Age shrine at West Hill, Uley. The scale totals 300mm. [Photograph: S.P.Q. Rahtz]

were constructed inside the enclosure, and a number of infant burials were also inserted at this time. Finds from the enclosure include Dobunnic coins.

Other ritual sites are more difficult to ascribe to this period. A collection of carved stone heads from the Forest of Dean are poorly provenanced and what little is known of their recent history casts doubt on their authenticity.[70] If genuine, they may indicate the presence of a Celtic shrine on the site. It is also worth noting that classical writers suggest that during the late Iron Age a caste or class of revered and very powerful ritual leaders, known as the Druids, operated in Britain, and that their shrines were often set in natural oak groves, or at springs and wells.[71]

The arrival of the Romans

On the eve of the Roman conquest, the Gloucestershire area was fairly densely occupied by communities living in hillforts, dyke-system enclosures, palisaded enclosures, and open settlements. Most people were engaged in farming, but some craftsmen probably specialized in their trade full-time, and privileged classes of leaders and priests may also be suspected. Some knowledge of the Roman way of life was probably widespread, if limited by the kinds of objects familiar through trade and exchange.

Much has been written about the political history of the conquest period,[72] but little of it can be confirmed or refuted by the archaeological evidence. It does, however, appear that in the years leading up to the conquest the kingdom of the Dobunni was split into a northern portion putatively under the rule of *Bodvoc*, and a southern portion under the rule of *Corio*.[73] Recent work suggests that, on the basis of pottery types, this division may be traced back into the middle Iron Age, perhaps hinting that the tribal group of the Dobunni was rather a confederacy of smaller units united politically at different times by alliances or strong leaders.[74]

Although the Roman invasion of Britain is traditionally dated to AD 43, it was some years before much presence was felt as far west as Gloucestershire. Traditionally it is thought that *Boduocus* (?*Bodvoc*) surrendered the northern Dobunni to Aulus Plautius, the commander of the invasion force, in AD 43, thereby assuring the peaceful subjugation of the area. In contrast, the southern Dobunni did not surrender and were apparently taken by force.[75] Whether this is a true account of what took place we shall probably never know, but by AD 49 the Romans were certainly present in the county and had established a frontier running roughly south-west to north-east through the area along a line which later became the Fosse Way. A cavalry unit was stationed in a fort of about 1.8ha at Cirencester[76] and at about the same time, or perhaps a little later, an army unit was stationed at Kingsholm just to the north of Gloucester.[77] The unit at Kingsholm was probably a detachment of the XXth legion transferred from Colchester (Essex).[78] Both forts underwent several episodes of rebuilding and refurbishment, not necessarily by the same units. Indeed it has proved most difficult to determine exactly which of the various legions known to have taken part in the invasion were stationed in this area at any one time.

A small fort of the invasion period is thought to have existed at Rodborough,[79] perhaps rather significantly, very close to the dyke-system enclosure at Minchinhampton.

Exactly how the communities in the Gloucestershire area reacted to the arrival of the Romans is not known. Traditionally, a rather placid picture of subjugation is portrayed, but equally likely is a period of turbulent resistance perhaps with harassment of garrisons, and attacks on supply convoys. It is known that the tribe of the Silures occupying the area west of the River Severn in south-eastern Wales were particularly troublesome and they apparently raided the Gloucestershire area in AD 47.[80]

It is hard to believe that army units of the size of those attested at Gloucester and Cirencester were not sent to the area without good cause, whether to launch attacks on the Silures or to control the Dobunni. One explanation for some of the imported pottery of types normally associated with military users, which has been found on farmstead settlements, is that it was spoil from attacks on military units. Likewise, the increased circulation of coinage at the time of the conquest may have resulted from payments being made to the supporters of the client kings.

After the invasion

Prehistory conventionally ends with the arrival of the Romans, but those people living at the time of the conquest must have been affected by Roman life, and it is interesting to see how they coped with the changes.

At Frocester very little effect of Romanization was felt at first.[81] The settlement apparently continued very much as before in terms of its structure and physical character, and the only perceivable change was that it ceased to be a wealthy farm with access to imported objects and high status materials. Instead it became a rather poor place with few of the luxuries, such as Samian ware, that might be expected, and indeed very few Roman coins were lost at the site until after about 200 AD when fortunes improved.

A completely different picture can be glimpsed at Claydon Pike in the upper Thames Valley.[82] Here, the late Iron Age settlement continued relatively unchanged until about AD 70 when it seems a major reorganization took place, not only of the settlement but also of the whole landscape around about. New roads and houses were built over the top of the late Iron Age settlement, new enclosures were established, and it is suggested that there was some kind of military control of the site.

Yet another pattern of change may be represented at The Ditches.[83] Here the late Iron Age and conquest period occupation within the hillfort was followed by the construction of a simple stone villa in a tradition quite alien to Britain but of course characteristic of Roman life in the Mediterranean. Again, the results of further excavation and post-excavation analysis must be brought together before the complete picture can be seen, but it is tempting to speculate that here is a case of a high status pre-Roman settlement emerging as a high status Romanized settlement.

The Samian ware from Bagendon suggests that the site was abandoned shortly after the middle of the 1st century AD,[84] presumably when the population moved to Cirencester to form a *vicus* or civilian settlement beside the military fort. Other late Iron Age settlements became Romano-British sites too, a small market town in the case of Wycomb, and perhaps a *mansio* and staging-post settlement in the case of Birdlip. The late Iron Age shrine at West Hill, Uley, became a Roman temple dedicated to Mercury;[85] no doubt other shrines in the area also became the temples of Roman gods.

By the end of the 1st century AD the army had left Cirencester and Gloucester, and civilian settlements on a scale previously unknown in this area had been established. At Gloucester the earlier base at Kingsholm was replaced first by a legionary fortress on the present site of the city centre and later, during the late 1st or early 2nd century, a *colonia* was created by the Roman authorities.[86] Cirencester became the administrative and economic centre of the former tribal area of the Dobunni,[87] and the stage was set for a way of life altogether different from that of the prehistoric period.

Appendix A – Select Radiocarbon Dates

The following radiocarbon dates relate to prehistoric sites in and around Gloucestershire which are mentioned in the text.[1] Each determination is given with its laboratory number and standard deviation, together with brief details of the material dated. All dates are in radiocarbon years BC based on the 5568 ± 30 half-life of carbon 14.

Ascott-under-Wychwood Long Barrow, Oxfordshire

Charcoal from pre-barrow pit	BM-491b	2943 ± 70 BC
Charcoal from old ground surface	BM-492	2785 ± 70 BC
Charcoal from within barrow	BM-832	2992 ± 74 BC
Charcoal from within barrow	BM-833	3070 ± 92 BC
Charcoal in primary fill of quarry	BM-835	3248 ± 225 BC
Charcoal from upper fill of quarry	BM-836	2495 ± 61 BC
Charcoal from upper fill of quarry	BM-837	2764 ± 166 BC

Beckford, Hereford and Worcester

Charcoal from large ditch	Birm-431	1410 ± 200 BC
Fill of pit 1842	Birm-432	160 ± 120 BC

Condicote Henge, Condicote, Gloucestershire

Charcoal from lower fill of inner henge ditch	HAR-3064	1770 ± 80 BC
	HAR-3067	1720 ± 100 BC

Crickley Hill, Coberley, Gloucestershire

Lowest tier of period 2 rampart	HAR-392	640 ± 60 BC
Gatepost from period 3B entrance	HAR-391	570 ± 90 BC
Charcoal from period 2 rampart lacing	HAR-394	400 ± 80 BC
Charcoal from period 2 rampart lacing	HAR-393	360 ± 70 BC

Frocester Court, Frocester, Gloucestershire

Shaft	HAR-2179	1120 ± 90 BC
Charcoal from fill of large ditch	HAR-4377	610 ± 80 BC

Hazleton North Long Barrow, Hazleton, Gloucestershire

Human rib from south entrance	OxA-383	2500 ± 90 BC
Human femur from north entrance*	OxA-643	2650 ± 120 BC
Human femur from north chamber	OxA-644	2890 ± 80 BC
Human femur from south chamber	OxA-645	2830 ± 80 BC
Human cranium from buried soil	OxA-646	2925 ± 80 BC
Cattle calcaneum from buried soil	OxA-738	3020 ± 80 BC
Pig humerous from buried soil	OxA-739	2965 ± 80 BC
Human femur from north entrance*	OxA-902	2870 ± 70 BC
Human femur from north entrance	OxA-903	2890 ± 60 BC
Human femur from north entrance	OxA-904	2910 ± 70 BC
Human femur from north chamber	OxA-905	3000 ± 70 BC

177

Human femur from south entrance	OxA-906	2930 ± 70 BC
Human femur from south entrance	OxA-907	3020 ± 60 BC
Human femur from south passage	OxA-908	2880 ± 60 BC
Human femur from south passage	OxA-910	3050 ± 70 BC
Human femur from south chamber	OxA-911	2880 ± 80 BC
Human femur from south chamber	OxA-912	3250 ± 150 BC
Cattle skull from the forecourt	OxA-913	3010 ± 70 BC
Cattle skull from the forecourt	OxA-914	3020 ± 70 BC
Cattle rib from south quarry	OxA-915	2890 ± 70 BC
Cattle femur from south quarry	OxA-916	2860 ± 70 BC
Human femur from north entrance★	OxA-643/902	2810 ± 60 BC

★ samples from the same bone

Holm Castle, Tewkesbury, Gloucestershire

Carbonized grain from pre-rampart occupation	HAR-1192	360 ± 70 BC

Midsummer Hill, Eastnor, Hereford and Worcester

Wood from quarry ditch associated with first gate	Birm-142	420 ± 190 BC
Carbonized grain associated with destruction of eighth gate	Birm-143	50 ± 100 BC

Peak Camp, Cowley, Gloucestershire

Animal bone in phase 2 enclosure ditch	OxA-416	2680 ± 110 BC
Animal bone in phase 2 enclosure ditch	OxA-417	2710 ± 80 BC
Animal bone in phase 2 enclosure ditch★	OxA-445	2720 ± 90 BC
Animal tooth in phase 2 enclosure ditch★	OxA-446	2860 ± 90 BC
Animal bone in phase 2 enclosure ditch	OxA-444	2840 ± 80 BC
Animal bone in phase 4 enclosure ditch	OxA-638	2340 ± 80 BC

★ Samples taken from the same mandible

Rollright, Oxfordshire

Charcoal from remation associated with round cairn near the King Stone	BM-2427	1420 ± 40 BC
Charcoal from cremation in area of the round cairn near the King Stone	BM-2428	1530 ± 50 BC
Charcoal with cremation associated with a collared urn in areas of the round cairn near the King Stone	BM-2429	1370 ± 90 BC
Charcoal from beside the round cairn near the King Stone	BM-2430	1540 ± 70 BC

Roughground Farm, Lechlade, Gloucestershire

Bone from pit 1260 (beaker pottery)	HAR-5499	1760 ± 100 BC
Bone from pit 962 (grooved ware)	HAR-5500	1990 ± 80 BC
Bone from pit 962 (grooved ware)	HAR-5501	1870 ± 90 BC
Bone from pit 784 (grooved ware)	HAR-5498	2150 ± 100 BC
Bone from crouched burial in F1157	HAR-5503	890 ± 80 BC
Bone from burial in a ditch F1215	HAR-5502	180 ± 120 BC
Bone from pit 1001	HAR-5504	1090 ± 100 BC

Swell 8 Round Barrow, Cow Common, Swell, Gloucestershire

Burnt timbers over burial pit	HAR-1325	1480 ± 80 BC
	HAR-1326	1440 ± 80 BC

Tormarton Bronze Age Burial, Tormarton, Avon

Bone from body with lodged bronze spearhead	BM-542	977 ± 90 BC

Uley Bury Hillfort, Uley, Gloucestershire

Carbonized grain in rampart construction	HAR-2289	300 ± 80 BC

Appendix B – Places to Visit

I MUSEUMS

The following museums in the county display prehistoric material from the area. Opening hours vary greatly and sometimes alter during the year; prospective visitors are advised to check by telephone in advance.

Cheltenham Museum and Art Gallery, Clarence Street, Cheltenham. (Cheltenham 37431)
Corinium Museum, Park Street, Cirencester. (Cirencester 5611)
Dean Heritage Centre, Camp Hill, Soudley, Cinderford. (Dean 22170)
Gloucester City Museum and Art Gallery, Brunswick Road, Gloucester. (Gloucester 24131)
Lydney Park Site Museum, Lydney Park, Lydney. (Dean 42844)
Stroud District Museum, Lansdown, Stroud. (Stroud 3394)
The Town House Museum, Barton Street, Tewkesbury (Tewkesbury 297174)

There is also some Gloucestershire material in the Ashmolean Museum (Beaumont Street, Oxford), Birmingham Museum and Art Gallery (Chamberlain Square, Birmingham), The British Museum (Great Russell Street, London WC1), and City of Bristol Museum and Art Gallery (Queens Road, Clifton, Bristol).

II SITES AND MONUMENTS

The following selection represents a cross-section of sites of different periods and types which are open to the public, situated in a public open space, or visible from a public right of way. Monuments on private land are not accessible to the general public without permission from the landowner. National Grid References are provided to assist in the location of sites.

1. Bagendon Dykes, Bagendon, Gloucestershire (SP 018064)

Late Iron Age dyke system enclosing about 200ha. Traditionally interpreted as the tribal centre of the Dobunni. The best place to see the dykes is where they run alongside Cutham Lane.

2. Belas Knap Long Barrow, Sudeley, Gloucestershire (SP 020254)

Neolithic long barrow built about 3000 BC with four burial chambers. Restored by the Ministry of Public Building and Works in the 1930s following extensive excavations. The monument is a classic Cotswold-Severn lateral chambered tomb. Points to look for include the mound shape, chambers, horns, and forecourt.

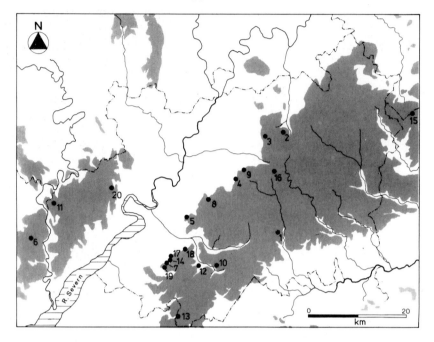

Map showing the position of sites mentioned in Appendix B.

3.   Cleeve Cloud Camp, Cleeve Common, Southam, Gloucestershire (SO 985255)
Small hillfort situated on the Cotswold escarpment, defined by two semicircular ramparts each
with external ditches. About 750m north of the fort is a linear earthwork running roughly east
to west across the hilltop. This is probably a boundary earthwork.

4.   Crickley Hill, Coberley, Gloucestershire (SO 927161)
This site was first occupied in the Neolithic period when a causewayed enclosure and later a
defended enclosure were constructed on the central knoll. After the destruction of the defended
enclosure a long earthen mound was constructed over the razed ramparts. The site was then
abandoned until about 650 BC when a larger area was fortified by a single ditch and rampart.
The site has been extensively excavated since 1969.
   Both the Neolithic and the Iron Age defences can be seen as earthworks, so too the long
mound. Within the Iron Age fort, coloured posts have been set in the ground to mark the
position of postholes forming the walls of the main houses.

5.   Haresfield Beacon, Haresfield, Gloucestershire (SO 823090)
An Iron Age hillfort of about 4ha enclosed by a single rampart running round Haresfield
Beacon and Ring Hill. Heavily disturbed by quarrying. To the east is a rampart known as the
Bulwarks which cuts off the Haresfield promontory.

6.   Harold's Stones, Trelleck, Gwent (SO 498051)
Stone row comprising three large upright blocks of local stone. Probably beaker period or
early Bronze Age in date.

7.   Hetty Pegler's Tump, Uley, Gloucestershire (SO 789004)
Neolithic long barrow probably built about 2900 BC with a transepted terminal chamber. The

Interior of Hetty Pegler's Tump, Uley. [Photograph: Stephen Dorey]

site was excavated in the last century when the remains of at least 15 skeletons were found. Although the site has been partly restored it still retains a great deal of atmosphere. Best visited with a candle to provide light in the chamber.

8. Kimsbury Hillfort, near Painswick, Gloucestershire (SO 869121)
A multivallate Iron Age hillfort of about 2.8ha on a prominent spur of Cotswold escarpment. The interior of the site is much damaged by quarrying and a golf course, but the ramparts are still visible on the east, west and south sides.

9. Leckhampton Hillfort, Leckhampton, Gloucestershire
(SO 948183)
Iron Age hillfort of about 2.8ha enclosed on the south and east sides by a single ditch and rampart. The north and west sides are formed by later quarry faces. A round mound set in a square shaped enclosure lies to the south-east of the entrance to the hillfort.

10. Long Stone, Minchinhampton, Gloucestershire (ST 883999)
A large standing stone about 2.3m high, possibly a marker stone for a Bronze Age cemetery. A rather smaller upright stone has been incorporated into the field boundary nearby. Among the folklore attached to this site is that the stone runs round the field when it hears the clock at Minchinhampton strike midnight.

11. Long Stone, Staunton, Gloucestershire (SO 559120)
A large standing stone about 2.5 m high beside the A4136 south of Staunton. Possibly a marker stone for a Bronze Age cemetery.

12.   Minchinhampton Common, near Stroud, Gloucestershire
(*c*.SO 8501)
Many earthworks can be seen on this common, including a Neolithic long barrow known as Whitefield's Tump, a possible Bronze Age round barrow, and a series of Iron Age dykes known as the Bulwarks.

13.   Nan Tow's Tump, Didmarton, Gloucestershire (ST 803893)
A large Bronze Age round barrow about 3m high and nearly 30m in diameter now covered in trees. Local folklore holds that Nan Tow was a witch who lived nearby and was buried upright in the barrow. Visible from the A46.

14.   Nympsfield Long Barrow, Coaley Peak, Frocester, Gloucestershire (SO 793013)
Neolithic long barrow dating to about 2900 BC with a transepted terminal chamber. The site was been excavated in 1937 and 1974 and has since been partly restored. Remains of at least 13 skeletons were found in the chambers.

15.   Rollright Stones, Rollright, Oxfordshire (SP 296308)
Well preserved stone circle with a diameter of about 31.6m. To the north is a single outlier, the King Stone, probably a Bronze Age standing stone marking the site of a cemetery. About 350m to the east is the remains of a Neolithic portal dolmen tomb known as the Whispering Knights. Much folklore attaches to this group of monuments.

16.   St Paul's Epistle Round Barrow, Dowdeswell, Gloucestershire (SP 002181)
Tree-covered Bronze Age round barrow visible from the road.

17.   The Soldier's Grave, Coaley Peak, Frocester, Gloucestershire (SO 793015)
Round cairn probably of late Neolithic or beaker period date. Excavations revealed a central boat-shaped pit lined with dry- stone-walling. The pit contained the remains of at least 28 individuals.

18.   The Toots Long Barrow, Selsley Common, near Stroud, Gloucestershire (SO 827031)
Grass covered long barrow probably dating to about 2900 BC. No visible chamber.

19.   Uley Bury Hillfort, near Uley, Gloucestershire (ST 784989)
Iron Age hillfort probably constructed about 300 BC. This is one of the largest in the county, enclosing about 13ha. The ramparts can be traced all round the hill, and entrances are visible at the south and east corners. There is no public access to the interior of the site.

20.   Welshbury Camp, Blaisdon, near Flaxley, Gloucestershire (SO 677155)
An Iron Age hillfort of about 1.7ha defended by a single bank and ditch across the north and east sides and a triple rampart on the south and west sides. The entrance is at the south-east corner.

Notes

CHAPTER 1 – In search of Gloucestershire's prehistory

[1] See Champion 1984 for review of the later prehistoric period as revealed by the classical sources.

[2] Local folklore relating to burial monuments is summarized in O'Neil & Grinsell 1960, 50–3.

[3] The first edition of *Britannia* was published in 1586. It went through many later editions, of which the most famous are Gibson's of 1695 and Gough's of 1789.

[4] Fowles 1982

[5] See Piggott 1950 for biography of William Stukeley, and notes in O'Neil & Grinsell 1960, 55–57 on early travellers in Gloucestershire. See also Gray 1981 for short biographies of many Gloucestershire antiquaries.

[6] Crawford 1925, 136–7

[7] Thurnam 1854

[8] Greenwell 1877, 445–457 and 513–549 for work in Gloucestershire.

[9] Rolleston 1876

[10] Grinsell 1964; Grinsell & Janes 1966

[11] For an account of the history of the Bristol and Gloucestershire Archaeological Society and the events leading up to its formation see Ralph 1976.

[12] Witts 1881, 201–2

[13] Witts 1883

[14] See Daniel 1943 on the origins and development of the Three Age System, and Rolleston 1878 for the publication of a lecture to the Bristol and Gloucestershire Archaeological Society in which the implications of the Three Age System were discussed.

[15] Biographical essays on Elsie Clifford and Helen O'Neil are provided by Reece 1984 and M.U.Jones 1984 respectively.

[16] Crawford 1925

[17] O'Neil & Grinsell 1960; Grinsell 1957; Leslie Grinsell pers. comm.

[18] See Hart 1967

[19] The development of archaeology during the late 1960s and early 1970s – the rescue era as it is often known – is well described in Rahtz (ed) 1974, and B.Jones 1984.

[20] Fowler 1979

[21] See Gillespie 1984 for more detailed account of radiocarbon dating and further bibliography.

[22] See Coles 1972 for a general survey of techniques and methods.

[23] Darvill 1984a

[24] Marshall 1985

[25] Information from Mr B.Walters.

[26] Leech 1977 for summary of work in the upper Thames Valley; see also Webster & Hobley 1964 for reconnaissance over the Warwickshire Avon.

[27] See Tite 1972, 7–56, for an introduction to geophysical surveying.

[28] See Evens, Smith & Wallis 1972, with earlier references.

[29] Peacock 1970

[30] Tylecote 1962

[31] See Clarke 1978 for detailed treatment and further references.

[32] Brown 1982; Brown & Barber 1985

[33] Brown 1982, 94–6
[34] Brown & Barber 1985, 93; Brown 1983
[35] Shotton 1978
[36] Bell 1984, 87
[37] Evans 1971, 31–40; Dimbleby & Evans 1974
[38] Hazelden & Jarvis 1979
[39] Taylor 1975
[40] Harding (ed) 1982

CHAPTER 2 – The earliest inhabitants (to *c* 3500 BC)

[1] Saville 1984a; Sparks & West 1972
[2] West 1968
[3] Wymer 1968; Roe 1981
[4] Wymer 1974
[5] Roe 1981, Ch. 5
[6] Wills 1938 on the Severn Valley gravels; Sandford 1965 on the upper Thames area.
[7] Saville 1984b
[8] Saville 1984a, 66
[9] Grinsell 1960
[10] Lacaille 1954; Roe 1974
[11] Clifford *et al* 1954
[12] Clifford *et al* 1954, 180
[13] Clifford *et al* 1954, fig. 2, no. 16
[14] Clifford 1937a
[15] Gloucester City Museum Accession No. A3125
[16] Saville 1984a, 62–4
[17] Viner 1978
[18] Gloucester City Museum Accession No. A3124
[19] Grinsell 1966
[20] Corinium Museum, Cirencester, Accession No. 1976/363
[21] Corinium Museum, Cirencester, Accession No. 1976/364
[22] Whitehead 1979
[23] Whitehead 1979, 118
[24] O'Neil 1965
[25] Roe 1981, 253 (note 1); Cook *et al* 1982
[26] See Gamble 1986, 32–42 on models of hunter-gatherer life-styles.
[27] West 1968, Ch. 13; Wymer 1981
[28] See Gamble 1986, 110–112 and Ch. 8
[29] Mellars 1974, 62–65; Roe 1981, Ch. 6
[30] Clifford 1939
[31] Clifford *et al* 1954, fig. 2, no. 12
[32] Clifford 1936a; Clifford *et al* 1954
[33] Roe 1981, 233
[34] Green 1984
[35] Cook *et al* 1982
[36] Campbell 1977 for general account of the upper Palaeolithic in Britain.
[37] Clifford *et al* 1954, 180–2; Campbell 1977, vol. 2, 104
[38] Gardiner 1932
[39] Burkitt 1938
[40] Symonds 1871
[41] Taylor 1928
[42] Jacobi 1979a, 28–37 on discontinuity in the west of Britain.
[43] Summarized in Simmons *et al* 1981.
[44] Simmons *et al* 1981, 83–9
[45] To what extent this paucity of evidence is real and to what extent it simply reflects

difficulties in finding and recognizing sites and objects of early post-glacial date is not clear.

[46] Taylor 1928, fig. 4
[47] Rogers *et al* 1981
[48] Sieveking 1981
[49] Campbell 1977
[50] Sykes & Whittle 1965
[51] Sykes & Whittle 1965, fig. 2
[52] Saville 1984a, 69
[53] Gloucester City Museum Accession No. A3674
[54] Cheltenham Museum Accession No. 1946/57
[55] Found by Mr Beveringe while fieldwalking; Wilfred Cox pers. comm.
[56] Mellars 1974, 87–8 on changes in flintwork.
[57] Eg. Care 1982
[58] Witchell 1973
[59] Palmer 1970
[60] Gracie 1942
[61] Saville 1984a, 71
[62] Saville 1984a, 71–2
[63] Saville 1984c, 19
[64] Evans 1971, 31–40
[65] Saville 1979a, 105
[66] Saville 1981,
[67] Summary reports in Walters (ed) 1985.
[68] Walters 1985; Saville 1986
[69] See Mellars 1976 and Jacobi 1978 for discussion of variations in the size and form of Mesolithic settlements.
[70] Simmons *et al* 1981, 110–124

CHAPTER 3 – The first farmers in Gloucestershire (*c* 3500 – *c* 2500 BC)

[1] For convenience the Neolithic period is divided into three phases, the early Neolithic (3500–3000 BC), the middle Neolithic (3000–3500 BC) and the late Neolithic (2500–2000 BC). This Chapter deals only with the first two of these phases. For general background to the Neolithic of southern England see Whittle 1977a.
[2] See Bender 1978; Whittle 1985
[3] De Laet (ed) 1976; Whittle 1977a, 99; Darvill 1987, 48–9
[4] Rackham 1976, 39
[5] Birks *et al* 1975
[6] Catt 1978
[7] Brown 1982, 96
[8] Evans 1971, 31–40
[9] Saville 1984c, 19
[10] Saville *et al* 1987
[11] O'Neil (1966, 20) suggests that the timber structure in the forecourt was built after the barrow had fallen into decay. Plate I of the report shows the gully which forms part of structure running under the stonework of the barrow, and examination of the site records suggests that Roman quarrying of the barrow for stone removed part of the cairn to expose the buried soil in the forecourt area (and see Darvill 1982a, 60–1).
[12] Greenwell 1877, 514; Darvill 1984b, fig. 2
[13] Selkirk 1971, 10
[14] Clifford 1936b, 125
[15] O'Neil 1966, 20 where the possible rotunda grave is designated grave 2.
[16] Lawrence & Winterbotham 1866
[17] See Powell 1973, 30–38 and Lynch 1976, 66–67 for general accounts of portal dolmen.

[18] Portal dolmen were seemingly never covered by cairns. Access was from the sides of the chamber.

[19] Crawford 1925, 166; and see Lambrick 1983, 36–37, and Lambrick 1988, for recent work at the site.

[20] Portal dolmen in Oxfordshire listed in Corcoran 1969, 289–290.

[21] O'Neil & Grinsell 1960, 89

[22] Excavations summarized in Crawford 1925, 69–70.

[23] See Lynch 1976, 75 for account of simple passage graves in England Wales (therein called small chamber-and-passage tombs).

[24] O'Neil 1966, 15 where the possible simple passage grave on this site is incorrectly referred to as a 'rotunda'.

[25] Greenwell 1877, 448 for account of the excavation; Crawford 1925, 91 for plan (Greenwell's 217).

[26] See Whittle 1977a, 58

[27] Dixon 1979, 143

[28] The most recent interim accounts are Dixon 1979 and 1981.

[29] See Saville 1984c for interim report; final account of excavations in preparation.

[30] Whittle 1977b with earlier references.

[31] Palmer 1976, 184, sites 4–6

[32] Information from Mr W.Nash of Oxford who has collected flintwork, Neolithic pottery and over 60 fragments of polished stone and flint axes from the ploughed ditches and interior of this site.

[33] Barker & Webley 1978, see esp. fig. 3 for Crickley Hill.

[34] Dixon 1979, 147

[35] Savage 1986, 231

[36] For interim accounts see Darvill 1981 and 1982b; final report in preparation.

[37] Darvill 1986, 122

[38] The flintwork from Peak Camp is predominantly a narrow flake based industry.

[39] Marshall 1985

[40] See Holgate 1985, and Bradley *et al* 1984, for summaries of fieldsurvey in the upper Thames Valley (in both papers the early and middle Neolithic of this Chapter is subsumed within their early Neolithic).

[41] Marshall 1985, 42

[42] See Hurst 1972, 38 for interim note; final report in preparation.

[43] One major problem with finding early prehistoric settlements in the major river valleys is that large areas were covered by alluvium during later prehistoric and more recent times. Reports of bone and pottery being found at a depth of 9.0m or more in alluvial clay at Tewkesbury (Symonds 1865, 38), and antler within peat at a considerable depth in a valley bottom at Woodchester (Walrond 1971, 15) suggests that there is much yet to be discovered about riverside and valley-bottom settlement.

[44] For general account of subsistence resources see section by G.Hillman and C.Grigson in Smith 1981.

[45] Eg. Smith 1965, 42 notes knife marks on cattle bones which may have resulted from skinning.

[46] Grimes 1960, 75

[47] A.S.Kennard in Clifford 1938a, 210

[48] Burton 1980

[49] Clifford 1950a

[50] Darvill 1983, Appendix XV on the analysis of Neolithic pottery assemblages.

[51] For a general discussion of the use of wood in prehistoric times see Coles *et al* 1978.

[52] See Drewett 1977, 225 for summary of evidence for human bones at causewayed enclosures.

[53] Crawford 1925

[54] See Renfrew (ed) 1983 for recent overview of megalithic monuments in western Europe. Daniel 1950 provides a review of chamber tombs in England and Wales.

[55] Corcoran 1969; Darvill 1982a

[56] The long barrows of the county are listed by O'Neil & Grinsell (1960), Corcoran (1969),

and Saville (1980, 6–8).

[57] For Heston Brake see Bagnall-Oakley 1889, 18–20, and for Herefordshire sites see Crawford 1925, 147–150.

[58] Bell 1984, 87

[59] Crawford 1922, 5; Darvill 1982a, 95

[60] See Saville 1984c, 12–14 for Hazleton evidence. Quarries are known at other sites from excavations, fieldsurveys, and geophysical survey.

[61] Startin & Bradley 1981

[62] See Corcoran 1972 for discussion of multi-period tombs.

[63] Clifford 1936b, 125 wherein the rotunda grave is called 'the central dome'.

[64] O'Neil 1966 for original excavation report.

[65] Saville 1984c, 19–21

[66] Grimes 1960, 41–90

[67] See Greenwell 1877, 524 for Pole's Wood East, and Witts 1881 for West Tump.

[68] Darvill 1982a

[69] Clifford & Daniel 1940

[70] Grimes 1939, 139; 1960, 90–101

[71] Corcoran 1969, 100–104; Darvill 1982a, 17–30

[72] Fleming 1973,

[73] See Piggott 1954, table III for list of recorded interments; O'Neil & Grinsell 1960, 89 on Belas Knap; Saville *et al* 1987, 116 on Hazleton; and Chesterman 1977, and Benson & Clegg 1978 on Ascott-under-Wychwood (Oxfordshire).

[74] Piggott 1954, 139

[75] Atkinson 1968; Saville *et al* 1987, 117

[76] Cameron 1934; L.H.Wells in Piggott 1962; Brothwell 1973

[77] Brothwell & Sandison 1967, 426–7

[78] Crawford 1925, 80 with earlier references.

[79] Clifford 1950a

[80] Saville 1984c, 17–19

[81] Eg. Clifford 1938a, 201 for details of forecourt features at Nympsfield.

[82] Clifford 1936b, 135

[83] Saville *et al* 1987, 115–118

[84] Renfrew 1976; 1983

[85] The dating of trackways is very difficult. Wooden timber tracks of Neolithic date have been discovered in the Somerset Levels and elsewhere (Coles & Coles 1986). See Grimes 1951 on the Jurassic Way.

[86] Saville 1982

[87] See papers in Clough & Cummins (eds) 1979 for background.

[88] Both axes are unpublished. The Bredon Hill example is in Birmingham City Museum (Accession No. 319), the Colwall Tunnel axe is in Hereford Museum (Accession No. 1306).

[89] Campbell-Smith 1965

[90] Cox 1969

[91] See Clark 1965, and Hodder & Lane 1982 for discussion of flint and stone axe trade in Britain.

[92] Tyler 1976, 77

[93] K.C.Durham in Grimes 1960, 75

[94] Clifford 1950a, 26

[95] A.S.Kennard in Clifford 1938a, 210

CHAPTER 4 – War and peace (*c* 2500–*c* 1600 BC)

[1] Bradley & Hodder 1979

[2] Dixon 1979, 147; 1981, 146

[3] Peterborough ware is traditionally divided into three broadly successive sub-styles: Ebbsfleet ware, Mortlake ware and Fengate ware. Peterborough ware is thought to have developed about 2500 BC.

[4] Clifford 1938a, 202

[5] See Clifford 1936b, 138; Grimes 1960, 72; Crawford 1925, 85; O'Neil 1966, 26; Crawford 1925, 128 respectively.

[6] Piggott 1963, 26–30

[7] Britnell 1984, 90–3

[8] Saville 1984c, 11–12

[9] Whittle 1978

[10] Smith 1968

[11] Hurst 1972, 38

[12] Clifford 1934a, 231

[13] T.C.Darvill in Garrod & Heighway 1984, 72

[14] Hannan 1972; Alan Hannan pers. comm..

[15] Dunning 1976, 77

[16] Dunning 1932

[17] Case 1986, 30–1

[18] Phillips 1971; Bernard Phillips pers. comm..

[19] Grinsell 1964, 8; Saville 1979a, 94 respectively.

[20] Darvill *et al* 1986

[21] Darvill forthcoming

[22] Garrod & Heighway 1984, 22–5

[23] Darvill & Timby 1986

[24] Smith 1946, 58

[25] Clark 1934

[26] Dunning 1932, 280

[27] For general discussion of Neolithic round barrows see Kinnes 1979.

[28] Clifford 1938b

[29] O'Neil & Grinsell 1960, 97–8

[30] Smith 1972, 164

[31] Vatcher 1966

[32] For interim account see Moore 1985.

[33] Benson & Miles 1974, 27, and research by T.C.Darvill and R.Locke 1986.

[34] Webster & Hobley 1964, 5–7, and information supplied by Hereford and Worcester County Museum Service.

[35] Dixon 1979, 147

[36] F.E.S.Roe in Smith 1968, 22–4

[37] Evens *et al* 1972, 265

[38] Saville & Roe 1984, 21

[39] Clarke 1970; Lanting & Van der Waals 1972

[40] Whittle 1981

[41] Case 1977 with earlier references.

[42] Dixon 1971, fig. 8.15

[43] Roe 1979

[44] Saville & Roe 1984, 19. A battle-axe from Oatground, Sinwell, Wotton-under-Edge, may be another early example from the county, but because its nearest parallels are with Danish battle-axes it has been reported as a modern import (Saville & Roe 1984, 20). The possibility that it is an ancient import must nevertheless remain.

[45] Needham 1979

[46] Ellison 1984, fig. 2

[47] Needham & Saville 1981

[48] Gardiner 1937; Dent 1877, 9; Hart 1967, 11 respectively.

[49] Darvill 1983, Appendix VII, schedule 10

[50] O'Neil 1966, 31

[51] Clifford 1964a

[52] Darvill forthcoming

[53] Smith & Cox 1985

[54] Stanford 1981, 137–8

[55] Taylor 1928, 65; Clarke 1970, 483

[56] Fell 1961, 30–1

[57] Dixon 1971, fig. 8.15

[58] Dunning 1932, fig. 2

[59] T.C.Darvill in Garrod & Heighway 1984, 73; Hurst 1972, 38; Darvill & Timby 1985; O'Neil & Grinsell 1960, 133; Williams 1947, 63

[60] Clifford 1937b, 159

[61] O'Neil 1966, 24

[62] Clifford 1930, 218–22

[63] Dunning 1937

[64] Clifford 1938c

[65] O'Neil & Bunt 1966

[66] Clifford 1937b, 162

[67] Else 1943

[68] Clifford 1950b

[69] O'Neil & Grinsell 1960, 119

[70] O'Neil & Grinsell 1960, 114

[71] Thomas 1967

[72] Barnett 1964

[73] Hannan 1972, 34; Alan Hannan pers. comm..

[74] Grimes 1960, 131–4

[75] Summary of 1931 excavation in O'Neil & Grinsell 1960, 106.

[76] Greenwell 1877, 446–7

[77] Green 1949

[78] Clifford 1937b, with additions.

[79] Hart 1967, 7; Crawford 1925, 209–10

[80] Burl 1969

[81] Witts 1883, 15

[82] Saville 1983a

[83] Saville 1980, 27; Harding & Lee 1987, 159–60

[84] Atkinson 1949; Benson & Miles 1974, 33

[85] Smith 1972, 164

[86] Information from Hereford and Worcester County Museum Service.

[87] Burl 1976

[88] Lambrick 1983; Lambrick 1988

[89] M.Bell in Saville 1983a, 44

[90] Brown 1982, 96

[91] Eg. Bradley *et al* 1984 on upper Thames Valley ritual centres.

CHAPTER 5 – The green and pleasant land (c 1600–c 700 BC)

[1] The Bronze Age is traditionally divided into three phases: the early Bronze Age (1900–1400 BC), which overlaps a little with the currency of beaker pottery, the middle Bronze Age (1400 –1000 BC), and the late Bronze Age (1000–700 BC).

[2] Tinsley 1981, 210–12

[3] Bradley 1984, 68–73

[4] For a general discussion of round barrows see Ashbee 1960; for Gloucestershire barrows see O'Neil & Grinsell 1960.

[5] See Grinsell 1941 for terminology.

[6] Smith 1972, and subsequent aerial reconnaissance by T.C.Darvill and R.Locke.

[7] Benson & Miles 1974; Leech 1977; Webster & Hobley 1964

[8] See Fleming 1971 for discussion of barrow cemeteries in Wessex.

[9] Piggott 1938

[10] See ApSimon 1954; Gerloff 1975 for background.

[11] Greenwell 1890, 70–2

[12] ApSimon 1954, 42

[13] O'Neil & Grinsell 1960, 125

[14] Scott-Garrett 1955
[15] Scott-Garrett 1955, 27
[16] O'Neil & Grinsell 1960, 109
[17] Gerloff 1975, 169
[18] Saville 1979a, 110
[19] Information from Corinium Museum, Cirencester.
[20] O'Neil & Grinsell 1960,123
[21] Longworth 1984, 19–24
[22] Dunning 1932, 277
[23] Grimes 1960, 101–14
[24] O'Neil & Grinsell 1960, 113
[25] Longworth 1984, 200
[26] O'Neil & Grinsell 1960, 20 and fig. 4
[27] Longworth 1984, 200 (no. 599)
[28] O'Neil & Grinsell 1960, 138
[29] O'Neil 1967
[30] Saville 1979a
[31] O'Neil & Grinsell 1960, 109 and 102
[32] Summarized in O'Neil & Grinsell 1960, 132.
[33] O'Neil & Grinsell 1960, 132
[34] Greenwell 1877, 446–7
[35] Grimes 1960, 110
[36] O'Neil 1977, 15–17
[37] O'Neil 1967
[38] O'Neil & Grinsell 1960, 133
[39] Bradley 1981, 101
[40] Dunning 1935
[41] O'Neil & Grinsell 1960, 131
[42] O'Neil & Grinsell 1960, 107; this urn is displayed in the site museum at Chedworth Roman villa.
[43] Timothy Allen pers. comm..
[44] Wilson 1983
[45] Crawford 1925, 113–4; and see O'Neil & Grinsell 1960, 52–3 for associated folklore.
[46] Lambrick 1983; Lambrick 1988
[47] Hart 1967, 8
[48] Hart 1967, 8
[49] Linnell 1971 where recorded as Neolithic.
[50] Darvill *et al* 1986, 36
[51] City of Bristol Museum Accession No. F3902
[52] Evens *et al* 1972, 264
[53] Herdman 1933
[54] Marshall 1985, 47
[55] Clifford 1933, 331–2
[56] Price 1983, 141
[57] Hannan 1976
[58] Britnell 1974, 297
[59] Richard Hingley pers. comm.; report in Allen *et al* forthcoming.
[60] Bradley 1978, 83 and 4; Christopher Young pers. comm..
[61] Darvill & Timby 1985
[62] ApSimon 1969, 45
[63] RCHME 1976, 62
[64] Information from Gloucester City Museum.
[65] Price 1983, 141
[66] Richard Hingley pers. comm.; GCC no date figs. 2 and 3
[67] Richard Hingley pers. comm.; report in Allen *et al* forthcoming.
[68] Bradley 1978, 83–4; Christopher Young pers. comm..
[69] Hall & Gingell 1974

[70] Burgess 1980

[71] Bradley 1978, 83–4; Christopher Young pers. comm..

[72] Thomas 1986, 12 correcting Pritchard 1906, 281–2

[73] Fisher 1919

[74] Hart 1967, 11; Green 1935, 197–8; Hart 1967, 11; Needham 1979, 267; Megaw & Hardy 1938, 283 respectively.

[75] Britton 1963, 316 with earlier references.

[76] Rowlands 1976

[77] Rowlands 1976, 347 (no. 1080)

[78] Burgess 1968

[79] Information from Corinium Museum, Cirencester.

[80] Clifford 1937d, 162–3

[81] Information from Corinium Museum, Cirencester; Hart 1967, 11; Information from Gloucester City Museum and John Smith pers. comm..

[82] Ellison 1984, 123

[83] Pritchard 1906

[84] Oswald 1972, 14

[85] Dunning 1932, 284; Green 1935, 196

[86] Hall & Gingell 1974

[87] Bradley 1979; Ehrenberg 1977; Ehrenberg 1980

[88] See for example Burgess *et al* 1972, 240–3 for Broadward hoards in upper Severn Valley.

[89] Terry 1953

[90] Ashmolean Museum Accession No. 1927.2579

[91] Information from Corinium Museum, Cirencester and Mr J.Peel.

[92] Information from Gloucester City Museum and John Smith pers. comm.

[93] Hart 1967, 11

[94] Bradley 1979

[95] Saville 1979a, 115–6

[96] Green 1980, 161–4

[97] David Miles pers. comm..

[98] RCHME 1976, xxvii

[99] RCHME 1976, 66 where Icomb earthwork is claimed as the remains of a probable hillfort; RCHME 1976, 107 (6); RCHME 1976, 45 (1), respectively.

[100] Brown & Barber 1985, 93

[101] Brown 1983; Shotton 1978

[102] Hazelden & Jarvis 1979

[103] Knight *et al* 1972

CHAPTER 6 – The age of the hillforts (*c* 700 – *c* 100 BC)

[1] Cunliffe 1978, Ch. 13

[2] Robinson 1984, 7–8

[3] Cunliffe 1986

[4] Bradley 1984, 129–32

[5] The RCHME (1976) survey of Iron Age and Romano-British monuments in the Gloucestershire Cotswolds provides a wealth of detail about sites and finds from the eastern part of the county.

[6] Forde-Johnson 1976, 42

[7] Eg. Cunliffe 1984a

[8] Harding 1972, 86–96; Saville 1984d, 152–5

[9] RCHME 1976, 59

[10] Hall & Gingell 1974

[11] RCHME 1976, 87

[12] Saville 1983b

[13] Gent 1983, with earlier references.

[14] Cunliffe 1984a, 18; Wainwright 1967, 57

[15] RCHME 1976, xxvii
[16] Dixon 1972; 1973; 1976; 1979
[17] Dixon 1979, 150
[18] Burrow *et al* 1925; Champion 1976 respectively.
[19] RCHME 1976, 109
[20] Fell 1961
[21] The presence of human bones in pits is attested at numerous hillforts in Wessex. This case is especially interesting as a study of the bones by D.R.Brothwell revealed cut-marks on two fragments which may have been caused by a blow from a sword (Fell 1961, 23).
[22] RCHME 1976, 106
[23] RCHME 1976, 22
[24] RCHME 1976, 86
[25] Bayne 1957; Leeds 1931 respectively. The position of the Oxfordshire early Iron Age hillforts is interesting, however, as they are not situated in naturally defensible locations like those of the Gloucestershire Cotswolds.
[26] Stanford 1981
[27] Hencken 1938
[28] Cunliffe 1978, 252–3 for reinterpretation of the evidence from this site.
[29] Hencken 1938, 23; Ross 1967, 61–126
[30] Christopher Young pers. comm.; Dunning 1933; Webster & Smith 1982, 137; and RCHME 1976, 102 respectively.
[31] Darvill *et al* 1986
[32] Richard Hingley and Timothy Allen pers. comm.; Moore 1985
[33] Dixon 1979, 150 on Crickley Hill.
[34] Harding 1972, 97–102; Saville 1984d, 155–9
[35] Cunliffe 1978, 273
[36] See Cunliffe 1978, 249
[37] RCHME 1976, 121
[38] Saville & Ellison 1983
[39] Hampton & Palmer 1977
[40] RCHME 1976, 91
[41] RCHME 1976, 17–19
[42] Dunning 1976
[43] Hart 1967, 16–19
[44] RCHME 1976, 103
[45] Ross 1970, 63–70
[46] RCHME 1976, 106 and 86; Hart 1967, 16–17; Hart 1967, 16
[47] Stanford 1981
[48] Cunliffe 1978, 252–3
[49] Wheeler & Wheeler 1932
[50] cf. Leech 1977
[51] Saville 1979b
[52] Reynolds 1974
[53] Gascoigne 1973
[54] Smith & Cox 1985, 8–9
[55] See Saville 1984d, 158 and Marshall 1978b, 11 for list of some examples.
[56] Darvill & Hingley 1984
[57] Darvill & Locke forthcoming
[58] cf. Perry 1986
[59] Price 1983; Eddie Price pers. comm..
[60] Spry & Wingham 1979
[61] Britnell 1974
[62] Smith 1946
[63] Miles & Palmer 1982; 1983
[64] Miles & Palmer 1983
[65] Hingley & Miles 1984
[66] Hingley & Miles 1984

[67] B.Wilson in Saville 1979b, 141–44.

[68] Darvill *et al* 1986, 43

[69] RCHME 1976, 19

[70] Fell 1961, 34

[71] B.Levitan in Saville & Ellison 1983.

[72] Saville & Ellison 1983, C4

[73] Dixon 1979, 148

[74] Smith & Cox 1985, 9

[75] Miles & Palmer 1983, 89

[76] Miles & Palmer 1983, 89; Price 1983, 140

[77] RCHME 1976, 2; RCHME 1976, 51; Saville 1980, 21; Spry & Wingham 1979, 30 respectively. The RCHME survey (1976, xlviii and elsewhere) also reports faint traces of celtic fields in several other parishes including: Stinchcombe, Frocester, Compton Abdale, Bagendon, Barnsley, Bibury, Duntisbourne Rouse, North Cerney and Rendcombe.

[78] Fowler, Bennett & Hill, 1976, 56

[79] Miles & Palmer 1983, 89

[80] Brown & Barber 1985, 92–3

[81] Marshall 1978b, 17

[82] Peacock 1968

[83] Morris 1982

[84] Cunliffe 1984a, 25

[85] Information from Dr J.Timby and Mr P.Garrod.

[86] Morris 1985

[87] Eddie Price pers. comm.; Gascoigne 1973, 204

[88] Allen 1967, 328–9

[89] Dunning 1976, 111

[90] Trow 1984

[91] Saville & Ellison 1983, B8–9

[92] Britnell 1974, 296

[93] Harbison & Laing 1974

[94] Information from Gloucester City Museum.

[95] Harbison & Laing 1974, 12

[96] Whimster 1981

[97] Gascoigne 1973; Fell 1961, 23; Dunning 1976,82

[98] Rawes 1984

[99] Darvill *et al*1986, 43

[100] Saville 1983b, 42

[101] Timothy Allen pers. comm..

[102] Clifford 1930, 224

[103] Green 1942

[104] Clifford 1944

[105] Burrow *et al* 1925

[106] O'Neil & Grinsell 1960, 121

[107] Ellison 1980; Ann Ellison pers. comm..

[108] Cunliffe 1984a, 27; 1984b, 8–9

[109] Hingley 1984

CHAPTER 7 – The kingdom of the Dobunni (*c* 100 BC–*c* AD 50)

[1] Cunliffe 1984c

[2] See papers in Macready & Thompson (ed) 1984

[3] Cunliffe 1981; Kent 1981

[4] Cunliffe 1982

[5] Cunliffe 1976; 1978, 334–341

[6] Champion 1984

[7] Caesar, *Gallic wars* BK V.12; see Allen 1944
[8] Hachmann 1976; Champion 1979, 417
[9] Haselgrove 1982
[10] Cunliffe 1984b
[11] *Strabo* IV, 5.2
[12] Haselgrove 1976,43
[13] Allen 1961
[14] Collis 1972
[15] Sellwood 1984 for latest studies.
[16] British R series coins
[17] Allen 1961
[18] Price 1983, 141; Eddie Price pers. comm..
[19] Miles & Palmer 1982; 1983
[20] Hingley & Miles 1984, 65
[21] RCHME 1976, 125
[22] RCHME 1976, Pl. 48 lower
[23] RCHME 1976, 60
[24] Garrod 1985; Patrick Garrod pers. comm..
[25] Clifford 1930; 1934a
[26] Clifford 1964b, 146
[27] Allen 1961, 136
[28] F.A. Ruddock in Clifford 1961, 186.
[29] Cunliffe 1976, 145
[30] Trow 1983
[31] Trow 1982a, 323
[32] RCHME 1976, 17–19
[33] Cunliffe 1976, 148
[34] Dunning 1976
[35] Dunning 1976, 105–8
[36] K.Green in Dunning 1976, 103.
[37] Jane Timby pers. comm..
[38] Saville & Ellison 1983
[39] Hampton & Palmer 1977
[40] A third possible dyke-system enclosure is the site at High Brotheridge, Cranham. Clifford (1961, 157) first draw attention to this possibility, and subsequent fieldwork by Gordon Harding has located earthworks to the north and south of the cross-ridge dyke on Coopers Hill, Brockworth (1977). Further possibilities have been explored by Wingham (1985). The estimated area given by Harding (1977,20) is nonsensical as it stands, although if the figure of 250 acres (101ha) is correct then this site is smaller in extent than either Bagendon (202ha) or Minchinhampton (120ha). If High Brotheridge is indeed another dyke-system enclosure there is no reason why the earthworks should not be discontinuous, as the field evidence suggests.
[41] Cunliffe 1976, 149–153
[42] Witts 1883, 3
[43] Clifford 1961; Reece 1981; Trow 1982b
[44] Peacock 1971, 180
[45] Clifford 1961
[46] Dannell 1977
[47] RCHME 1976, 81–3
[48] Clifford 1937c
[49] See Rivet 1966, 102
[50] J.W.Jackson in Clifford 1961, 268–71.
[51] Trow 1983, 2
[52] RCHME 1976, 19
[53] Dunning 1976, 112
[54] F.A.Ruddock in Clifford 1961, 186–194.
[55] Clifford 1934b

[56] Dunning 1976, 112–4
[57] Wheeler & Wheeler 1932, fig. 11.9
[58] British Museum 1925, fig. 169
[59] Clifford 1930, 232
[60] Clifford 1934a
[61] Clifford 1961, 155
[62] Clifford 1961, 268
[63] Dunning 1976, 116
[64] Staelens 1982 with earlier references.
[65] Staelens 1982, 21
[66] Darvill 1984a, 36 and 54; Courtney 1986
[67] Staelens 1982, 27
[68] Staelens 1982, 27
[69] Ellison 1980; Ann Ellison pers. comm..
[70] Information from Gloucester City Museum.
[71] Piggott 1968
[72] C.F.C.Hawkes in Clifford 1961.
[73] C.F.C.Hawkes in Clifford 1961.
[74] Cunliffe 1984a
[75] C.F.C.Hawkes in Clifford 1961; Manning 1976
[76] Wacher & McWhirr 1982
[77] Hurst 1985
[78] Hurst 1985, 119
[79] Rennie 1959
[80] Wacher & McWhirr 1982, 65; Dudley 1974
[81] Price 1983, 141
[82] Miles & Palmer 1983, 91
[83] Trow 1986, 243
[84] Dannell 1977
[85] Ellison 1980
[86] McWhirr 1981, 22–8
[87] McWhirr 1981, 28–9

APPENDIX A – Select list of Radiocarbon dates

[1] Four ostensibly prehistoric radiocarbon dates from sites in Gloucestershire must for the time being be rejected because of sample contamination or technical difficulties with the determination. These are: 3300 ± 90 BC (HAR-1010) and 3180 ± 80 BC (HAR-116) from cremated bone in a Roman grave in the Bath Gate cemetery at Cirencester; and 4830 ±110 BC (HAR-1320) and 1830 ±100 BC (HAR-1323) from charcoal in Iron Age pits at Guiting Manor Farm, Guiting Power.

Further Reading and Bibliography

Further reading

For those readers wishing to discover more about the prehistory of the Gloucestershire area and its wider context, the following brief list of books will hopefully provide a useful starting place. Full titles, together with the date and place of publication, can be found in the bibliography.

Archaeology in Gloucestershire edited by Alan Saville provides a wide-ranging conspectus of archaeological work in the county up until 1984. The archaeology of the area west of the Severn is summarized in *Archaeology in Dean* by Cyril Hart, while the archaeology of the part of Gloucestershire which in 1974 became part of Avon has recently been brought together in *The archaeology of Avon* edited by Mick Aston and Rob Iles. The Iron Age period in eastern Gloucestershire was the subject of a detailed survey by the Royal Commission on the Historical Monuments of England (RCHME), and their report entitled *Iron Age and Romano-British Monuments in the Gloucestershire Cotswolds* includes many plans and photographs.

Neighbouring counties are variously served by general accounts of their archaeology; one book, dealing with Avon, has already been mentioned. Parts of Gwent and Hereford and Worcester are included in *The archaeology of the Welsh Marches* by Stan Stanford, while the upper Thames Valley and Oxfordshire Cotswolds are dealt with in *The archaeology of the Oxford Region* edited by Grace Briggs, Jean Cook and Trevor Rowley.

On a national scale, the most recent general account of British prehistory is *Prehistoric Britain* by Timothy Darvill. For environmental changes during prehistory the various papers in *The environment in British Prehistory* edited by Ian Simmons and Michael Tooley provide a valuable summary, while for a discussion of prehistoric society and social change see *The social foundations of prehistoric Britain* by Richard Bradley.

Books dealing with specific periods of prehistory tend to be fairly technical, but of course bring together a great deal of otherwise disparate information. Up-to-date accounts include: *The lower and middle Palaeolithic periods in Britain* by Derek Roe, and *The upper Palaeolithic of Britain* by John Campbell which together cover the period up to 10,000 BC; a paper entitled 'The early Holocene settlement of Wales' by Roger Jacobi in *Culture and environment in prehistoric Wales* edited by J.A. Taylor for the period

10,000–3500 BC; *The earlier Neolithic of Southern Britain and its continental background* by Alasdair Whittle for the period 3500–2500 BC; *The Age of Stonehenge* by Colin Burgess for the period 2500–1000 BC; and *Iron Age communities in Britain* by Barry Cunliffe for the period 1000 BC – AD 43.

The most useful guidebooks to sites in the Gloucestershire area are: *Prehistoric and Roman sites of the Cheltenham area* by Wilfred Cox, *Discovering regional archaeology: The Cotswolds and upper Thames* by James Dyer, and *Guide to prehistoric England* by Nicholas Thomas.

Two periodicals report recent finds in the county and contain detailed discussions of specific topics: the *Transactions of the Bristol and Gloucestershire Archaeological Society*, published annually by the Bristol and Gloucestershire Archaeological Society since 1876, and *Glevensis*, published annually by the Gloucester and District Archaeological Research Group since 1966.

Later periods of Gloucestershire's past are covered by other volumes in the County Library Series; readers wishing follow on from where this book finishes may be especially interested in *Roman Gloucestershire* by Alan McWhirr.

Bibliography

The following abbreviations are used:

BAR	British Archaeological Reports
CBA	Council for British Archaeology
CRAAGS	Committee for Rescue Archaeology in Avon, Gloucestershire, and Somerset
DAMHB	Directorate of Ancient Monuments and Historic Buildings
MPBW	Ministry of Public Building and Works
OUCA	Oxford University Committee for Archaeology
PCNFC	Proceedings of the Cotteswold Naturalists Field Club
RCHME	Royal Commission on the Historical Monuments of England
TBGAS	Transactions of the Bristol and Gloucestershire Archaeological Society
WAT	Western Archaeological Trust

Allen, D., 1944, The Belgic dynasties of Britain and their coins. *Archaeologia*, 90, 1–46
Allen, D., 1961, A study of the Dobunnic coinage. In E.M. Clifford, *Bagendon: A Belgic oppidum*. Cambridge. 75–147
Allen, D., 1967, Iron currency bars in Britain. *Proc Prehist Soc*, 33, 307–335
Allen, T., Darvill, T.C., & Jones, M.U., forthcoming, *Excavations at Roughground Farm, Lechlade, Gloucestershire: A prehistoric and Roman landscape*. Place of publication to be determined
Apsimon, A.M., 1954, Dagger graves in the 'Wessex' Bronze Age. *University of London Institute of Archaeology Ann Rep*, 10, 37–62
Apsimon, A.M., 1969, 1919–1969: Fifty years of archaeological research–The Spelaeological Society's contribution to archaeology. *Proc Univ Bristol Spelaeological Soc*, 12.1, 31–56
Ashbee, P.A., 1960, *The Bronze Age round barrow in Britain* London

Aston,M. & Iles,R. (eds), 1987, *The archaeology of Avon*. Bristol. Avon County Council

Atkinson, R.J.C., 1949, A henge monument at Westwell, near Burford, Oxon. *Oxoniensia*, 14, 84–7

Atkinson, R.J.C., 1968, Old mortality: Some aspects of burial and population in Neolithic England. In J. Coles & D.D.A. Simpson (eds), *Studies in Ancient Europe*. Leicester. 83–94

Bagnall-Oakley, M.E., 1889, *An account of some of the rude stone monuments and ancient burial mounds in Monmouthshire*. Newport

Barker, G. & Webley, D., 1978, Causewayed camps and early Neolithic economies in central southern England. *Proc Prehist Soc*, 44, 161–186

Barnett, C., 1964, A Beaker cist at Beachley. *Monmouthshire Antiquary*, 1, 112–6

Bayne, N., 1957, Excavations at Lyneham Camp, Lyneham, Oxon. *Oxoniensia*, 22, 1–10

Bell, M., 1984, Environmental archaeology in south-west England. In H.C.M. Keeley (ed), *Environmental archaeology: A regional Review* (= DAMHB Occasional Paper 6). London. 43–133

Bender,B., 1978, Gatherer-hunter to farmer: A social perspective. *World Archaeol*, 10, 204–22

Benson, D. & Clegg, I., 1978, Cotswold burial rites? *Man* (ns), 13, 134–7

Benson, D. & Miles, D., 1974, *The upper Thames Valley: An archaeological survey of the river gravels* (= Oxford Archaeological Unit Survey 2). Oxford

Birks, H.J.B., Deacon, J. & Pegler, S., 1975, Pollen maps for the British Isles 5000 years ago. *Proc Royal Soc London*, B, 189, 87–105

Bradley, R., 1978, *The prehistoric settlement of Britain*. London

Bradley, R., 1979, The interpretation of later Bronze Age metalwork from British rivers. *International J of Nautical Archaeol and Underwater Exploration*, 8.1, 3–6

Bradley, R., 1981, Various styles of urns: Cemeteries and settlement in southern England c 1400–1000 BC. In R. Chapman, I. Kinnes & K. Ransborg (eds), *The archaeology of death*. Cambridge. 93–104

Bradley, R., 1984, *The social foundations of prehistoric Britain*. London

Bradley, R. & Hodder, I., 1979, British prehistory: An integrated view. *Man* (ns), 14, 93–104

Bradley, R., Holgate, R. & Ford, S., 1984, The Neolithic sequence in the upper Thames Valley. In R. Bradley & J. Gardiner (eds), *Neolithic studies* (= BAR 133). Oxford. 107–134

Briggs, G., Cook, J. & Rowley, T. (eds), 1986, *The archaeology of the Oxford Region*. Oxford. Oxford University Press of External Studies

British Museum, 1925, *A guide to antiquities of the early Iron Age* (2nd ed). London

Britnell, W.J., 1974, Beckford. *Curr Archaeol*, 4, 293–7.

Britnell, W.J., 1984, The Gwernvale long cairn, Crickhowell, Brecknock. In W.J. Britnell & H.N. Savory, *Gwernvale and Penywyrlod: Two Neolithic long cairns in the Black Mountains of Brecknock* (= Cambrian Archaeological Monograph 2). Bangor. 43–154

Britton, D., 1963, Traditions of metalworking in the late Neolithic and early Bronze Age of Britain: Part 1. *Proc Prehist Soc*, 29, 258–325

Brothwell, D., 1973, The human biology of the Neolithic population of Britain. In I. Schwidetzky (ed), *Die Anfange des Neolithikums vom orient bis Nordeuropa – Teil VIIIa (Anthropologie)*. Koln. 280–299

Brothwell, D. & Sandison, A.T., 1967, *Diseases in Antiquity*. London

Brown, A.G., 1982, Human impact on the former floodplain woodlands of the Seven. In M. Bell & S. Limbrey (eds), *Archaeological aspects of woodland ecology* (= BAR S146). Oxford. 93–104

Brown, A.G., 1983, Floodplain deposits and accelerated sedimentation in the lower Severn basin. In K.J. Gregory (ed), *Background to palaeohydrology*. London. 375–97

Brown, A.G. & Barber, K.E., 1985, Late Holocene palaeoecology and sedimentary history of a small lowland catchment in central England. *Quaternary Research*, 24, 87–102

Burgess, C., 1968, The late Bronze Age in the British Isles and north-western France. *Arch J*, 125, 1–45

Burgess, C., 1980, *The age of Stonehenge*. London

Burgess, C., Coombs, D. & Davies, D.G., 1972, The Broadward complex and barbed spearheads. In F. Lynch & C. Burgess (eds), *Prehistoric Man in Wales and the west*. Bath. 211–83

Burkitt, M.C., 1938, Description of a flint implement from a digging in the gravel of the

Eastington pit. *PCNFC*, 26, 296–7

Burl, A., 1969, Henges: Internal features and regional groups. *Arch J*, 126, 1–28

Burl, A., 1976, *The stone circles of the British Isles*. London & New York

Burrow, E.J., Paine, A.E.W., Knowles, W.H. & Gray, J.W., 1925, Excavations on Leckhampton Hill, Cheltenham, during the summer of 1925. *TBGAS*, 47, 81–112

Burton, J., 1980, Making sense of waste flakes: new methods for investigating the technology and economies behind chipped stone assemblages. *J Archaeol Sci*, 7, 131–48

Cameron, J., 1934, *The skeleton of British Neolithic Man*. London

Campbell, J.B., 1977, *The upper Palaeolithic of the British Isles: A study of Man and nature in the late Ice Age*. Oxford. (2 vols)

Campbell-Smith, W., 1965, The distribution of jadeite axes in Europe. *Proc Prehist Soc*, 31, 25–33

Care, V., 1982, The collection and distribution of lithic raw materials during the Mesolithic and Neolithic periods in southern England. *Oxford J Archaeol*, 1, 269–85

Case, H.J., 1977, The beaker culture in Britain and Ireland. In R.Mercer (ed), *Beakers in Britain and Europe* (= BAR S26). Oxford. 71–101

Case, H.J., 1986, The Mesolithic and Neolithic in the Oxford region. In G. Briggs, J. Cook & T. Rowley (eds), *The archaeology of the Oxford region*. Oxford. 18–37

Catt, J.A., 1978, The contribution of loess to soils in lowland Britain. In S. Limbrey & J.G. Evans (eds), *The effect of Man on the landscape: the Lowland Zone* (= CBA Research Report 21). London. 12–20

Champion, S.T, 1976, Leckhampton Hill, Gloucestershire, 1925 and 1970. In D.W. Harding (ed), *Hillforts: Later prehistoric earthworks in Britain and Ireland*. London. 177–90 and 430–5

Champion, T.C, 1979, The Iron Age: Southern Britain and Ireland. In J.V.S. Megaw & D.D.A. Simpson (eds), *Introduction to British Prehistory*. Leicester. 344–445

Champion, T.C., 1984, Written sources and the study of the European Iron Age. In T.C. Champion & J.V.S. Megaw (eds), *Settlement and Society: Aspects of west European prehistory in the 1st millennium BC*. Leicester. 9–22

Chesterman, J.T., 1977, Burial rites in a Cotswold long barrow. *Man* (ns), 12, 22–23

Clark, J.G.D., 1934, Derivative forms of the *petit tranchet* in Britain. *Arch J*, 91, 32–58

Clark, J.G.D., 1965, Traffic in stone axe and adze blades. *Economic Hist Rev*, 18, 1–28

Clarke, D.L., 1970, *Beaker pottery of Great Britain and Ireland*. Cambridge. (2 vols)

Clarke, D.L., 1978, *Analytical Archaeology* (2nd ed). London

Clifford, E.M., 1930, A prehistoric and Roman site at Barnwood near Gloucester. *TBGAS*, 52, 210–54

Clifford, E.M., 1933, The Roman villa, Hucclecote. *TBGAS*, 55, 323–76

Clifford, E.M., 1934a, An early Iron Age site at Barnwood, Gloucestershire. *TBGAS*, 56, 227–35

Clifford, E.M., 1934b, An early British fragment. *Antiq J*, 14, 59–61

Clifford, E.M., 1936a, A palaeolith found near Gloucester. *Antiq J*, 16, 91

Clifford, E.M., 1936b, Notgrove long barrow, Gloucestershire. *Archaeologia*, 86, 119–62

Clifford, E.M., 1937a, A palaeolith from Gloucestershire. *Proc Prehist Soc*, 3, 465–6

Clifford, E.M., 1937b, The Beaker folk in the Cotswolds. *Proc Prehist Soc*, 3, 159–63

Clifford, E.M., 1937c, The earthworks at Rodborough, Amberley, and Minchinhampton. *TBGAS*, 59, 287–307

Clifford, E.M., 1937d, Archaeological objects of special interest in Gloucestershire. *PCNFC*, 26.2, 159–168

Clifford, E.M., 1938a, The excavation of Nympsfield long barrow, Gloucestershire. *Proc Prehist Soc*, 4, 188–213

Clifford, E.M., 1938b, The Soldier's Grave, Frocester, Gloucestershire. *Proc Prehist Soc*, 4, 214–8

Clifford, E.M., 1938c, Beaker found at Prestbury, Gloucestershire. *TBGAS*, 60, 348–51

Clifford, E.M., 1939, Palaeolith from the upper Thames. *Antiq J*, 19, 193

Clifford, E.M., 1944, Graves found at Hailes. *TBGAS*, 65, 187–198

Clifford, E.M., 1950a, The Cotswold megalithic culture: The grave goods and their background. In C. Fox & B. Dickins (eds), *The early cultures of north-west Europe*. Cambridge. 21–40

Clifford, E.M., 1950b, The Ivy Lodge round barrow. *TBGAS*, 69, 59–77

Clifford, E.M., 1964a, Two finds of Beaker pottery from Gloucestershire. *TBGAS*, 83, 34–39

Clifford, E.M., 1964b, Early Iron Age pottery from Rodborough Common and Duntisbourne Abbots. *TBGAS*, 83, 145–6

Clifford, E.M., 1961, *Bagendon: A Belgic Oppidum*. Cambridge

Clifford, E.M. & Daniel, G.E., 1940, The Rodmarton and Avening portholes. *Proc Prehist Soc*, 6, 133–65

Clifford, E.M., Garrod, D.A.E. & Gracie, H.S., 1954, Flint implements from Gloucestershire. *Antiq J*, 34, 178–87

Clough, T.H.McK. & Cummins, W.A. (eds), 1979, *Stone axe studies* (= CBA Research Report 23). London.

Coles, B. & Coles, J., 1986, *Sweet Track to Glastonbury: The Somerset Levels in prehistory*. London

Coles, J., 1972, *Field archaeology in Britain*. London

Coles, J.M., Heal, S.V.E. & Orme, B.J., 1978, The use and character of wood in prehistoric Britain and Ireland. *Proc Prehist Soc*, 44, 1–46

Collis, J., 1972, Functional and theoretical interpretations of British coinage. *World Archaeol*, 3, 71–84

Cook, J., Stringer, C.B., Currant, A.P. Schwarcz, H.P. & Wintle, A.G., 1982, A review of the chronology of the European middle pleistocene hominid record. *Yearbook of Physical Anthropology*, (1982), 19–65

Corcoran, J.X.W.P., 1969, The Cotswold-Severn Group. In T.G.E. Powell, J.X.W.P. Corcoran, F. Lynch & J.G. Scott, *Megalithic enquiries in the west of Britain*. Liverpool. 13–106 and 273–295

Corcoran, J.X.W.P., 1972, Multi-period construction and the origin of the chambered long cairn in western Britain and Ireland. In F. Lynch & C. Burgess (eds), *Prehistoric Man in Wales and the west*. Bath. 31–64

Courtney, T., 1986, Birdlip Bypass Project. In B. Rawes (ed), Archaeological Review No 10, 1985. *TBGAS*, 104, 234

Cox, W.L., 1969, Jadeite axe, Beckford. *TBGAS*, 88, 205–6

Cox, W.L., 1981, *Prehistoric and Roman sites of the Cheltenham Area* (2nd ed). Cheltenham. Gloucestershire County Library

Crawford, O.G.S., 1922, *The long barrows and stone circles in the area covered by Sheet 8 of the quarter-inch Map* (= Ordnance Survey professional Papers (ns) 6). Southampton.

Crawford, O.G.S., 1925, *The long barrows of the Cotswolds*. Gloucester

Cunliffe, B., 1976, The origins of urbanization in Britain. In B. Cunliffe & T. Rowley (eds), *Oppida in barbarian Europe* (= BAR S11). Oxford. 135–62

Cunliffe, B., 1978, *Iron Age communities in Britain* (2nd ed). London

Cunliffe, B., 1981, Money and society in pre-Roman Britain. In B. Cunliffe (ed), *Coinage and society in Britain and Gaul: Some current problems* (= CBA Research Report 38). London. 29–39

Cunliffe, B., 1982, Britain, the Veneti and beyond. *Oxford J Archaeol*, 1, 39–65

Cunliffe, B., 1984a, Iron Age Wessex: Continuity and change. In B. Cunliffe & D. Miles (eds), *Aspects of the Iron Age in central Southern Britain* (= OUCA Monograph 2). Oxford. 12–46

Cunliffe, B., 1984b, Gloucestershire and the Iron Age of southern Britain. *TBGAS*, 102, 5–16

Cunliffe, B., 1984c, Relations between Britain and Gaul in the first century BC and early first century AD. In S. Macready & F.H. Thompson (eds), *Cross-channel trade between Gaul and Britain in the pre-Roman Iron Age* (= Society of Antiquaries Occasional Paper (ns) 4). London. 3–23

Cunliffe, B., 1986, Iron Age. In T. Darvill, *The archaeology of the uplands: A rapid assessment of archaeological knowledge and practice*. London. 30–3

Daniel, G.E., 1943, *The Three Age System*. Cambridge

Daniel, G.E., 1950, *The prehistoric chamber tombs of England and Wales*. Cambridge

Dannell, G.B., 1977, The samian from Bagendon. In J. Dore & K. Greene (eds), *Roman pottery studies in Britain and beyond* (= BAR S30). Oxford. 229–34

Darvill, T.C., 1981, Excavations at the Peak Camp, Cowley, Gloucestershire – An interim note. *Glevensis*, 15, 52–6

Darvill, T.C., 1982a, *The megalithic chambered tombs of the Cotswold-Severn region* (= Vorda

Research Series 5). Highworth

Darvill, T.C., 1982b, Excavations at the Peak Camp, Cowley, Gloucestershire – Second interim report. *Glevensis*, 16, 20–5

Darvill, T.C., 1983, *The Neolithic of Wales and the mid-west of England: A systemic analysis of social change through the application of action theory.* Unpublished PhD thesis. University of Southampton

Darvill, T.C., 1984a, *Birdlip Bypass project – First report: Archaeological assessment and field survey.* Bristol. Western Archaeological Trust

Darvill, T.C., 1984b, Neolithic Gloucestershire. In A. Saville (ed), *Archaeology in Gloucestershire: From the earliest hunters to the Industrial Age.* Cheltenham. 80–112

Darvill, T.C., 1986, Prospects for dating Neolithic sites and monuments in the Cotswolds and adjacent areas. In J.A.J. Gowlett & R.E.M. Hedges (eds), *Archaeological results from accelerator dating* (= OUCA Monograph 11). Oxford. 119–24

Darvill, T.C., 1987, *Prehistoric Britain.* London

Darvill, T.C., forthcoming, The early prehistoric period. In T. Allen, T. Darvill & M.U. Jones, *Excavations at Roughground Farm, Lechlade, Gloucestershire: A prehistoric and Roman landscape.* Place of publication to be determined

Darvill, T.C. & Hingley, R.C., 1982, A 'banjo' type enclosure at Northleach. *TBGAS*, 100, 249–51

Darvill, T.C., Hingley, R., Jones, M. & Timby, J., 1986, A Neolithic and Iron Age site at The Loders, Lechlade, Gloucestershire. *TBGAS*, 104, 27–48

Darvill, T.C. & Locke, R., forthcoming, Aerial photography in eastern Gloucestershire and the upper Thames Valley 1986.

Darvill, T.C. & Timby, J., 1985, Excavations at The Buckles, Frocester, 1984: Second interim report. *Glevensis*, 19, 24–8

Darvill, T.C. & Timby, J., 1986, Excavations at Saintbridge, Gloucester. *TBGAS*, 104, 49–60

Dent, E, 1877, *Annals of Winchcombe and Sudeley.* London

De Laet, S.J. (ed), 1976, *Acculturation and continuity in Atlantic Europe* (= Dissertationes Archaeologicae Gandenses 16). Brugge

Dimbleby, G.W. & Evans, J.G., 1974, Pollen and land snails analysis of calcareous soils. *J Archaeol Sci*, 1, 117–133

Dixon, P.W., 1971, *Crickley Hill, Gloucestershire: Third interim report.* Cheltenham. Privately published

Dixon, P.W., 1972, Crickley Hill 1969–71. *Antiquity*, 46, 49–52

Dixon, P.W., 1973, Longhouse and roundhouse at Crickley Hill. *Antiquity*, 47, 56–9

Dixon, P.W., 1976, Crickley Hill 1969–72. In D.W. Harding (ed), *Hillforts: Later prehistoric earthworks in Britain and Ireland.* London. 161–75, 424–29, and 507–8

Dixon, P.W., 1979, A Neolithic and Iron Age site on a hilltop in Southern England. *Scientific American*, 241.5, 142–150

Dixon, P.W., 1981, Crickley Hill. *Curr Archaeol*, 7, 145–7

Drewett, P., 1977, The excavation of a Neolithic causewayed enclosure on Offham Hill, East Sussex, 1976. *Proc Prehist Soc*, 43, 201–42

Dudley, D.R., 1974, Tacitus and the Roman conquest of Wales. In E. Birley & B. Dobson (eds), *Roman frontier studies 1969* (= Proceedings of the 8th International Congress on Limesforchung). Cardiff. 27–33

Dunning, G.C., 1932, Bronze Age settlements and a Saxon Hut near Bourton-on-the-Water, Gloucestershire. *Ant J*, 12, 279–93

Dunning, G.C., 1933, Report on pottery found in the Crypt Grammar School grounds, Gloucester, during excavations made 1931–2. *TBGAS*, 55, 227–91

Dunning, G.C., 1935, Late Bronze Age Urn From Lower Swell, Gloucestershire. *Antiq J*, 15, 471–3

Dunning, G.C., 1937, A beaker from Bourton-on-the-Water, Gloucestershire. *Proc Prehist Soc*, 3, 163–4

Dunning, G.C., 1976, Salmonsbury, Bourton-on-the-Water, Gloucestershire. In D.W. Harding (ed), *Hillforts: Later prehistoric earthworks in Britain and Ireland.* London. 75–118, 373–401 and 488–94

Dyer, J., 1970, *Discovering regional archaeology: The Cotswolds and the upper Thames.* Tring. Shire

Publications

Ellison, A., 1980, *Excavations at West Hill Uley: 1977–9 – 2nd Interim report* (= CRAAGS Occasional Paper 9). Bristol

Ellison, A., 1984, Bronze Age Gloucestershire: Artefacts and distributions. In A. Saville (ed), *Archaeology in Gloucestershire: From the earliest hunters to the Industrial Age*. Cheltenham. 113–127

Else, W.J., 1943, Bronze Age pottery at Moor near Fladbury. *Trans Worcestershire Natur Club*, 9, 53–6

Ehrenburg, M., 1977, *Bronze Age spearheads from Berkshire, Buckinghamshire, and Oxfordshire* (= BAR 34). Oxford

Ehrenburg, M., 1980, The occurrence of Bronze Age metalwork in the Thames: An investigation. *Trans London Middlesex Archaeol Soc*, 31, 1–15

Evans, J.G., 1971, Habitat change on the calcareous soils of Britain: The impact of Neolithic Man. In D.D.A. Simpson (ed), *Economy and settlement in Neolithic and Bronze Age Britain and Europe*. Leicester. 27–73

Evans, E.D., Smith, I.F. & Wallis, F.S., 1972, The petrological identification of stone implements from south-western England: Fifth report of the sub-committee of the south-western Federation of Museums and Art Galleries. *Proc Prehist Soc*, 38, 235–75

Fell, C.I., 1961, Shenberrow Hill Camp, Stanton, Gloucestershire. *TBGAS*, 80, 16–41

Fisher, C.H., 1919, Two bronze spearheads from Rodborough, near Stroud. *PCNFC*, 13, 85–7

Fleming, A., 1971, Territorial patterns in Bronze Age Wessex. *Proc Prehist Soc*, 37.1, 138–166

Fleming, A., 1973, Tombs for the living. *Man* (ns), 8, 177–93

Forde-Johnston, J., 1976, *Hillforts of the Iron Age in England and Wales*. Liverpool

Fowler, P.J., 1979, Archaeology and the M4 and M5 motorways, 1965–78. *Arch J*, 136, 12–26

Fowler, P.J., Bennett, J. & Hill, V.S., 1976, Archaeology and the M5 Motorway: Fourth Report. *TBGAS*, 94, 47–91

Fowles, J. (ed), 1982, *John Aubrey's Monumenta Britannica*. Sherbourne. (2 vols)

Gamble, C., 1986, *The Palaeolithic settlement of Europe*. Cambridge

Gardiner, C.I., 1932, Recent discoveries in the Stroud Valley. *PCNFC*, 24.3, 163–80

Gardiner, C.I., 1937, Bronze celt from a field near Waterlane, S.E. of Bisley. *PCNFC*, 26.2, 206

Garrod, A.P., 1985, Gloucester/Longford, Gambier Parry Lodge development. In B.Rawes (ed), Archaeological Review No 9, 1984. *TBGAS*, 102, 234–5

Garrod, A.P. & Heighway, C., 1984, *Garrod's Gloucester: Archaeological observations 1974–81* (= WAT Excavation Monograph 6). Bristol

Gascoigne, P.E., 1973, Iron Age pit, Guiting Power. *TBGAS*, 92, 204–7

GCC, no date, *An Archaeological strategy for the upper Thames gravels in Gloucestershire and Wiltshire*. Gloucester. Gloucestershire County Council and Wiltshire County Council

Gent, H., 1983, Centralized storage in late prehistoric Britain. *Proc Prehist Soc*, 49, 243–68

Gerloff, S., 1975, *The early Bronze Age daggers in Great Britain* (= Prahistorische Bronzefunde, Abteilung VI, Band 2). Munchen

Gillespie, R., 1984, *Radiocarbon user's handbook* (= OUCA Monograph 3). Oxford

Gracie, H.S., 1942, Surface flints from Long Newton, Gloucestershire. *TBGAS*, 63, 172–189

Gray, I., 1981, *Antiquaries of Gloucestershire and Bristol*. Bristol

Green, C., 1935, Some bronze implements from Gloucestershire. *Antiq J*, 15, 196–8

Green, C., 1942, An Iron Age cremation burial in the Cotswolds. *Antiq J*, 22, 216–8

Green, C., 1949, A round barrow near Haresfield, Gloucestershire. *Antiq J*, 29, 80–1

Green, S., 1980, *The flint arrowheads of the British Isles* (= BAR 75). Oxford. (2 vols)

Green, S., 1984, *Pontnewydd Cave: A lower Palaeolithic hominid site in Wales*. Cardiff

Greenwell, W., 1877, *British Barrows*. Oxford

Greenwell, W., 1890, Recent researches in barrows in Yorkshire, Wiltshire, Berkshire etc.. *Archaeologia*, 52, 1–72

Grimes, W.F., 1939, The excavation of Ty-isaf long cairn, Brecknockshire. *Proc Prehist Soc*, 5, 119–142

Grimes, W.F., 1951, The Jurassic Way across England. In W.F. Grimes (ed), *Aspects of archaeology in Britain and beyond*. London. 144–71

Grimes, W.F., 1960, *Excavations on defence sites 1939–45: I – mainly Neolithic–Bronze Age* (= MPBW Reports 3). London

Grinsell, L.V., 1941, The Bronze Age barrows of Wessex. *Proc Prehist Soc*, 7, 73–113

Grinsell, L.V., 1957, Cotswold Antiquities. *The Youth Hosteller*, February 1957, 4

Grinsell, L.V., 1960, A Palaeolithic implement from Beckford, Worcestershire. *Antiq J*, 40, 67–8

Grinsell, L.V., 1964, The Royce collection at Stow-on-the-Wold. *TBGAS*, 83, 5–23

Grinsell, L.V., 1966, A Palaeolithic implement from Poole Keynes. *TBGAS*, 85, 207–8

Grinsell, L.V. & Janes, D., 1966, The Royce collection of Cotswold antiquities: Supplement. *TBGAS*, 85, 209–213

Hackmann, R., 1976, The problem of the Belgae seen from the continent. *Bull Inst Archaeol*, 13, 117–37

Hall, M. & Gingell, C., 1974, Nottingham Hill, Gloucestershire, 1972. *Antiquity*, 48, 306–9

Hampton, J.N. & Palmer, R., 1977, Implications of aerial photography for archaeology. *Arch J*, 134, 157–93

Hannan, A., 1972, Tewkesbury, Oldbury Road. *Archaeol Rev*, 7, 34–5

Hannan, A., 1976, Holm Castle, Tewkesbury: Excavations during 1975. *Glevensis*, 10, 10–11

Harbison, P. & Laing, L., 1974, *Some Iron Age Mediterranean imports in England* (= BAR 5). Oxford

Harding, A.F. & Lee, G.E., 1987, *Henge monuments and related sites of Great Britain* (= BAR 175). Oxford.

Harding, A.F. (ed), 1982, *Climatic change in later prehistory*. Edinburgh

Harding, D.W., 1972, *The Iron Age in the upper Thames basin*. Oxford

Harding, G.T., 1977, High Brotheridge: The account of a survey and speculations. *Glevensis*, 11, 17–22

Hart, C., 1967, *Archaeology in Dean*. Gloucester

Haselgrove, C., 1976, External trade as a stimulus to urbanization. In B. Cunliffe & T. Rowley (eds), *Oppida in barbarian Europe* (= BAR S11). Oxford. 25–50

Haselgrove, C., 1982, Wealth, prestige and power: The dynamics of late Iron Age political centralization in south-east England. In C. Renfrew & S. Shennan (eds), *Ranking, resource and exchange*. Cambridge. 79–88

Hazelden, J. & Jarvis, M.G., 1979, Age and significance of alluvium in the Windrush Valley, Oxfordshire. *Nature*, 282, 291–2

Hencken, T.C., 1938, The excavation of the Iron Age camp on Bredon Hill, Gloucestershire, 1935–1937. *Arch J*, 95, 1–111

Herdman, D.W., 1933, Prehistoric vessel from Hawling. *TBGAS*, 55, 381–2

Hingley, R., 1984, Towards social analysis in archaeology: Celtic society in the Iron Age of the upper Thames Valley. In B. Cunliffe & D. Miles (eds), *Aspects of the Iron Age in central Southern Britain* (= OUCA Monograph 2). Oxford. 72–88

Hingley, R. & Miles, D., 1984, Aspects of Iron Age settlement in the upper Thames Valley. In B. Cunliffe & D. Miles (eds), *Aspects of the Iron Age in central Southern Britain* (= OUCA Monograph 2). Oxford. 52–71

Holgate, R., 1985, Neolithic settlement in the upper Thames. *Curr Archaeol*, 8, 374–5

Hodder, I. & Lane, P., 1982, A contextual examination of Neolithic axe distribution in Britain. In J.E. Ericson & T.K. Earl (eds), *Contexts for prehistoric exchange*. London. 213–35

Hurst, H., 1972, Excavations at Gloucester, 1968–1971: First interim report. *Antiq J*, 52, 24–69

Hurst, H., 1985, *Kingsholm* (= Gloucester Archaeological Reports 1). Gloucester

Jacobi, R.M., 1978, The settlement of northern Britain in the 8th millennium BC. In P. Mellars (ed), *The early post-glacial settlement of northern Europe*. London. 295–332

Jacobi, R.M., 1979a, The upper Palaeolithic in Britain, with special reference to Wales. In J.A. Taylor (ed), *Culture and environment in prehistoric Wales* (= BAR 76). Oxford. 15–99

Jacobi, R.M., 1979b, The early Holocene settlement of Wales. In J.A. Taylor (ed), *Culture and environment in prehistoric Wales* (= BAR 76). Oxford. 131–206

Jones, B., 1984, *Past imperfect: The story of rescue archaeology*. London

Jones, M.U., 1984, Helen O'Neil: A personal appreciation. In A. Saville (ed), *Archaeology in Gloucestershire: From the earliest hunters to the Industrial Age*. Cheltenham. 31–37

Kent, J.P.C., 1981, The origins of coinage in Britain. In B. Cunliffe (ed), *Coinage and society in*

Britain and Gaul: Some current problems (= CBA Research Report 38). London. 41–3

Kinnes, I., 1979, *Round barrows and ring-ditches in the British Neolithic* (= British Museum Occasional Paper 7). London

Knight, R.W., Browne, C. & Grinsell, L.V., 1972, Prehistoric skeletons from Tormarton. *TBGAS*, 91, 14–17

Lacaille, A.D., 1954, Palaeoliths from the lower reaches of the Bristol Avon. *Antiq J*, 34, 1–27

Lambrick, G., 1983, *The Rollright Stones*. Oxford. Oxford Archaeological Unit

Lambrick, G., 1988, *The Rollright Stones: Archaeological investigations 1981–1986*. English Heritage

Lanting, J.N. & van der Waals, J.D., 1972, British beakers as seen from the continent. *Helinium*, 12, 20–46

Lawrence, W.L. & Winterbotham, L., 1866, Examination of a chambered long barrow in Gloucestershire. *Proc Soc Antiq London*, 3, 375–82

Leech, R., 1977, *The upper Thames Valley in Gloucestershire and Wiltshire: An archaeological survey of river gravels* (= CRAAGS Survey 4). Bristol

Leeds, E.T., 1931, Chastleton Camp, Oxfordshire, a hillfort of the early Iron Age. *Antiq J*, 11, 382–98

Linnell, E., 1971, Tewkesbury: Oldbury. *Archaeol Rev*, 6, 15

Longworth, I.H., 1984, *Collared urns of the Bronze Age in Great Britain and Ireland*. Cambridge

Lynch, F.M., 1976, Towards a chronology of megalithic tombs in Wales. In G.C.Boon & J.M.Lewis (eds), *Welsh Antiquity*. Cardiff. 63–79

Macready, S. & Thompson, F.H., 1984, *Cross-channel trade between Gaul and Britain in the pre-Roman Iron Age* (= Society of Antiquaries Occasional Paper (ns) 4). London

Manning, W.H., 1976, The conquest of the West Country. In K. Branigan & P.J. Fowler (eds), *The Roman West Country*. Newton Abbot. 15–41

Marshall, A.J., 1978a, The pre-Belgic Iron Age in the northern Cotswolds. *TBGAS*, 96, 9–16

Marshall, A.J., 1978b, Material from Iron Age sites in the northern Cotswolds. *TBGAS*, 96, 17–26

Marshall, A.J., 1985, Neolithic and earlier Bronze Age settlement in the northern Cotswolds: A preliminary outline based on the distribution of surface scatters and funerary areas. *TBGAS*, 103, 23–54

McWhirr, A., 1981, *Roman Gloucestershire*. Gloucester

Megaw, B.R.S. & Hardy, E.M., 1938, British decorated axes and their diffusion during the earlier part of the Bronze Age. *Proc Prehist Soc*, 4, 272–307

Mellars, P., 1974, The Palaeolithic and Mesolithic. In C.Renfrew (ed), *British prehistory – a new outline*. London. 41–92

Mellars, P., 1976, Settlement patterns and industrial variability in the British Mesolithic. In G.de G. Sieveking, I.H. Longworth & K.E. Wilson (eds), *Problems in economic and social archaeology*. London. 375–399

Miles, D. & Palmer, S., 1982, *Figures in a landscape: Archaeological investigations at Claydon Pike, Fairford/Lechlade, Gloucestershire – Interim report 1979–81*. Oxford. Oxford Archaeological Unit

Miles, D. & Palmer, S., 1983, Claydon Pike. *Curr Archaeol*, 8, 88–91

Moore, J., 1985, Lechlade: Hambridge Lane. *Oxford Archaeol Unit Newsletter*, 12.3, 2

Morris, E.L., 1982, Iron Age pottery from western Britain: Another petrological study. In I. Freestone, C. Johns & T. Potter (eds), *Current research in ceramics: Thin-section studies* (= British Museum Occasional Paper 32). London. 15–28

Morris, E.L., 1985, Prehistoric salt distributions: Two case studies from western Britain. *Bull Board Celtic Stud*, 32, 336–79

Needham, S., 1979, The extent of foreign influence on early Bronze Age axe development in southern Britain. In M. Ryan (ed), *The origin of metallurgy in Atlantic Europe: Proceedings of the fifth Atlantic colloquium*. Dublin. 265–93

Needham, S. & Saville, A., 1981, Two early Bronze Age flat bronze axeheads from Oddington. *TBGAS*, 99, 15–20

O'Neil, H.E., 1965, A Palaeolithic flint implement from Bourton-on-the-Water. *PCNFC*, 34.4, 225–7

O'Neil, H.E., 1966, Sale's Lot long barrow Withington, Gloucestershire, 1962–1965.

TBGAS, 85, 5–35

O'Neil, H.E., 1967, Bevan's Quarry round barrow, Temple Guiting, 1964. *TBGAS*, 86, 16–41

O'Neil, H.E., 1977, Salmonsbury, Bourton-on-the-Water. Some aspects of archaeology in Bourton Vale. *TBGAS*, 95, 10–23

O'Neil, H.E. & Bunt, J.S., 1966, A beaker from Leckhampton, Cheltenham, Gloucestershire. *TBGAS*, 85, 216–7

O'Neil, H.E. & Grinsell, L.V., 1960, Gloucestershire barrows. *TBGAS*, 79.1, 5–149

Oswald, A., 1972, Excavations at Beckford. *Trans Worcestershire Archaeol Soc.* (3rd ser), 3, 7–54

Palmer, R., 1976, Interrupted ditch enclosures in Britain: The use of aerial photography for comparative studies. *Proc Prehist Soc*, 42, 161–186

Palmer, S., 1970, The Stone Age industries of the Isle of Portland, Dorset, and the utilization of Portland Chert as artefact material in southern England. *Proc Prehist Soc*, 36, 82–115

Peacock, D.P.S., 1968, A petrological study of certain Iron Age pottery from western England. *Proc Prehist Soc*, 34, 414–27

Peacock, D.P.S., 1970, The scientific analysis of ancient ceramics: A review. *World Archaeol*, 1, 375–389

Peacock, D.P.S., 1971, Roman amphorae in pre-Roman Britain. In M. Jesson & D. Hill (eds), *The Iron Age and its hillforts*. Southampton. 161–88

Perry, B.T, 1986, Excavations at Bramdean, Hampshire, 1983 and 1984, with some further discussion of the 'banjo' syndrome. *Proc Hampshire Fld Club Archaeol Soc*, 42, 35–42

Phillips, B., 1971, Blunsdon St Andrew, Home Farm. *Archaeol Rev*, 6, 17

Piggott, S., 1938, The early Bronze Age in Wessex. *Proc Prehist Soc*, 4, 52–106

Piggott, S., 1950, *William Stukeley*. Oxford

Piggott, S., 1954, *The Neolithic cultures of the British Isles*. Cambridge

Piggott, S., 1962, *The West Kennet long barrow: Excavations 1955–56* (= MPBW Reports 4). London

Piggott, S., 1968, *The Druids*. London

Powell, T.G.E., 1973, Excavation of the megalithic chambered cairn at Dyffryn Ardudwy, Merioneth, Wales. *Archaeologia*, 104, 1–50

Price, E.G, 1983, Frocester. *Curr Archaeol*, 8, 139–45

Pritchard, J.E., 1906, Archaeological Notes for 1905. *TBGAS*, 29, 265–283

Rackham, O., 1976, *Trees and woodland in the British landscape*. London

Rahtz, P.A. (ed), 1974, *Rescue archaeology*. Harmondsworth

Ralph, E., 1975, The Society 1876–1976. In P. McGrath & J. Cannon (eds), *Essays in Bristol and Gloucestershire History*. Bristol. 1–49

Rawes, B., 1984, Observations at Salmonsbury Camp, 1983. *TBGAS*, 102, 215–9

Rchme, 1976, *Ancient and historical monuments in the county of Gloucestershire volume I: Iron Age and Romano-British monuments in the Gloucestershire Cotswolds*. London

Reece, R., 1981, Bagendon. In B. Rawes (ed), Archaeological Review No 5, 1980. *TBGAS*, 99, 173

Reece, R., 1984, Elsie M. Clifford: The person and the work. In A. Saville (ed), *Archaeology in Gloucestershire: From the earliest hunters to the Industrial Age*. Cheltenham. 19–25

Renfrew, C., 1976, Megaliths, territories and populations. In J. DeLaet (ed), *Acculturation and continuity in Atlantic Europe* (= Dissertationes Archaeologicae Gandenses 16). Brugge. 198–220

Renfrew, C. (ed), 1983, *The megalithic monuments of western Europe*. London

Rennie, D.M., 1959, The excavation of an earthwork on Rodborough Common in 1954–5. *TBGAS*, 8, 24–43

Reynolds, P. 1974, Experimental Iron Age storage pits: An interim report. *Proc Prehist Soc*, 40, 118–131

Rivet, A.L.F., 1966, Summing-up: Some historical aspects of the civitates of Roman Britain. In J.S. Wacher (ed), *The civitas capitals of Roman Britain*. Leicester. 101–113

Robinson, M., 1984, Landscape and environment of central southern Britain in the Iron Age. In B. Cunliffe & D. Miles (eds), *Aspects of the Iron Age in central southern Britain* (= OUCA Monograph 2). Oxford. 1–11

Roe, D.A., 1974, Palaeolithic artefacts from the River Avon terraces near Bristol. *Proc Univ*

Bristol Spelaeological Soc, 13.3, 319–26

Roe, D.A., 1981, *The lower and middle Palaeolithic periods in Britain*. London

Roe, F.E.S., 1979, Typology of stone implements with shaftholes. In T.H. McK.Clough & W.A. Cummins (eds), *Stone axe studies* (= CBA Research Report 23). London. 23–48

Rogers, T., Pinder, A. & Russell, R.C., 1981, Cave art discoveries in Britain. *Illustrated London News*, January 1981, 32–4

Rolleston, G., 1876, On the people of the long barrow period. *J Anthropol Inst*, 5, 120–73

Rolleston, G., 1878, On the three periods known as the Iron, the Bronze and the Stone Ages. *TBGAS*, 2, 128–150

Ross, A., 1967, *Pagan Celtic Britain*. London

Ross, A., 1970, *Everyday life of the pagan Celts*. London

Rowlands, M.J., 1976, *The organization of middle Bronze Age metalworking in southern Britain* (= BAR 31). Oxford. (2 vols)

Sandford, K.S., 1965, Notes on the gravels of the upper Thames floodplain between Lechlade and Dorchester. *Proc Geol Assoc*, 76.1, 61–76

Savage, R., 1986, Badgeworth-Coberley: Crickley Hill excavations 1983–1985. In B. Rawes (ed), Archaeological Review No 10, 1985. *TBGAS*, 104, 231

Saville, A., 1979a, *Recent work at Cow Common Bronze Age cemetery, Gloucestershire* (= CRAAGS Occasional Paper 6). Bristol

Saville, A., 1979b, *Excavations at Guiting Power Iron Age site, Gloucestershire, 1974* (= CRAAGS Occasional Paper 7). Bristol

Saville, A., 1979c, Further excavations at Nympsfield chambered tomb, Gloucestershire, 1974. *Proc Prehist Soc*, 45, 53–92

Saville, A., 1980, *Archaeological sites in the Avon and Gloucestershire Cotswolds* (= CRAAGS Survey 5). Bristol

Saville, A., 1981, Mesolithic industries in central England: An exploratory investigation using microlith typology. *Arch J*, 138, 49–71

Saville, A., 1982, Carrying cores to Gloucestershire: Some thoughts on lithic resource exploitation. *Lithics*, 3, 25–8

Saville, A., 1983a, Excavations at Condicote henge monument, Gloucestershire. *TBGAS*, 101, 21–48

Saville, A., 1983b, Excavations at Norbury Camp, Gloucestershire, 1977. In A. Saville, *Uley Bury and Norbury Hillforts* (= WAT Excavation Monograph 5). Bristol. 25–45

Saville, A., 1984a, Palaeolithic and Mesolithic evidence from Gloucestershire. In A. Saville (ed), *Archaeology in Gloucestershire: From the earliest hunters to the Industrial Age*. Cheltenham. 59–79

Saville, A., 1984b, A Palaeolith presumed to be from Charlton Abbots, Glos.. *TBGAS*, 102, 219–221

Saville, A., 1984c, Preliminary report on the excavation of a Cotswold-Severn tomb at Hazleton, Gloucestershire. *Antiq J*, 64, 10–24

Saville, A., 1984d, The Iron Age in Gloucestershire: A review of the evidence. In A. Saville (ed), *Archaeology in Gloucestershire: From the earliest hunters to the Industrial Age*. Cheltenham. 140–78

Saville, A., 1986, Mesolithic finds from west Gloucestershire. *TBGAS*, 104, 228–30

Saville, A. (ed), 1984, *Archaeology in Gloucestershire: From the earliest hunters to the Industrial Age*. Cheltenham. Cheltenham Art Gallery and Museums & the Bristol and Gloucestershire Archaeological Society

Saville, A. & Ellison, A., 1983, Excavations at Uley Bury hillfort Gloucestershire 1976. In A. Saville, *Uley Bury and Norbury hillforts* (= WAT Excavation Monograph 5). Bristol. 1–24

Saville, A., Gowlett, J.A.J. & Hedges, E.M., 1987, Radiocarbon dates from the chambered tomb at Hazleton (Glos.): A chronology for Neolithic collective burial. *Antiquity*, 61, 108–19

Saville, A. & Roe, F., 1984, A stone battle-axe from Wotton-under-Edge, and a review of battle-axe and macehead finds from Gloucestershire. *TBGAS*, 102, 17–22

Scott-Garrett, C., 1955, Tidenham Chase barrow. *TBGAS*, 74, 15–35

Selkirk, A., 1971, Ascott-under-Wychwood. *Curr Archaeol*, 3, 7–10

Sellwood, L., 1984, Tribal boundaries viewed from the perspective of numismatic evidence. In B. Cunliffe & D. Miles (eds), *Aspects of the Iron Age in central southern Britain* (= OUCA

Monograph 2). Oxford. 191–204

Shotton, F.W., 1978, Archaeological inferences from the study of alluvium in the lower Severn-Avon Valleys. In S. Limbrey & J.G. Evans (eds), *The effect of Man on the landscape: The lowland zone* (= CBA Research Report 21). London. 27–31

Sieveking, G., 1981, A visit to Symond's Yat, 1981. *Antiquity*, 55, 123–5

Simmons, I.G., Dimbleby, G.W. & Grigson, C., 1981, The Mesolithic. In I.G. Simmons & M.J. Tooley (eds), *The environment in British prehistory*. London. 82–124

Simmons, I.G. & Tooley, M.J. (eds), 1981, *The environment in British prehistory*. London

Smith, A.G., 1981, The Neolithic. In I.G. Simmons & M.J. Tooley (eds), *The environment in British prehistory*. London. 125–209

Smith, C.N.S., 1946, A prehistoric and Roman site at Broadway. *Trans Worcestershire Archaeol Soc*, 23, 57–74

SMITH, I.F., 1965, *Windmill Hill and Avebury: Excavations by Alexander Keiller 1925–1939*. Oxford

Smith, I.F., 1968, Report on late Neolithic pits at Cam, Glos.. *TBGAS*, 87, 14–28

Smith, I.F., 1972, Ring-ditches in eastern and central Gloucestershire. In P.J.Fowler (ed), *Archaeology and the landscape*. London. 157–67

Smith, R. & Cox, P., 1985, *The past in the pipeline: Archaeology of the Esso Midline*. Salisbury

Sparks, B.W. & West, R.G., 1972, *The Ice Age in Britain*. London

Spry, N. & Wingham, H., 1979, Withington, Casey Compton and Churcham, Long Brook Camp. *Glevensis*, 13, 30–1

Staelens, Y.J.E., 1982, The Birdlip cemetery. *TBGAS*, 100, 19–31

Stanford, S., 1980, *The archaeology of the Welsh Marches*. London

Stanford, S., 1981, *Midsummer Hill: An Iron Age hillfort on the Malverns*. Leominster. Privately published

Startin, B. & Bradley, R., 1981, Some notes on work organization and society in prehistoric Wessex. In C.L.N. Ruggles & A.W.R. Whittle (eds), *Astronomy and society in Britain during the period 4000–1500 BC* (= BAR 88). Oxford. 289–96

Sykes, C.M. & Whittle, S.L., 1965, A flint-chipping site on Tog Hill near Marshfield. *TBGAS*, 84, 5–14

Symonds, F.G.S, 1865, On the drifts of the Severn, Avon, Wye and Usk. *PCNFC*, 3, 31–39

Symonds, W.S., 1871, On the contents of a Hyaena's Den on the Great Doward, Whitchurch, Ross. *Geol Mag*, 8, 433–88

Taylor, H., 1928, King Arthur's Cave, near Whitchurch, Ross-on-Wye. *Proc Univ Bristol Spelaeological Soc*, 3.2, 59–87

Taylor, J.A., 1975, The role of climatic factors in environmental and cultural changes in prehistoric times. In J.G.Evans, S.Limbrey & H.Cleere (eds), *The effect of Man on the landscape: The highland zone* (= CBA Research Report 11). London. 6–19

Terry, W.N., 1953, A bronze spearhead from Moreton-in-Marsh. *TBGAS*, 72, 150–1

Tinsley, H.M., 1981, The Bronze Age. In I.G. Simmons & M.J. Tooley (eds), *The environment in British prehistory*. London. 210–49

Tite, M., 1972, *Methods of physical examination in archaeology*. London

Thomas, N., 1967, A double beaker burial on Bredon Hill, Worcs. *Trans Birmingham Archaeol Soc*, 82, 58–76

Thomas, N., 1976, *A guide to prehistoric England* (2nd ed). London

Thomas, N., 1986, J.E. Pritchard and the archaeology of Bristol. *TBGAS*, 104, 7–25

Thurnam, J., 1854, Description of a chambered tumulus, near Uley, Gloucestershire. *Arch J*, 11, 315–27

Trow, S., 1982a, An early intaglio found near Cirencester. *Britannia*, 13, 322–3

Trow, S., 1982b, Bagendon. In B. Rawes (ed), Archaeological Review No 6, 1981. *TBGAS*, 100, 258–9

Trow, S., 1983, *Excavations at 'The Ditches' hillfort, North Cerney, Gloucestershire (Second interim report)*. London. Privately published

Trow, S., 1984, North Cerney, Ditches hillfort. In B. Rawes (ed), Archaeological review No 8, 1983. *TBGAS*, 102, 231

Trow, S., 1985, An interrupted-ditch enclosure at Southmore Grove, Rendcomb, Gloucestershire. *TBGAS*, 103, 17–22

Trow, S., 1986, North Cerney, Ditches hillfort and villa. In B.Rawes (ed), Archaeological Review No 10, 1985. *TBGAS*, 104, 243

Tylecote, R.F., 1962, *Metallurgy in archaeology*. London

Tyler, A., 1976, *Neolithic flint axes from the Cotswold Hills* (= BAR 25). Oxford

Vatcher, F., 1966, Lechlade cursus. *Excavations Annual Report 1965*. London. MPBW. 5

Viner, D.J., 1978, A Palaeolithic implement from Cerney Wick. *TBGAS*, 96, 69–70

Wacher, J. & McWhirr, A., 1982, *Early Roman occupation at Cirencester* (= Cirencester Excavations I). Cirencester

Wainwright, G.J., 1967, The excavation of an Iron Age hillfort on Bathampton Down, Somerset. *TBGAS*, 86, 42–59

Walters, B., 1985, Nedge Cop, Bearse Farm, St Briavels. *The New Regard*, 1, 21

Walters, B, 1985, (ed), Archaeological Notes. *The New Regard*, 1, 21–38

Walrond, L.F.J., 1971, Woodchester. *Archaeol Rev*, 6, 15

Webster, G. & Hobley, B., 1964, Aerial reconnaissance over the Warwickshire Avon. *Arch J*, 121, 1–22

Webster, G. & Smith, L., 1982, The excavation of a Romano-British rural settlement at Barnsley Park: Part II. *TBGAS*, 100, 65–190

West, R.G., 1968, *Pleistocene geology and biology*. London

Wheeler, R.E.M. & Wheeler, T.V., 1932, *Report on the excavation of the prehistoric, Roman and post-Roman site in Lydney Park, Gloucestershire* (= Reports of the Research Committee of the Society of Antiquaries of London 9). Oxford

Whimster, R., 1981, *Burial practices in Iron Age Britain* (= BAR 90). Oxford. (2 vols)

Whitehead, P.F., 1979, An Acheulian handaxe from South Cerney, Gloucestershire. *TBGAS*, 97, 117–8

Whittle, A.W.R., 1977a, *The earlier Neolithic of Southern England and its continental background* (= BAR S35). Oxford

Whittle, A.W.R., 1977b, Earlier Neolithic enclosures in north-west Europe. *Proc Prehist Soc*, 43, 329–348

Whittle, A.W.R., 1978, Resources and population in the British Neolithic. *Antiquity*, 52, 34–42

Whittle, A.W.R, 1981, Later Neolithic society in Britain: A realignment. In C.L.N. Ruggles & A.W.R. Whittle (eds), *Astronomy and society in Britain during the period 4000–1500 BC* (= BAR 88). Oxford. 297–342

Whittle, A.W.R., 1985, *Neolithic Europe: A survey*. Cambridge

Williams, A., 1947, Excavations at Langford Downs, Oxon. (near Lechlade) in 1943. *Oxoniensia*, 11/12, 44–64

Wills, L.J., 1938, The Pleistocene development of the Severn from Bridgenorth to the sea. *Quarterly J Geol Soc*, 94, 161–242

Wilson, J.C., 1983, The standing stones of Anglesey: A discussion. *Bull Board Celtic Stud*, 30, 363–89

Wingham, H., 1985, Harding's High Brotheridge and Leggatt's legends. *Glevensis*, 19, 9–15

Witchell, A.N., 1973, Mesolithic evidence from Troublehouse, Cherington, Gloucestershire. *TBGAS*, 92, 12–20

Witts, G.B., 1881, Description of the long barrow called West Tump in the parish of Brimpsfield, Glos.. *TBGAS*, 5, 201–11

Witts, G.B., 1883, *Archaeological handbook of the county of Gloucester*. Cheltenham

Wymer, J., 1968, *Lower Palaeolithic archaeology in Britain as represented by the Thames Valley*. London

Wymer, J., 1974, Clactonian and Acheulian industries in Britain: Their chronological significance. *Proc Geol Assoc*, 85.3, 391–421

Wymer, J., 1981, The Palaeolithic. In I.G. Simmons & M.J. Tooley (eds), *The environment in British prehistory*. London. 49–81

Acknowledgements

This book is based upon a series of courses on prehistoric Gloucestershire which have been given in various parts of the county for the Department of Extra-mural Studies of the University of Bristol. Special thanks therefore go to all those students who patiently sat through the verbal presentations of the material covered here, and who helped improve the quality of the arguments and explanations by their questioning and discussion.

With an archaeological book of this sort much depends upon being able to draw upon evidence from a variety of excavation projects, fieldsurveys, and museum collections. Accordingly, I am especially grateful to all those who have generously provided information, access to finds or collections in their care, drawings, or photographs, especially: Alison Allden, Timothy Allen, Arthur ApSimon, Malcolm Atkin, Don Benson, Tony Brown, Stephen Clews, Wilfred Cox, Philip Dixon, Ann Ellison, Victoria Fenner, Patrick Garrod, Leslie Grinsell, John Gowlett, Frank Green, Mike Hall, Alan Hannan, Richard Hingley, Rupert Housley, Rodney Hudson, Henry Hurst, Roger Jacobi, Margaret Jones, George Lambrick, Peter Leach, Ian Longworth, Alan McWhirr, David Miles, Georgina Plowright, Eddie Price, Richard Reece, Richard Savage, Alan Saville, Andrew Sherratt, Isobel Smith, John Smith, Jane Timby, Stephen Trow, David Viner, Lionel Walrond, Bryan Walters, Malcolm Watkins, David Wilson, and Christopher Young. Naturally, the author accepts full responsibility for any remaining misinterpretations of the evidence summarized here.

The following individuals and organizations are thanked for allowing the reproduction of figures or plates: Academic Press (14 and 137), Antiquity (118), W. Baker (90), Birmingham University Field Archaeology Unit (174), Bristol and Gloucestershire Archaeological Society (151 and 169), T. Brown (14), Cheltenham Museum and Art Gallery (140), Corinium Museum, Cirencester (19B, 19E, 91, 102C, 116B, 116C, 158 and 167), Crickly Hill Archaeological Trust (Front cover, 44, 77, 130) Gloucester City Museum and Art Gallery (61, 147, 148, 150 and 173), Gloucestershire County Planning Department (181), M. Hall (118), Hazleton Excavation Project (57), R. Hingley (153), P. Garrod (147), Ministry of Defence (75), Newport Museum and Art Gallery (87), Oxford Archaeological Unit (92, 98 lower, 112, 144 lower, 161), Oxford Radiocarbon Accelerator Unit (9), Prehistoric Society (56 and 74), E. Price (114 lower and 142), Royal

Commission on the Historical Monuments of England (50, 127, 128 lower, 135, 138, 145, 165,), S. Trow (163), The Trustees of the British Museum (149), and H. Wingham (129, 132 and 136).

The following figures were prepared by Jane Timby, except where indicated from original drawings made especially for this book: 19 (B and E based on drawings by S. Morris, D after Clifford *et al* 1954 fig 2); 22 (after Clifford *et al* 1954 fig 2, and Clifford 1939); 23 (after Clifford *et al* 1954 fig 1, Campbell 1977 fig 97, and Burkitt 1938); 26 (after Saville 1984a fig 5, Campbell 1977 fig 134, and Sykes and Whittle 1965); 27; 30 (after Saville 1984a fig 5, Witchell 1973, and Gracie 1942); 36 (after Darvill 1984b fig 2, and O'Neil 1966 fig 4); 37; 45 (including material after Dixon 1971 fig 9, Tyler 1976 fig 1, and Grimes 1960 fig 32); 59 (after Clifford 1950b, figs 4–7 and Saville 1984c, fig 5); 64 (after Tyler 1976 figs 2 and 7); 67 (after Crawford 1925 128, Saville 1979c, fig 14, and Grimes 1960 fig 30); 70 (after Smith 1968 figs 2–3, Dunning 1976 fig 11, and drawings supplied by Alan Hannan); 72; 78; 81; 85 (after Clifford 1937b, O'Neil 1966, O'Neil & Bunt 1966, and Clarke 1970); 102 (A after Greenwell 1890, C from drawing supplied by Corinium Museum, Cirencester); 107 (after O'Neil & Grinsell 1960 fig 4, and Grimes 1960 fig 43); 109 (after O'Neil 1967 fig 3); 116 (B–D after drawing by Sandy Morris); 118 (after Hall & Gingell 1974 figs 2–4); 137 (after Dunning 1976 fig 24); 147; 171 (after figs in Clifford 1961). Figure 142 was drawn by Philip Moss, 103 by Sandy Morris, 144 upper and 161 by the Oxford Archaeological Unit, 14 by Tony Brown, 130 by Philip Dixon 77 by Liz Wilczynska, and 44 by Liz Wilczynska based on Philip Dixon's original. Figures 11, (after Darvill 1984a, fig 17) 13, 20, 25, 28, 39 (based on Crawford 1925, 91), 41, 43 (based on Darvill 1984b, fig 4 with additional plots by T. Darvill and R. Hingley, and from Trow 1985), 47, 51 (data from O'Neil & Grinsell 1960), 52 (data from O'Neil & Grinsell 1960), 53 (based on O'Neil 1966, fig 2), 54, 63, 68, 82, 93, 95 (data from O'Neil & Grinsell 1960 with additions), 97 (data from O'Neil & Grinsell 1960), 100 (based on O'Neil & Grinsell 1960, figs 1 and 5), 105 (based on O'Neil 1967, fig 1), 111, 114 upper, 125, 127 (after RCHME 1976, op. xxvi), 128 lower (after RCHME 1976, op xxvi), 138 (after RCHME 1976, op xxvi), 145 (after RCHME 1976, 1), 153 (based on plots supplied by R. Hingley), 157, 160, 165 (after RCHME 1976, xxviii), and 180 were prepared by the author.

Finally, special thanks go to Leslie Grinsell and Jane Timby for critically reading sections of the text in draft, and to Richard Bryant, the series editor, and the staff of Alan Sutton Publishing Ltd for seeing this volume through the press so speedily and efficiently.

The Long Stone, Staunton. [Photograph: Author]

Index of Places

Illustrations are shown separately in brackets at the end of each entry

212